Continuity and Discontinuity in Criminal Careers

Paul E. Tracy

University of Texas
Dallas, Texas

and

Kimberly Kempf-Leonard

University of Missouri–St. Louis
St. Louis, Missouri

Plenum Press • New York and London

Library of Congress Cataloging-in-Publication Data

On file

ISBN 0-306-45347-9

© 1996 Plenum Press, New York
A Division of Plenum Publishing Corporation
233 Spring Street, New York, N. Y. 10013

10 9 8 7 6 5 4 3 2 1

Printed in the United States of America

Foreword

It takes courage to do research on crime and delinquency. Such research is typically conducted in an atmosphere of concern about the problem it addresses and is typically justified as an attempt to discover new facts or to evaluate innovative programs or policies. When, as must often be the case, no new facts are forthcoming or innovative programs turn out not to work, hopes are dashed and time and money are felt to have been wasted. Because they take more time, longitudinal studies require even greater amounts of courage. If the potential for discovery is enhanced, so is the risk of wasted effort. Long-term longitudinal studies are thought to be especially risky for other reasons as well. Theories, issues, and statistical methods in vogue at the time they were planned may not be in vogue when they are finally executed. Perhaps worse, according to some perspectives, the structure of causal factors may shift during the execution of a longitudinal project such that in the end its findings apply to a reality that no longer exists.

These fears and expectations assume an ever-changing world and a corresponding conception of research as a more or less disciplined search for news. Such ideas belittle the contributions of past research and leave us vulnerable to theories, programs, policies, and research agendas that may have only tenuous connections to research of any kind. As a result, a crucial function of crime research is actually to reconfirm previous studies, to remind us that what was true yesterday remains true today, to remind us that current programs face the same stubborn reality that resisted the programs of the past.

Research, of course, adequately performs this confirmatory function only when it conscientiously attends to prior research. Fortunately, the cogency of claims to new knowledge is also enhanced by careful attention to earlier findings. Thus, good crime research earns its name in the first instance by doing well what has been done before.

Paul Tracy and Kimberly Kempf-Leonard trace the rich history of research on the careers of offenders and clearly identify the distinctive contributions of their own effort. As a consequence, *Continuity and Dis-*

continuity in Criminal Careers is excellent research in the fundamental sense of both of these terms. It reminds us of facts we should not forget by thoroughly reviewing earlier work on criminal careers and the controversies surrounding it. It reminds us of the difficulties inherent in efforts to predict and control crime. At the same time, it offers hope and guidance for future research and crime control policy.

All of its lessons are reinforced by thorough analysis of a large and impressive body of longitudinal data describing the transition from juvenile delinquency to adult crime. A major virtue of the longitudinal design is that it actually requires researchers to replicate their own research, to do again what they have done before. By itself, the longitudinal design limits speculation about the offender's past and disciplines speculation about the offender's future. This discipline is particularly important when offenders move from the juvenile to the criminal justice system. With two systems dealing with offenders, especially systems based on different premises, invidious comparisons naturally follow. Thus, without longitudinal data, it is easy to suggest that the juvenile justice system fails to attend to the information available to it and that criminal activity in adulthood might easily have been prevented by appropriate intervention. At the same time, without outcome data, it is easy to assume the success of juvenile court interventions in preventing adult crime. In the absence of information on delinquent activity, it is easy to suggest that possession of such information would allow the criminal justice system to deal with offenders in a highly efficient and effective manner.

With relevant longitudinal data, none of these conclusions is easily reached, and emphasis shifts from invidious comparison to actual outcomes and feasible policies consistent with them. Tracy and Kempf-Leonard recognize that their design and data focus attention on the effectiveness of the juvenile justice system. (Discussion of criminal justice policy is inappropriate because the effects of this system are not assessed.) But their data also reduce the importance of the criminal justice system by showing that the bulk of serious offenders are identified before it comes into play. Of course their design and data also rule out focus on social reform as the key to the crime problem. To my mind, this is all well and good. The question at hand is the relative importance and value of the two justice systems. With abundant data on their side, the authors argue that it is time we recognized again the centrality of the juvenile justice system in dealing with the crime problem. It may be easier to treat children as adults, and more popular to advocate increased intervention at the adult level, but the evidence would seem to point in the other direction.

It also points to the role of research as a moderator of excessive enthusiasm for untested and untried ideas. It may take courage to do research on crime and delinquency, but as *Continuity and Discontinuity in Criminal Careers* reminds us, it takes more courage (and money) to tackle the crime problem without it.

TRAVIS HIRSCHI

Preface

During our doctoral training at the Sellin Center for Studies in Criminology and Criminal Law at the University of Pennsylvania, we benefited from a criminological tradition that exposed us to the phenomenon of criminal careers and introduced us to the advantages associated with the longitudinal study of such careers. Beyond these substantive and methodological perspectives, we were taught something much more important and enduring—that criminologists should provide, whenever feasible, viable policy perspectives on the problem of illegal behavior and the improvement of society's reaction to crime and criminals

Fortunately, the Sellin Center and its director, Marvin E. Wolfgang, gave us the unparalleled opportunity to work on the 1958 Philadelphia Birth Cohort Study and thereby study criminal careers through a major longitudinal study while at the same time, satisfying our interests in policy, especially juvenile justice policy.

Longitudinal research in criminology, and especially a large-scale birth cohort study like ours, requires an inordinate investment of time and energy. Tracy began his involvement with the 1958 birth cohort in 1978 and his work has continued for 18 years. Kempf-Leonard joined the study in 1982, and she has worked on the project for 14 years. Over these many years, we have been absorbed in a seemingly endless and very time-consuming array of research tasks.

The birth cohort first had to be identified using Philadelphia Board of Education computer files. After the eligible cohort (i.e., birth in 1958 and residency in Philadelphia from at least ages 10 through 17) had been secured, the delinquency of the cohort then had to be determined. This necessitated a laborious process of identifying the delinquents by their "j" number using the 3" × 5" cards contained in the files of the Philadelphia Juvenile Court system. The approximately 6,300 Juvenile Court "j" numbers subsequently lead us to the voluminous records of the Philadelphia Police Department. Here we secured the juvenile rap sheets, which in turn provided us with the identifying numbers for the offense investigation reports. There were some 20,000 investigation re-

ports that had to removed from file boxes in a warehouse, then photocopied, coded, keypunched (yes, keypunched, as personal computers
were not yet available), entered into a mainframe computer and then
verified.

When the Sellin Center decided to conduct a follow-up study, we
could have carefully drawn a sample, as most would have done, thus
making the investigation of which 1958 cohort members made the transition from youth to adult and from delinquency to crime that much easier. But instead, Tracy decided that expedience should be sacrificed in favor of assuring the generalizability and representativeness of the
follow-up study by collecting the adult crime data on the entire cohort.
Kempf-Leonard was highly supportive of this decision since she had become enchanted with the relationship between juvenile offending and
adult crime and wanted the luxury of an entire cohort at her disposal
like Tracy had for the juvenile stage of the research.

The laborious data collection process had to begin all over again. We
had to search the files of the Philadelphia District Attorney's Office and
the Court of Common Pleas to determine which cohort members had
been arrested as adults. We then located and photocopied their police
rap sheets. We returned to the police warehouse to locate the investigation reports and proceeded with the copying, coding, data entry, and
data cleaning for another six to seven thousand criminal offenses.

Suffice it to say, we have been highly committed to longitudinal research and have invested the majority of our professional energies in
this study. We were more than casual observers when, over the past
decade, a controversy arose concerning the benefits derived from longitudinal research and the value of studying criminal careers. One grandi-
ose viewpoint has characterized the criminal career agenda as providing
highly definitive information about careers in crime and even possible
solutions that could be adopted by the criminal justice system. Another
stance has dismissed the potential achievements and has severely criticized the unwarranted allocation of scarce research funding and resources to such endeavors, thus chastising criminologists for the hegemony enjoyed by criminal careers and longitudinal designs.

Unfortunately, polemics, however genuine they may be on either
side of a debate, are often distracting—and perhaps worse, can be counterproductive. This is especially the case when, with the benefit of hind-
sight, the critics turn out to have been quite correct in their characterization that criminal career research and longitudinal methods had not yet
produced a body of results which would confirm their favor among the
criminological community. In response, all the defenders can do is to

continue reiterating all the potential benefits that longitudinal research will produce someday.

With this volume, we hope to illustrate not merely the potential of longitudinal designs for criminology, but also to provide some important findings on the transition from youth to adult and from delinquency to crime that may not have been achievable through any other approach. We have carefully reviewed prior research on criminal careers and have incorporated measurement issues in this study that flow directly from prior studies.

We are aware of the criticisms levied at our birth cohort design, and we willingly concede that some of these observations are indeed valid. Yet we are fortunate because our cohort data depict a very large and diverse urban population, and our criminal history data are comprehensive in both their completeness and their coverage of a highly significant portion of the life cycle in crime—from delinquency onset through age 26.

Again, we recognize the inherent limitations in our data which are strong in criminal history measures but are generally deficient in their inability to measure and test many theoretically relevant factors. However, we anticipate that our subsequent work with a follow-up sample of the 1958 birth cohort will make a contribution to theory building that is beyond this investigation.

It has been our intention to produce a volume that would be both convincing and useful to criminologists but also interesting and valuable to juvenile justice professionals who are charged with the responsibility of reacting to juvenile delinquents. In the course of our writing, we continually found ourselves in situations where these two goals conflicted. On the one hand, many of the research questions in this study are complex, as are many of the measurement and analytical procedures necessary to search for answers. While providing sufficient detail about the techniques used in this study for our academic colleagues, the descriptions of the more technical aspects would be dreadfully boring to the many professional readers.

Our solution to this dilemma was to organize the book to suit both interests. The procedures we followed and the empirical results obtained are described in detail in Chapters 4 through 8. Although we summarize the results briefly at the conclusion of each chapter, many of the findings are interrelated. We decided, therefore, to provide an overview of the full body of findings in Chapter 9 and then a discussion of their implications in Chapter 10.

We anticipate some readers may actually wish to begin the book with these last two chapters. Regardless of order, we hope this work will interest both our colleagues and practitioners alike. Most important, rather than contribute further to the debate over the viability of criminal career research, we hope this research will redirect the discussion to the important measurement issues surrounding criminal careers and the significant policy implications that our results engender concerning the relationship between delinquency careers and later criminality.

Scholarly research, especially when it takes on the cast of a marathon as this study has, cannot be accomplished without the assistance, guidance, and even the patience of many people. We are especially thankful to Kathryn Tracy and Charlie Leonard, who indulged our distraction during the months of planning, analyses, and writing. They probably heard a lot more about criminal careers than they ever wanted. They each deserve considerable credit for putting up with long telephone conversations, hours at the computer, and the seemingly false promise that "this part of the cohort study will finally be done any day now."

We appreciate the cooperation of many agencies from the city of Philadelphia including the Board of Education, the District Attorney's Office, the Juvenile Court, the Court of Common Pleas, and most particularly, the Police Department. The professionals in these agencies never gave us the feeling that our research was intrusive in their daily work. But we know the truth, and we fully realize what a burden we were.

We also acknowledge the support and assistance of our program monitors, Pamela Swain, Wendy Wilson, and Barbara Allen-Hagen, of the Office of Juvenile Justice and Delinquency Prevention, United States Department of Justice.

We owe a permanent debt to the many graduate students and staff at the Sellin Center for Studies in Criminology and Criminal Law, the Department of Sociology, and the Wharton School at the University of Pennsylvania who carefully collected, coded, and helped prepare these data. Special thanks are due to Mark Keintz and Steven Aurand, computer programmers and statisticians extraordinaire.

We thank the series editors, Joseph G. Weis and James Alan Fox, for their early belief in our project and continued support in seeing it completed. Special thanks to Eliot Werner, our Plenum editor, for his faith in us despite the fact that this work has taken much longer than expected.

We also appreciate the helpful critique provided by anonymous reviewers of the first draft and the editorial advice we received from Whit Crowson.

We are thrilled beyond description that Travis Hirschi has provided the foreword for this volume. Given his vocal and long-standing criticisms of longitudinal research, we are truly appreciative of his comments.

Finally, we owe a considerable intellectual debt to Marvin Wolfgang, a debt that can neither be stated properly nor ever repaid. We thank him for inspiring us and reinforcing our interest in longitudinal research. We are eternally grateful for nurturing in us an appreciation of why the topic of criminal careers is so fundamentally important in criminology. We are especially fortunate that he has always willingly shared his wisdom and guidance.

PAUL E. TRACY
KIMBERLY KEMPF-LEONARD

Contents

Continuity and Discontinuity in Criminal Careers

1

Introduction

The research reported in this volume concerns a continuing longitudinal investigation of a birth cohort of persons who were born in 1958, and who continuously resided in the city of Philadelphia at least during the years in which they were at risk for delinquency (i.e., ages 10 through 17). The findings pertaining to the delinquency careers of the 27,160 persons that comprise the 1958 birth cohort have been previously reported (see Tracy, Wolfgang, and Figlio, 1985, 1989, 1990). The research presented here is one of two follow-up investigations of the adult criminality committed by the cohort as the members made the transition from the legal status of juvenile to that of adult, and thus, from the delinquent acts that comprise their delinquency careers to the adult offenses through the age of 26 of the subsequent criminal careers.

This follow-up study of the continuity and discontinuity between the delinquent and criminal careers in the 1958 cohort is significant in three major respects. First, this is the largest group of subjects in the United States whose criminality has been studied longitudinally for any period of time, let alone such a lengthy period of time (onset through age 26). Second, unlike other sample-based studies, the criminal history data have been collected for the *entire population* in the cohort from the point of onset, either juvenile or adult, through age 26. Third, unlike other research which suffers from an overabundance of males, a racially uneven balance of subjects, or some other sample constraint or bias (e.g., in-school survey respondents), the 1958 birth cohort has a very well-balanced distribution of subjects by gender, race, and social class. Moreover, these data are consistently available for the entire cohort for the entire period under investigation.

In addition to this follow-up research concerning the official adult crime committed by the cohort as it ages and matures, we have a further follow-up study under way which concerns a comprehensive interview with a carefully selected stratified probability sample of the cohort. The interview component deals with such important topics as etiological factors in the development of delinquency and crime, victimization experience, self-reported delinquency and crime, and a multitude of health and developmental issues relating to critical life events and their relationship to behavior, both social and antisocial, over the life course.

This third volume of the 1958 cohort study will augment the official delinquency and adult criminal careers of the cohort with a myriad of survey-based data. These data, together with the complete criminal history data that we report on here, will permit etiological analyses of both risk factors and prosocial factors in the lives of the cohort. Such studies are not possible with the official offense archival data that we have been concerned with in this investigation.

This longitudinal study of delinquency and adult criminality must be viewed within a broader criminological context that has increasingly embraced the investigation of criminal careers and has undertaken the study of such careers using primarily longitudinal research methods. Indeed, over the past two decades, criminological research has increasingly focused on a particular category of offender and his or her associated criminal behavior. This particular focus has concerned what was originally referred to as the "chronic offender" (Wolfgang, Figlio, and Sellin, 1972). The contemporary focus, however, has evolved beyond the category of the habitual or chronic offender category itself to a much broader concern with topics such as "criminal careers" and "career criminals" (see Blumstein, Cohen, Roth, and Visher, 1986).

The research focusing on criminal careers has been quite varied in terms of fundamental research particulars, such as subject groups (general population versus known offenders), methodological approach (longitudinal versus cross-sectional), and especially the measurement of crime itself (official archival data versus self-report surveys). Despite design or measurement differences in past studies, research on criminal careers/career criminals has generally investigated a set of concepts that are represented to have theoretical and substantive significance to the discipline, as well as strategic policy importance to criminal justice practitioners and lawmakers. These criminal career research concepts range from the onset, duration, and cessation of criminal behavior to rates of participation in crime (usually referred to as *prevalence*) and measures of frequency (often referred to as *incidence, individual offense rates*, or *lambda*), and to the sociodemographic correlates of these concepts (race, sex, and social class have been the most usual correlates studied).

It is indisputable that this "criminal career paradigm" has dominated criminological research over at least the past 15 to 20 years. It is

also quite clear that, despite a widely held belief that this clearly delineated area of inquiry has been significant, desirable, worthwhile, and so
on, there have been a number of polemical publications (Blumstein, Cohen, and Farrington, 1988a, 1988b; Gottfredson and Hirschi, 1986, 1987,
1988; Hagan and Palloni, 1988; Tittle, 1988) that have spawned a debate
over the yield attained through criminal career research on the one
hand, and the value of or necessity for a longitudinal approach to studying criminal behavior on the other.

It is not our intention to engage in an argumentative exercise that
fuels this debate unnecessarily. The present context is inappropriate for
such a debate, and more important, such polemics generally accomplish
little in terms of resolving substantive concerns that confront researchers
interested in studying a particular phenomenon. Rather, given that the
criminal career paradigm is so central to our focus in this study, and the
longitudinal method is so crucial to the type of data we have collected
and to the type of analyses that we have conducted, it seems desirable to
provide a brief exposition on these matters.

Thus, we provide below a short but necessary commentary on the
origins of the concept of the *criminal career* followed by an exposition of
the evolution of this term in the literature of criminology. Next, we provide a synopsis of the debate surrounding the criminal career paradigm
by reviewing the arguments on both sides of the debate. In this way, we
can provide an appropriate context for our longitudinal birth cohort
study, while at the same time acknowledging and responding to the absence of consensus surrounding this particular research agenda.

Foundations of the Criminal Career Concept

The current use of the concept of *career* in contemporary criminological research may best be understood by looking at the scholarly progression through which this term has evolved. The developmental route
along which the concept of the criminal career evolved appears to have
originally begun in the early 1900s at the University of Chicago. Researchers at what has since become known as the "Early Chicago
School" employed extensive participant observation techniques to investigate the life histories of individuals in order to gain insight into urban life. The objective in this pursuit was to identify patterns of personal
adaptation or change in response to differing social circumstances. The
"life history" method of ethnographic investigation prospered through
the work of Robert Park, Ernest Burgess, and a host of students who

studied under these pioneering sociologists (see, Anderson, 1923; Park 1915; Park, Burgess, and McKenzie, 1925; Thrasher, 1927; and Zorbaugh, 1929).

Bursik (1989) has made the important observation that the contemporary interest in the concept of careers in crime and the phenomenon of the chronic offender can be attributed to the work of Shaw (1930, 1931, 1936) and his associates (e.g., Sutherland, 1937). Essentially, Shaw employed the life history or case study method to investigate the dynamic aspect of delinquency careers and how they may begin and evolve over the course of time. Thus, in the first sentence of *The Jack-Roller*, Shaw writes: "The subject matter of this volume is limited to the case study of the *career* of a young male delinquent. . . ." (1930: 1; emphasis added) and the title of Shaw's next work, *The Natural History of a Delinquent Career* (1931), also indicates that the concept of *career* was being used as an explanatory term to frame the focus of the investigation. A review of these two works of Shaw as well as his later work, *Brothers in Crime* (1936), and Sutherland's *Professional Thief* (1937), reveals that Shaw and Sutherland viewed crime as a form of all-encompassing activity that thoroughly dominated the routine activities of persons occupied in such careers.

The subsequent contribution made by Everett Hughes (1952), another student of Robert Park, in his study of occupations is seemingly responsible for the notion of *career* as an autonomous heuristic concept. In the traditional life history method, data were gathered to capture the essence of lives, whereas in the approach used by Hughes the focus was on types of occupations or activities associated with the progress of employment. In this model, *career* was essentially equivalent to *occupation* and, among others, the occupations of teachers (Becker, 1957), medical students (Becker, Geer, Hughes, and Strauss, 1961), and funeral directors (Habenstein, 1955) were explored by Hughes' students.

The career approach was considered an improvement because it focused on categories of behavior among occupational types rather than merely focusing on individuals. This permitted greater generalizability, while at the same time it preserved the objective of the life history method: identifying change and the patterns of behavior that ensue over time.

Bursik (1989) has made another important observation concerning the legacy of Shaw and Sutherland. Despite the value of the case study method, Bursik notes, "the growing popularity of survey research made many researchers increasingly skeptical of a study design that did not permit the statistical testing of hypotheses and in which the generalizability of the findings was problematic" (1989: 389). Accordingly, Bursik finds, "the empirical investigation of the development of careers in crime generally languished and was relegated to the sidelines of mainstream criminological research" (1989: 389–390).

The situation has fortunately changed, and the work of Shaw and Sutherland has fostered many recent efforts to examine the criminal career of specific offender types (see, for example, Akerstrom, 1985; Cameron, 1964; Cullen and Link, 1980; Irwin, 1970; Jackson, 1969; Klockars, 1976; Letkemann, 1973; Martin, 1952; Maurer, 1940, 1964; Miller, 1978; Polsky, 1969; Prus and Sharper, 1977; Wright and Decker, 1994). Research in this style has viewed crime as a form of work within which career options are available—options not unlike the more traditional career paths in law-abiding occupations. Thus, these studies were responsible for the introduction of terms such as *career contingencies, turning points, recruitment, sequences, stages,* and the *professional criminal,* terms that are consistent with a career metaphor.

The early research on criminal or delinquent careers was not restricted to the Chicago school alone. At about the same time, during the 1930s, the Gluecks began their pioneering investigations of delinquency. The research of the Gluecks resulted in 13 books and almost 300 articles, and many of these publications concerned delinquent or criminal careers (see, for example Glueck and Glueck, 1930, 1934, 1937, 1940, 1943, 1945, 1950, 1968). Overviews of the research can be found in Glueck and Glueck (1964, 1974), and a recent review of the Gluecks' research and results from reanalyses of some of the data can be found in Laub and Sampson (1988) and Sampson and Laub (1990, 1993).

Lemert (1951) continued the focus on the career concept by introducing the notion of the deviant career. In Lemert's classic formulation, primary deviance, depending on the nature of the ensuing societal reaction, can lead to a process of secondary deviance and ultimately to the development and maintenance of a deviant career. Subsequently, Lemert (1962) focused on the interactional nature of this sequence by addressing the process by which the labelled deviant recognizes and accepts the deviant label conferred by the societal reaction and pursues the deviant career as the sole alternative available.

Becker (1963) continued this interactionist perspective and sought to identify the process through which the deviant label was affixed by the social audience, secondary deviance occurred, and was subsequently followed by career commitment to a deviant life-style. By focusing on the deviant careers followed by the marijuana users among the dance musicians he was studying, Becker was led to acknowledge that careers, whether legitimate or deviant, sometimes include exodus. Thus, unsuccessful career progression, or the inability to continue the particular career or life-style, was recognized as another, and perhaps the final, dimension of the criminal or deviant career.

Goffman further extended the career concept to include what he called a "moral career" (1961, 1963). Goffman offered the following explanation for his use of the concept.

> Traditionally, the term career has been reserved for those who expect to enjoy the raises laid out within a respectable profession. The term is coming to be used, however, in a broadened sense to refer to any social strand of any person's course through life. (1961: 127)

An important dimension to longitudinal research on delinquency and crime emerged with the appearance of *Delinquency in a Birth Cohort* in 1972. In this pioneering research with the 1945 Philadelphia birth cohort, Wolfgang and his associates used a retrospective birth cohort design to investigate the delinquency careers of 9,945 boys who were born in 1945 and who had lived in Philadelphia throughout the course of their juvenile years at risk (ages 10–17). With the benefit of a longitudinal cohort design, Wolfgang et al. (1972) were the first to report population-based data concerning the onset, offense patterns, offense specialization, age variations, and the severity and duration of juvenile careers.

Among the most significant findings of the research was that a very small fraction of the birth cohort, those offenders who had accumulated at least five police contacts before becoming adults, had committed a far greater share of the delinquency in the birth cohort than their proportionate representation in the birth cohort might have suggested. Specifically, the 627 chronic delinquents constituted just 6% of the cohort (n = 9,945) and 18% of the delinquent subset (n = 3,475), yet these chronic offenders were responsible for a total of 5,305 offenses, or 52% of all the delinquency in the cohort through age 17. With regard to the subset of serious index crimes, Wolfgang et al. (1972) found that the chronics had committed 63% of the Uniform Crime Reports index offenses, including 71% of the homicides, 73% of the rapes, 82% of the robberies, and 69% of the aggravated assaults.

These results of the 1945 birth cohort study concerning the chronic offenders have very probably become the most important and enduring findings of the research. Although criminologists had long suspected that rates of offending were skewed—that a small group of habitual offenders were committing crimes at a high rate—the Philadelphia birth cohort study showed just how small the chronic offender group actually was, and just how skewed their rates of offending actually were.

Since the emergence of the 1945 cohort study, several studies have replicated the juvenile career approach pioneered by Wolfgang. For example, in his work with three Racine birth cohorts Shannon (1980, 1988) has also found evidence of a chronic delinquency career. In the 1942 cohort, 1% of the males had four or more felony contacts, but this group was responsible for 29% of all such felony contacts. In the 1949 cohort, the chronic offenders comprised only 3% of the total group, but had accumulated 50% of the felony contacts. In the last cohort, 1955, the 6% with four or more felony contacts accounted for 70% of this type of police contact. Similarly, Hamparian, Schuster, Dinitz, and Conrad (1978) also reported that in an Ohio cohort of violent delinquents, chronic offending was restricted to 31% of the offenders.

Other studies have confirmed that the disproportionate volume of crime attributable to chronic offenders is not restricted to juveniles, and that despite the familiar inverse trend evident in age-specific arrest rates, the habitual offender or chronic recidivism effect is observable among adult criminals. The Rand inmate surveys have found that a relatively small group of offenders report the commission of a substantial proportion of crime. For example, Peterson, Braiker, and Polich (1980) have found that 25% of a group of California inmates could be classified as career criminals, and this group of chronics reported committing approximately 60% of the armed robberies, burglaries, and auto thefts, and about one-half of the assaults and drug sales reported by the full sample of inmates. Visher (1986) has reanalyzed Rand's second inmate survey (prison and jail inmates in California, Michigan, and Texas) and has found that one-half of the inmates reported committing fewer than four robberies per year, while the very high-rate offenders, who constituted just 5% of all the inmates, reported committing more than 180 robberies per year.

These results concerning the chronic delinquency career and the few studies that have confirmed the same effect for adult careers, have demonstrated that skewed rates of illegal behavior are a problem in both the juvenile and adult reference periods. But there is now good evidence to suggest that the problem of the career offender is longitudinal, and in fact can begin very early in a delinquent's career and can continue into adulthood. This situation is most clearly evidenced by the follow-up study of the 1945 Philadelphia birth cohort.

Wolfgang, Thornberry, and Figlio (1987) followed up a representative sample of 974 members of the 1945 birth cohort to age 30 using Philadelphia police and court records. The data indicated that chronic offenders constituted 15% of the cohort and these criminals were found to have committed 74% of all the official crime, and accounted for 84% of the personal injury offenses and 82% of the property offenses recorded from the onset of the career up to age 30.

Further evidence of longitudinal chronicity comes from the continuing Cambridge Study in Delinquent Development (Farrington, 1981). Farrington has reported that up to age 24, the chronic offenders constituted just 6% of the sample and 17% of the convicted youths, yet these chronics were responsible for one half of the convictions. The Farrington results thus provide cross-cultural evidence of chronicity and its prolonged tenure.

The research reviewed above provides sufficient evidence that in any group or cohort of subjects there is an uneven distribution of offenses. Most people will never commit or be arrested for a crime; they do not have offense careers. Some individuals will commit only one or two crimes and then desist, thus pointing to a short or limited career. Other persons will accumulate many offenses, while still others will recidivate very frequently indeed, thus indicating a prolonged or extensive career in crime.

Contemporary Perspective on the Criminal Career Concept

Polsky was one of the first commentators to address the need for the career perspective in the study of deviance and crime. Polsky noted that, "career criminals, whose importance to any theorist of human behavior, not to mention the rest of society, is so disproportionate to their numbers." He went on to say that "criminology falls flat on its face" when it comes to "providing well-rounded, contemporary, sociological descriptions and analyses of criminal lifestyles, subcultures, and their relation to larger social processes and structures" (1969: 114)

A decade later, Petersilia's comments indicate that void in criminology remained.

> Little is known about how and when the criminal career begins, or how long it is likely to last, why criminal careers persist, and why some persons abandon criminal careers early, others continue into adult crime, and still others begin crime careers late in life. . . . Little is known about the extent and types of crime committed at different stages of criminal careers. (1980: 325–26)

More recently, the concept of the criminal career has come to be defined along the dimensions suggested above by Petersilia. One of the first attempts to characterize the substantive focus offered by the criminal career concept has been provided by Blumstein, Cohen, and Hsieh (1982). They noted:

> [It] is useful to conceptualize individual criminal activity in terms of a "criminal career," with entry into a career at or before the first crime committed and drop-out from the career at or after the last crime committed. During a criminal career, the offender has a continuing propensity to commit crimes, accumulates some arrests, is sometimes convicted and less frequently is incarcerated. (1982: 2)

Blumstein and his associates have also provided a noteworthy caution concerning the possible misinterpretations that could ensue from an improper conceptualization of the career concept. They offered the following clarification of its heuristic value:

> This characterization of an individual's criminal activity as a "career" is not meant to imply that offenders derive their livelihood exclusively or even predominantly from crime. The concept of a "criminal career" is intended only as a means of structuring the longitudinal sequence of criminal events associated with an individual in a systematic way. This notion of a criminal career can be applied to all crimes committed by an offender, or it can be restricted to sub-sequences of crimes which focus on selected crime types. (Blumstein et al., 1982: 5)

The criminal career, according to Blumstein and his colleagues, is thus a multifaceted phenomenon identified according to the onset of the illegal behavior and ultimately by possible desistance from crime involvement. The commission of crime is not necessarily the only focus, or even the most prevalent activity, of persons involved in a criminal career. Moreover, the criminal career can be characterized either by the total offenses that an offender commits or by specific crime types, such as predatory violence, during the entire life course or in just significant portions of it (e.g., early versus late juvenile years; early adulthood versus middle age, and so on).

Blumstein (1983) provided further clarification by making an important distinction between variants of the concept, that is, the "criminal career" versus the "career criminal," which could engender much confusion and misunderstanding.

> The term "careers" does not necessarily mean that the individual earns his living primarily or even significantly through criminal activity. That characterization may be more appropriate to the group noted as career criminals. Here, the concept of career simply recognizes the fact that individuals start their criminal activity at some age (most often in the mid-teens) engage in crime at some individual crime rate (that may be high or low and may change over time), commit a mixture of crimes (that may also change over time) and, for the most part, eventually stop committing crimes or drop out of their careers. (1983: 5–6)

The research on criminal careers and career criminals became central to the research agenda of both the academic research community and governmental policy-makers alike. Walker has provided the following assessment of the Wolfgang et al. 1945 Philadelphia birth cohort study: "Their landmark study *Delinquency in a Birth Cohort* is the single most important piece of criminal justice research in the last 25 years and has become a major influence on crime control thinking" (1985: 39). With reference to the chronic offender data in the cohort, Walker remarked, "since Wolfgang first identified them, those 627 juveniles have inspired the freshest and most important thinking in criminal justice (1985: 39).

One significant reason for this praise of the Wolfgang cohort study is that it established a research agenda that bridged the two spheres of academic research and governmental policy. That is, in response to the criminological fact of life represented by the chronic offender, many researchers and government officials recognized that the group of habitual or career criminals represented a special category of offender that held great promise for research. For the academician, the chronic offender and the criminal career became a delineated focus of both substantive and methodological developments in criminology. For the policy-maker, the criminal career and the career criminal became the focus of special criminal justice intervention, such as targeted law enforcement and prosecution procedures, to be followed by selective incapacitation strategies and stringent sentencing guidelines. These are just a few of the most popular measures being implemented to combat career criminals and their excessive and prolonged involvement in crime.

Barnett, Blumstein, and Farrington (1987) have captured this multiple appeal of the career criminal phenomenon and have acknowledged that there is indeed a distinct policy-related interest in career criminal research. They have observed, "It has been argued that, if prosecution resources and institutional and other treatment facilities could be used more selectively for these high-rate offenders, this might prevent a significant number of crimes" (1987: 83).

However, Barnett et al. have also made the crucial observation that the substantive importance of criminal career information goes beyond the mere identification of career criminals for criminal justice policy purposes because:

> Detailed information about criminal careers is fundamental to isolating the different facets of the career—initiation, the pattern of offending during the active period, and termination. It is necessary to separate these different facets in order to test various approaches to the prevention or reduction of

crime and to investigate different ways in which possible "causes of crime" affect these different aspects of criminal careers (1987: 83–84).

Critique of the Criminal Career Paradigm

This characterization of the value of research on criminal careers has been strongly rejected by Gottfredson and Hirschi[1] beginning in 1983 with their paper, "Age and the Explanation of Crime." In this early critique of the career criminal approach and longitudinal research designs, Hirschi and Gottfredson develop a series of theses concerning the relationship between age and crime. Fundamentally their point is that because the age distribution of crime is practically invariant over many social conditions and demographic factors, the use of age as an explanation for crime, as well as research that depends on an age effect, is not justified.

Specifically, Hirschi and Gottfredson argue that the presumed age effects were an instrumental factor in the rise of longitudinal studies and contributed to their consequent preferred status among criminological researchers. They further argue:

> This research emphasis gains much of its attractiveness from the association between age and such concepts as "career criminal," "recidivism," and "desistance," all of which are thought to be of considerable theoretical and practical import and all of which are thought to require, by definition, longitudinal designs for their study. (1983: 553)

After determining that the presumed age effects, which are so fundamentally necessary as a justification for a longitudinal criminal career approach, are generally not supported by the empirical evidence, Hirschi and Gottfredson are led to conclude that:

> The alleged necessity of the longitudinal study is apparently based on a combination of substantive and methodological considerations. The major substantive consideration appears to be the age effect. The methodological considerations derive from the experimental model, because of which it is claimed that the longitudinal design is unique in its ability to resolve the question of causation. Our critique here focuses on the substantive justification for the longitudinal study. At the same time however, we are not convinced that the longitudinal study offers solutions to causal questions commensurate with its costs. As we have shown, the conceptual apparatus

---

[1] In all fairness to Michael Gottfredson and Travis Hirschi, the reader is advised to consult and evaluate the various Gottfredson–Hirschi arguments in their original form. The particular positions quoted here are meant to serve illustrative purposes only.

generated by longitudinal thinking has been very misleading. This design
has been oversold to criminology at high substantive and economic costs.
(1983: 582)

Gottfredson and Hirschi continued their dissatisfaction with the
criminal career paradigm in a second paper, "The True Value of Lambda
Would Appear to be Zero" (1986), a paper which they have described
elsewhere as an effort to "introduce some small degree of tension into an
otherwise complacent system that had, we thought, limited thinking
about crime to the repetition of pretentious slogans, ignored research
contrary to its assumptions, and proposed to lead public policy about
crime in the wrong direction" (1988: 37).

The substance of this second Gottfredson-Hirschi critique can be
evidenced with a few select passages that highlight their concerns. Although the argument proceeds from a substantive examination of the
evidence surrounding various aspects of the criminal career paradigm,
there seems to be a distinctly political undertone.

First, with reference to the relationship between criminal career research and federal funding they write, "the criminal career notion so
dominates discussion of criminal justice policy and so controls expendi-
ture of federal research funds that it may now be said that criminal justice research in this country is centrally planned" (1986, p.213). Second,
with respect to the terminology of the academic community, they observe that, "the language of criminology is now saturated with the vo-
cabulary of this perspective—with terms like lambda, prevalence and
incidence, onset and desistance, chronicity and selective incapacitation"
(1986: 214). Third, after reviewing the research evidence they assert that,
"the evidence is clear that the career criminal idea is not sufficiently substantial to command more than a small portion of the time and effort of
the criminal justice practitioner or academic community" (1986: 231).

In a third polemical paper, Gottfredson and Hirschi (1987) turn
their attention to the adequacy of longitudinal research designs to investigate not only criminal careers, but also, crime in general. After reviewing the evidence from a host of studies concerning the two presumed
benefits of longitudinal research (i.e., methodological and substantive
superiority), they offer the following interesting conclusions.

First, concerning the hegemony enjoyed by longitudinal perspectives, Hirschi and Gottfredson maintain that, "neither the results of current longitudinal research in criminology nor reasonable expectations
about proposed longitudinal research in the area justifies the dominance
this design has achieved" (1987: 610).

Second, given this arguable absence of either current findings or future potential, Gottfredson and Hirschi finally assert:

> Attention to longitudinal designs diverts attention from policy-relevant and theoretically important issues. Indeed, current advocates of longitudinal studies blur the distinction between theory and method to such an extent that they seem to be making important substantive and logical assertions when in fact they are merely repeating an extremely narrow conception of crime and its causation. As a consequence, the cost of longitudinal thinking to the study of crime is not restricted to the large sums necessary for its execution (1987: 610).

These Gottfredson and Hirschi commentaries stimulated a necessary and very worthwhile debate in the literature, which subsequently witnessed a comment by Blumstein et al. (1988a), a reply by Gottfredson and Hirschi (1988), a further rejoinder by Blumstein et al. (1988b), and two other thoughtful commentaries (Hagan and Palloni, 1988; and Tittle, 1988).

We published the juvenile careers volume of the 1958 cohort study in the wake of the debate surrounding longitudinal research, and included in that volume a brief exposition of the preceding issues. In particular, one of the present authors noted that, "Scientific disagreement is healthy, and criminology will surely benefit from the exchange of ideas stimulated by the career criminal controversy" (Tracy et al. 1990: 18). Although it was duly acknowledged that cross-sectional research is not incapable of examining important topics surrounding criminal careers, it was nonetheless maintained that the longitudinal approach, especially the birth cohort method, is the most viable and productive way to study many issues that surround delinquent and adult careers in crime and the transition between the two.

In support of this position that there are distinct advantages to the use of longitudinal methods in the study of delinquency and crime, Tracy et al. presented the following excerpts from the literature:

> [L]ongitudinal research can show when criminal careers begin, when they end, and how long they last. It can also show the prevalence and incidence of offending, the cumulative prevalence rate, and the seriousness and diversity of offending, at different stages of a criminal career (Farrington, Ohlin, and Wilson, 1986: 25); and

> [T]he main advantage of such surveys of crime and delinquency lies in their ability to provide detailed information about the natural history and course of development of offending. In particular, longitudinal surveys can show the extent of continuity or discontinuity between offending at different ages, the extent to which one event precedes or follows another in developmental sequences, and how well later events can be predicted by earlier ones. They can also provide information about the time ordering of different events, which can be useful in drawing conclusions about cause and effect, and they can show the effects of different events on the course of development of criminal careers (Blumstein et al. 1988b: 67)

In retrospect, it is important to set the record straight and acknowledge here that the Gottfredson–Hirschi position was not without merit. That is, up to a particular historical point, prior to 1990, longitudinal research, especially research focusing on the continuity between delinquent careers and adult criminal careers, had not produced a substantial yield of findings. It was a method with the potential, perhaps even high potential, to reveal significant aspects of the ways in which delinquent careers, once begun, follow certain routes that present discernible and significant risks of continuing when the delinquent becomes an adult.

Thus, Gottfredson and Hirschi were correct in their analyses, and they were quite justified in their commentaries which argued that longitudinal research had not produced a yield commensurate with its apparent dominance in the field.

Ultimately, the potential of a research approach has to be realized in order for confidence in and reliance on the technique to continue. Fortunately, the present research fulfills the promise of longitudinal designs and reveals findings about the continuity between delinquent and adult careers that would not be possible with cross-sectional methods.

The present research effort adheres to the expansive definition of criminal career research offered by Blumstein et al. (1982) described previously, and the various research foci discussed immediately above (Blumstein et al., 1988a). The specific objective of this investigation was to determine, first, whether juvenile delinquents are more likely than their nondelinquent peers to commit crime as adults. Once this objective is attained, then we sharpen our focus to address whether the tendency to commit crime as an adult can be further differentiated across important pathways that characterize the delinquency career.

Thus, questions such as the following are illustrative of our focus. Are delinquents with a long list of delinquencies more likely than others to engage in adult crime? If delinquents abandon crime late in their adolescence, will they be involved again later as adults? Do youth who exhibit patterns of crime specialization and/or serious offending also commit adult crime? Last, does the way in which juvenile courts dispose of delinquency cases affect the delinquent's chances of becoming an adult criminal?

In accordance with these research issues, this monograph is organized as follows.

In Chapter 2 we present an overview of the theoretical and policy considerations subsumed in this research. We will address the value that investigations such as this one hold for theory development and the various administrative policy concerns generally inherent in criminal career research. We also will provide extensive commentary on our prevailing emphasis on the patterns of constancy and change within the delinquency career paths, and thus the criminological value of focusing on the continuity and discontinuity that characterizes some careers in crime but not others.

Chapter 3 provides a discussion of the results from previous empirical research concerning the various dimensions of delinquent careers and puts into perspective the particular dimensions of interest in this investigation and further identifies important methodological concerns subsumed therein.

Chapter 4 discusses the limitations of prior research, describes the 1958 Philadelphia Birth Cohort study, and explains the data collection efforts and variable measurements that have been employed and the methodology used in this study. We also give some attention to the limitations inherent in the data and the methods we use.

The findings of the study will be reported in Chapters 5 through 8. Chapter 5 contains basic descriptive tables such as cross-tabulations, frequencies, and means concerning the transition from juvenile delinquency status to adult crime status. These statistics serve to highlight the extent of continuity and discontinuity in the delinquency-to-adult career transitions in the 1958 cohort. They further serve to justify the other specific analyses that will follow.

Chapter 6 uses a series of logistic regression models to analyze the demographic variables and select juvenile offense career differences (frequency of offenses, age-at-onset, age-at-last-offense, and court dispositions) in making the transition from juvenile status to adult crime.

Chapter 7 extends the analyses of Chapter 6 and concerns the topic of juvenile offense types and the related issue of delinquency "specialists." We also examine the association between these measures and the likelihood of making the transition from delinquency to crime.

Chapter 8 reports the prediction models based on logistic regression analyses of juvenile offense seriousness. Here we address the crucial issue of whether juvenile careers escalate in seriousness, and whether particular intervention points are predictive of adult crime.

Chapter 9 provides a summary of the salient findings that raise particular issues of relevance for the juvenile justice policy arena. With these findings as an empirical referent, we then provide in Chapter 10 a discussion of the contemporary policy context surrounding juvenile offenders generally, and an extensive discussion of the juvenile justice policy implications of our results in particular. Last, we offer a set of specific recommendations for specific policy initiatives concerning the treatment of delinquency in order to prevent or deter the continuation of the criminal career.

2

Theoretical and Policy Considerations

Public concern about juvenile justice and the apparently alarming rates of juvenile violence has reached a point of greater public policy significance than at any time in the last decade. Hardly a week goes by without the national media reporting on some violent episode involving juveniles somewhere across the country. Crime, especially juvenile crime, has not only captured the public's attention but has also preoccupied legislative bodies at all levels of government. The 103rd Congress passed the *Violent Crime Control and Law Enforcement Act of 1994* (P.L. 103-322) which ushered in sweeping changes in federal criminal law, including changes pertinent to juveniles.

Because crime is such a major public policy concern, and because elected officials are hurriedly attempting to develop laws and procedures to respond to the public's fear and anxiety, a war metaphor is often used to emphasize the significance of the reform ideas and policy recommendations. Many of these efforts reveal a concern about career offenders in general, or address specific aspects in the development of criminal careers. The popular "three strikes and you're out" sentencing policies, for example, make the accumulation of a prior record the principal determinant of society's response. The "get tough" stance of many juvenile code reforms, especially those which remove the confidentiality provisions of juvenile records, also show the extent to which career offending is being considered in crime control policies.

It is important that research on crime should inspire the development of sound theory and effective policy. Unfortunately, the current state of criminal justice policies reflects neither insight nor comprehensiveness. Don Gottfredson has suggested that "weak or poorly defined concepts steer major criminal justice policies" (1989: 1). Policy reforms also are criticized for constituting mere political posturing without reasonable forecasts for effectiveness. For example, the Congressional debate in 1994 to extend capital punishment to more than 50 relatively uncommon offenses is indicative of political displays taking precedence over substance and realistic opportunities for effective strategies. Moreover, Jacob has commented that the war rhetoric is exaggerated; the war is characterized more by skirmishes than by battles, and consists of much marching to and fro as officials seek to position their resources for optimal effect (1984: 59).

If society is ever to reduce the problem of crime, the phenomenon must first be better understood, and such understanding requires the accumulation and dissemination of findings from extensive research. The criminal career research agenda can assist in this effort. Thus, this chapter will discuss the plausible contributions to both theory building and offender processing that are likely to be obtained from criminal career research in general and, in particular, from this study.

Explanations for crime that have relevance for understanding aspects of criminal career development will be identified from within both the classical and positive schools of criminology. Further, the recent efforts at integrating perspectives to advance theory will also be reviewed. The chapter will conclude with a discussion of how information on offending over the life course can improve the effectiveness of criminal justice policy responses. It is important to focus strategic intervention during the juvenile stage in order to prevent adult crime altogether, or at least reduce the propensity for juveniles to continue their delinquency as adults.

Theoretical Considerations

Theories of crime and offending traditionally have adhered to strict boundaries within the classical and positive schools. Theories within the classical school assume that rationality influences behavior, and such theories often focus on the achievement of crime control through either deterrence or "just desert" measures. They further justify state action as achieving retributive functions. Alternatively, the positive school is based on the premise that persons offend not because of an expression of free will to engage in crime, but rather, because of one or more inducing, facilitating, or predisposing factors or elements within the individual's personality structure or socioenvironmental context. Within both the classical and positive schools, explanations have been advanced to understand overall criminal career development or clarify the existence of specific career dimensions.

Theorists within each perspective have generally hoped that their work would influence those in authority to improve society and thereby reduce criminal proclivities whatever their genesis. However, having a direct policy relevance has not been the sine qua non of most theories. Instead, the scientific merits of specific theories have been debated almost exclusively. Explanations for crime have been criticized for their omission of important factors, inadequate testing of theoretical tenets on restricted samples, and explanatory outcomes which represent a minor achievement no better than chance occurrences.

Fortunately, the need for theoretical development, including better conceptualization, more rigorous testing, and policy relevance, is now widely recognized. There are recent independent advances within the classical and positive traditions, as well as important theoretical explanations integrating components from each school of thought. To the extent that our theories are better able to explain crime in general, offending of certain types, or criminality during specific periods of life, criminology will be in a stronger position to offer society more definitive data with which to assist in crime control efforts.

The Classical Perspective

The classical school of thought fundamentally contends that people are rational creatures who are capable of reason and have freely motivated behavior. According to the classical school, individuals become involved with crime in order to pursue specific objectives, and offenders may consequently be held accountable for their behavior and the specific intent to violate the law contained therein. Through utilitarian assumptions of deterrence, Beccaria, Bentham, and the Enlightenment thinkers of the mid-18th century advocated reforms of jurisprudence and criminal law to reduce crime. They made no provision for differential culpability by age or sequence of offending. These omissions, together with advances in the scientific method, led to diminished popularity of the classical school by the mid-19th century.

Classical explanations for crime have recently experienced a resurgence. The theoretical contribution within the classical perspective offered by R. Clarke and Cornish (1985) shows the important role that research over the life course can have in helping to achieve a better understanding of why crime occurs. This theory of offender decision making embraces the sentiments of rationality and freely motivated behavior and, with acknowledgement of Matza's (1964) notion of "soft determinism," includes situational factors and developments from several disciplines to justify the rational decision-making synthesis.

The Clarke and Cornish framework offers a diagram of the criminal event and specifies three stages of offender involvement—initial involvement, continuation, and desistance. Clarke and Cornish further require that crime-specific models, such as those they provide for burglary in a middle-class suburb, be developed for each decision process because rational choices are likely to differ according to offense type. Their continuation model, therefore, is premised on the notion that a particular crime type is repeated, such as occurs in the criminal career with offense specialization. In this model, persons are allowed the simultaneous careers and sequential career stages that were identified in the definition of a criminal career provided in Chapter 1.

Likewise, rationality and choice are components of the life-style explanation for crime found in routine activity theory. According to this theory, crime occurs when suitable targets of crime are available, motivated offenders are present, and guardians capable of deflecting crime are absent (Cohen and Felson, 1979). Crime is considered both offense-specific and offender-specific (Phillip and Votey, 1987). Life-styles and situations tend to differ by age and career paths; therefore, crime involvement may vary accordingly. Older offenders, for example, may desist from crime when the risks finally exceed the potential gain (Shover, 1985).

Utilitarian assumptions of classical thought also prevail among economic explanations for crime. The attendant econometric equations of crime involvement include measures of risk assessment, expenditures, and potential gains (Becker, 1968; Ehrlich, 1973; Loftin and McDowell, 1981). These models have been offered as being relevant for understanding the "choices" surrounding the continuation of criminal careers.

Crime explanations rooted in rationality and choice influence punitive responses and strategies for crime prevention. Murray and Cox (1979), for example, have contended that punishment-oriented programs can be more effective in preventing future crime than interventions stressing treatment and rehabilitation. These theories and the corresponding policies aimed at holding offenders more accountable currently enjoy great popularity in American society. The relevance of the classical perspective to criminal career development is evident both in scholarly work and public perception.

For example, in his critique of juvenile justice reforms, Bernard (1992) points out that crime policies must distinguish offenders by age because most delinquents are best described as "naive risk-takers" who lack the ability of adults to understand the consequences of their actions. Wright, Logie, and Decker (1995) have reported experimental results indicating that active burglars demonstrate cognitive skills concerning memory retention different from nonoffenders. Such differential functioning appears to be directly related to their experiences in targeting sites for residential burglaries. Meanwhile, public concern surrounding crime responds to media images of diabolical, calculating, and hedonistic career offenders who are unable to restrain their criminal conduct.

Advocates of classical crime explanations are not without critics, however. For example, Stott and Wilson (1977) contend that addiction to a criminal life-style cannot be simply explained as the choice of a criminal way of life for economic reasons, because it is obvious, at least to the ordinary citizen, that the criminal acts against his own interests. Many such criticisms of a free will offender, one who is exercising a "rational choice," are espoused by advocates of deterministic explanations for crime, largely from the theorists aligned with the positive school.

The Positive Perspective

Among the myriad of theories within the positive school, a common feature is the application of the scientific method to the investigation of antecedent factors, which are hypothesized to propel persons in the direction of crime. Many disciplines have contributed to a deterministic theory of crime, but sociology has dominated such efforts and has targeted social structure and socialization processes as the primary sources of crime.

Social structure theories tend to explain crime either as the result of disorganization or competing values and interests within society. Following Durkheim's views, social disruption and the attendant structural disadvantages cause some persons in society to offend and violate even the laws in which they believe. Social disorganization as explained by Shaw and McKay (1942), anomie theories of crime from Merton (1938), more recently, Messner and Rosenfeld's (1994) depiction of the "American dream," and notions of an "urban underclass" (Jencks, 1992; Wilson, 1987), follow this tradition.

These theories are important to patterns of career offending because the effects of strain may differ in their saliency depending on other influences and particular stage of life. For example, several theorists identify adolescence as the most vulnerable time of life. Cloward and Ohlin (1960) elaborate that delinquency is not only the result of blocked access to legitimate means to achieve shared objectives, but may also be due to differential access to illegitimate means to evade the strain. Cohen (1955) sees a subcultural reaction among youths to their strain, manifested in "negativistic, malicious, and nonutilitarian" behaviors. Miller (1958) argues that the focal concerns of lower-class boys create an autonomous subculture.

Other theoretical explanations contend that within heterogeneous societies, especially one as ethnically diverse as the United States, conflict between values (Sellin, 1938; Wolfgang and Ferracuti, 1967) or interests (Chambliss and Seidman, 1971; Quinney, 1970; Vold, 1958) account for most crime. Gibbons (1975) suggests that criminal careers evolve due to risk taking in response to value conflict. Culture conflict and a variety of subcultural explanations have been used to investigate whether different norms of behavior exist for criminal career offenders (Gibbons, 1975; Glaser, 1979; Robins, 1966; Shaw, 1930; Shaw and McKay, 1942; Thrasher, 1927). Most often, the variety of theoretical perspectives has led to contradictory conclusions rather than to a widespread consensus.

Shaw (1930), Shaw and McKay (1942) and Thrasher (1927) interpreted life histories of offenders which conveyed the impression that it is normal for a slum boy to become delinquent. Their thesis was that delinquent subcultures are shared and transmitted by almost all slum youths and are nurtured by the visibility of much adult professional crime which operates more openly there than in better residential areas. Elsewhere, Robins minimizes the social structure explanation, reporting that: "low social status, in short, is neither a predictor of sociopathy in its own right, nor the mechanism by which sociopathic fathers produce sociopathy in their children" (1966: 184).

Theories of social development identify differential associations, societal reaction, or inadequate control as responsible for crime. Sutherland's theory that crime is learned from differential associations that vary in frequency, intensity, duration and priority has important potential for understanding different stages and potential paths of criminal career development. Unfortunately, his concepts of social learning and differential associations are difficult to operationalize, and the theory seems to defy appropriate testing. The research generally reduces the nine propositions of Sutherland's theory to a limited measure of peer influence.

With regard to crime and life stages, the argument has been advanced that peer group associations might be responsible for criminal careers (Glaser, 1978: 126–127), may assist in explaining onset, frequency, and persistence (Smith, Visher, and Jarjoura, 1991), and might also promote offense specialization (Klein, 1979). The relationship between delinquents and their peers also has been refuted as a cause of crime (Stott and Wilson, 1977; West, 1969). Stott and Wilson argue in favor of a psychological explanation based on personal instability of the offender. Other variations of differential association theory, including differential anticipation (Glaser, 1978: 126–127; 1979: 217–218), situational factors (Clarke, 1980; Clarke and Mayhew, 1980; Gibbons, 1975), and integration with the opportunity structure (Klein, 1979); social learning (Sinclair and Clarke, 1982), and social control theory (Glaser, 1979) also have been proposed as explanations for career progression and the development of unique career patterns.

The theory of symbolic interaction, as it is conceptualized in criminology by the labeling perspective, also has been used as a plausible frame for understanding the development of criminal careers based on reciprocal action between individuals and the net of criminal justice (Blumstein et al., 1982; Chaiken and Chaiken, 1982a; Cicourel, 1968; Cline, 1980; Emerson, 1969; Empey and Rabow, 1961; Farrington, Osborn, and West, 1978; Frazier, Bock, and Henretta, 1980; Gibbons, 1975; Klein, 1984; Myerhoff and Myerhoff, 1964; Petersilia, 1980; Polk et al., 1981). The relevant assumption underlying the explanation of societal reaction is that a delinquent identity is reinforced due to official labeling, and variation is explainable by the nature of the intervention. An increase in the intensity of the label, for example, should correspond with a decrease in the probability of desistance.

Gibbons has summarized the application of the labeling perspective to dynamics of criminal careers as follows:

> They [labeling theorists] assert the importance of societal reactions, turning points, career contingencies, and the like, arguing that individual careers in deviance do not usually follow some kind of straight line progression of behavioral deviation. Instead, variability rather than regularity may be most characteristic of offenders; lawbreakers engage in flirtations with criminality; individuals get drawn into misconduct for a variety of reasons and many of them manage to withdraw from deviance. (1975: 152–153)

As we have identified, within the classical and positive schools of thought several theories have been touted as capable of distinguishing career offenders or specific patterns of offending. Moreover, other explanations exist in addition to the theories we have discussed. Many of these theories frequently are tested in competition with each other, but the outcomes have not been major improvements in our understanding of crime. Some theories suffer more than others, of course, but each has been judged as somehow incapable of providing an all-encompassing explanation for crime.

Fortunately, progress in conceptual development and measurement has helped our theories to become more robust. And, the disappointments resulting from the pursuit of a general theory of crime have helped scholars and policy-makers alike to appreciate better the smaller advances made, including assessments of the most worthy components of each theory. Even with these achievements, however, our ability to prevent crime or intervene effectively is not successful.

Integration Efforts

Largely due to the disillusionment with past theoretical achievements, the need for more specific and better explanations for crime recently has spawned renewed interest in theory building. In addition, the traditional boundaries between classical and positive explanations now seem more permeable. The result is that most current theoretical developments are integrated efforts. The potential for understanding criminal behavior improves with multifactor theories united with elements for understanding offender decision making. It is important that the explanations also be concise. Powerful and succinct theories are likely to target unique life stages or types of crime. Reliable descriptions of criminal career patterns, therefore, offer a foundation for such integrated theoretical speculation.

Of course, there is a strong tradition of multifactor approaches to understanding criminal careers. In their early research, for example, the Gluecks (1950; 1964) and Healy and Bronner (1926; 1936) tabulated the traits of offenders and nonoffenders across several years and accepted statistically significant bivariate differences as evidence of crime causation. In addition, typologies of criminal behavior, such as those developed by Clinard and Quinney (1967), Cloward and Ohlin (1960), Frum (1958), Gibbons (1975), Gottfredson (1975), and Reckless (1961) are the result of explanations for crime that acknowledge many individual determinants. According to Taylor, Walton, and Young (1973), typologies may be the best available models because the criminal career phenomenon defies parsimonious theory. They state:

> [T]he notion of identifiable careers in criminality may be an hypothesis about behavior which is too clinical. . . . Instead, it may be that many lawbreakers exhibit relatively unique combinations of criminal conduct and attitudinal patterns, or at least we may only be able to group them with considerable difficulty into some very general categories or types (1973: 150–166).

Recent efforts to advance theory provide detailed explanations about how important concepts interact and result in crime. This focus on conceptual development is an important sign of progress beyond earlier work, which labored to catalog statistically significant associations among criteria and impute causation. Contemporary theorists benefit from the results of the cumulative work and from methodological and computational advancements. The improved quality of new work also reflects general progress within criminology in understanding that theory and research must intermingle.

Hirschi (1985), for example, argues that his theory of social control can be reconciled with rational choice. He contends that control and choice theories merely differ in their respective targets. The objective of social control is to explain *involvement*—or criminality. Rational choice, as presented by Clarke and Cornish (1985), is concerned with specific *events*—or crime. Hirschi uses the lack of specialization reported by the Rand Corporation Habitual Offenders Program to illustrate the difference he sees between criminality and crime, and thus the divergence between social control and rational choice. This crime versus criminality argument also is addressed elsewhere (Gottfredson and Hirschi, 1986; 1987), but without specific attention to the compatibility of the two theories. Hirschi contends that careers in crime not only occur infrequently, but that the very notion of such a career defies the concept of criminality.

This effort by Hirschi is important for two reasons. First, if the argument holds that crime and criminality are constant, then the concept of a criminal career can be more likely set aside. Second, the conceptualization argument is noteworthy because it provides a vehicle for overcoming the exclusive boundaries between positive and classical explanations for crime. Social control is a popular theory within the positive school, and rational choice typifies the growing acceptance during this decade of the resurgence of classical thought. Therefore, if successful, Hirschi could provide a connection between the positive and classical schools of thought, which have traditionally appeared mutually exclusive. Moreover, Hirschi is not alone in investigating a plausible bridge between social control and rational choice theories. Felson (1986) also examines this relationship in an effort to integrate social control, routine activity, and rational choice theories.

Other recent efforts to understand crime through insightful integrative theories tend to remain within the positive school of thought. Weis and his associates (Weis and Hawkins, 1981; Weis and Sedenstrom, 1981) have proposed "social development theory," which integrates features of the social control and social structure theories in order to account for the processes of poor socialization and alienation, while also accounting for structural disadvantage arising from the community context. Similarly, Elliott and colleagues (see, for example, Elliott, Ageton, and Canter, 1979; Elliott, Huizinga, and Ageton, 1985) draw upon aspects of strain, social learning, and control theories to explain how strain, weak socialization, and living in socially disadvantaged areas lead to weak social bonds with conventional society. Such factors combine instead to foster bonding with delinquent peers. In his conception of shame and reintegration, Braithwaite (1989) combines elements of social control, labeling, and social structure theories to shape his explanation for individual criminality and societies in which it is more likely. Messner and Rosenfeld (1994) provide a macrolevel theory linking "anomic cultural orientations" with institutional structures.

Several recent efforts have recognized the need to explain delinquency and crime in a life-course perspective. For example, Hagan and Palloni (1988) adopt elements of social control and conflict of interests in their conceptualization of power-control theory. They recognize the important influence of unique life stages; as Hagan clearly reports, "Delinquency and criminal events are linked into life trajectories of broader significance, whether those trajectories are criminal or noncriminal in form" (1989: 200).

Similarly, Thornberry and colleagues (see, Thornberry, 1987; Thornberry, Lizotte, Krohn, Farnworth, Jang, 1991) have used a longitudinal research study to develop "interactional theory." Interactional theory blends features of the social control and social structure approaches, but more important, this theory also holds that delinquent youths are proactive. Their belief systems lead them to seek out others who share their beliefs and can reinforce a commitment to deviant conduct. Further, interactional theory recognizes that criminality is developmental, and as children mature, the causal process changes.

Another recent contribution helps identify not only the importance of integration, but also the necessity of applying theory to criminal careers. In developing their theory, Sampson and Laub (1993: 6–7) chastise criminology for its focus on the teenage years to the exclusion of other stages of life. Specifically, their criticism is that criminology has failed to understand the theoretical significance of childhood characteristics in general, as well as the connection between early childhood and adult experiences. In addition, they contend that criminologists have failed to consider the link between social structure and the mediating processes of informal social control.

Sampson and Laub argue the importance of understanding these connections at every phase of life. They use the Gluecks' longitudinal data to develop their theory that structural disadvantage; weakened informal social bonds to family, school, and work; and the disruption of social relations between individuals and institutions that provide social capital, are the causes of most crime.

While the future for criminology and our capability to understand crime and criminality remain unknown, if attempts to integrate deterministic and free will perspectives continue, it is evident that crime over the life course should constitute a major research interest.

Policy Considerations

In our society we tend to believe that social problems can be overcome with adequate information and proper action. The extant views on the genesis of offensive conduct and the policies that have been adopted to respond to crime reflect this belief. To accomplish the objectives of crime control, policy makers want information on the causes of crime and concrete solutions that are both practical and that will yield immediate results. Science, however, tends to be self-critical and more concerned with the process of getting results than with either the policy relevance of the results or the speed with which such results are produced. As a consequence, the policy arena often cannot wait for science to provide adequate answers or for scientists to reach consensus on which answers are best.

It is becoming clear that legislators and policy makers are adopting the idea that the crime problem—both in the genesis of the phenomenon and in the search for effective societal responses—is so complex and so elusive that it overwhelms social science's current capability for explanation and solutions. In addition, an escalating fear of crime has led the public, and thereby elected officials, to develop a "quick fix" mentality for crime control. Consequently, criminology and related disciplines are now at risk of playing a diminished role in informing the crime control debate.

Thus, it is critical, now more than ever, that criminologists conduct research and direct the results of their investigations to the important function of informing the debate over crime control measures, especially strategies for responding to the escalating problem of serious juvenile crime. Clearly, the recently accumulating findings with respect to the continuity between delinquent and adult criminal careers represent a significant opportunity for criminology to showcase its expertise in affecting policy initiatives.

Research-based knowledge about career offending patterns during various stages of the life cycle, and the differential risk factors that position some delinquents more than others for higher probabilities of moving on to adult crime, can inform criminal justice policy in a number of arenas. Research can be relevant to police investigation techniques, prosecutorial decisions, pretrial detention choices, the sentencing process, and particular correctional treatment approaches.

The dissemination of research findings can also help to alleviate a growing public panic, however misplaced, that we are in the midst of a crime wave that defies solution. Research can help to clarify the goals of intervention, such as crime prevention, deterrence, punishment, and public safety, by demonstrating the appropriateness and potential effectiveness of such measures depending on type of offender, life stage, rank order of the offense, and so on.

Clearly, information about career development can improve the effectiveness of both juvenile justice and criminal justice responses, but the juvenile justice venue appears to be of greatest relevance. Knowledge regarding the dynamics of the delinquency career could affect the procedures for apprehension, court referral or diversion, detention, and disposition of juvenile cases. More broadly, such knowledge could also influence the future philosophy of juvenile justice. For example, information about the parameters of juvenile careers would improve policies establishing the age of juvenile court jurisdiction and the criteria by which certification, transfer, or waiver to criminal court are made. Likewise, information about the differential transition of juveniles to adult crime could, and should, affect the use of juvenile records, targeted prosecution programs, and enhanced sentencing policies for such juveniles, whether they are tried as adults or face enhanced options in juvenile court.

The Juvenile Justice Policy Arena

Juvenile justice currently is the subject of considerable legislative debate because of public perception that it is too lenient and ineffective in its treatment of juvenile offenders. The widespread belief, especially among the public, is that, regardless of their particular recidivism status or the severity of their offenses, juveniles are all treated in a similar manner—a manner all too lenient, given the perceived severity of the delinquency problem. Juvenile crime has increased in recent years and it has become more lethal, while at the same time many "at risk" adolescent populations have decreased in number. One plausible explanation for this situation is that a small number of offenders is responsible for an enormous amount of the crime, and society has not responded effectively to these chronic juvenile offenders.

The public's concern over ineffectiveness is logical if not deserved, given that juvenile justice issues rank lowest in prestige and fall among the least desirable type of work for most police officers, attorneys, and judges (Bernard, 1992). Much of this criticism is unwarranted, but because of the provisions for confidentiality of juvenile proceedings and the records of juvenile courts, the system's response to juvenile crime and juvenile criminal matters are not effectively communicated to the community thereby enhancing the illusion that "nothing works."

The informal nature of juvenile proceedings, the operation of wide discretion, the absence of review mechanisms, and the opportunities for abuse in juvenile justice are unparalleled anywhere else in the legal system. These characteristics of juvenile justice make it an easy candidate for improvement through better training, more explicit policy directives, and incentives for career specialization among juvenile justice personnel. The process of training and policy development can be better informed by research describing patterns of offending across life stages. As the important role of juvenile justice in overall crime control becomes recognized and more fully appreciated, juvenile justice jobs and other attributes of the system will achieve greater primacy and enhanced respect.

Police encounters with juveniles have been the subject of several observational and survey studies, and the concluding theme is one of broad discretion (Black and Reiss, 1970; Lundman, 1974; Piliavin and Briar, 1964; Smith and Visher, 1981). Many sources also tell us that in addition to lower prestige and fewer opportunities for advancement associated with the work, inadequate training in how to interact with juveniles, and more important, the pursuit of juvenile justice as opposed to criminal justice objectives is a common problem (Brown, 1981; Kenney, Pate and Hamilton, 1990; Walker, 1983).

Juvenile units within police agencies tend to concentrate on intelligence gathering, to the exclusion of investigation of juvenile cases. Many special units emphasize gangs, but rather than reduce crime, this attention may have resulted in according gangs greater prestige, power, and influence within the community. There also is little consensus among officers on the appropriate procedures for handling juvenile cases, and there are seldom explicitly written policies on the subject within police departments. In many jurisdictions the lack of standards for policing results in encounters with adolescents that escalate beyond what is necessary, as well as more frequent court referral of minority youths than white youths involved in similar behaviors (Morash, 1984).

Suggestions to improve police work with juveniles typically involve the issue of structured discretion (Davis, 1975; American Bar Association, 1977; Kenney et al., 1990) or multicultural awareness training (Kempf-Leonard, Pope, and Feyerherm, 1995). While these are worthwhile suggestions, there are many ways in which knowledge about juvenile careers could improve police performance. For example, police departments could adopt as policy a differential response style of policing (Klein, 1975; Klein, Tielman, Styles, Lincoln, and Lubin-Rosenzweig, 1976). The policy could specify appropriate interventions depending on criteria associated with certain career paths. These at-risk factors might distinguish youths according to age-at-onset, likelihood of chronic offending, escalation from status offenses to minor and serious law violations, or types of crime in which specialization is more common.

Further, intensive police academy training about these juvenile career patterns could enable community policing patrols to be more effective at mediating situations involving youth. The intelligence and crime control efforts of special juvenile units could focus on identification of the potentially serious and chronic offenders. More intensive intervention and resources could be directed to the youths who are most at risk of subsequent serious or repetitive offending. Their apprehension and containment, and the prevention of future chronic offenders, would result in significant reduction of crime.

If police work with juveniles becomes better able to distinguish between those youths in need of early juvenile justice intervention and those who are less amenable to treatment opportunities in juvenile justice, and who consequently should be held more accountable in criminal justice, then similar advances could be made in juvenile courts. Traits associated with onset, desistance, and persistent careers could help clarify which youths are more likely to benefit from juvenile court assistance, when, and how. The development of crime specializations or escalating severity might be prevented more often. Knowing the dynamics of juvenile careers also could influence juvenile court dispositions and modes of treatment. A range of alternatives should be available and juvenile justice should expend more resources on those youths most in need, or upon those at greatest risk of additional problems.

Knowledge about features of juvenile careers could help to draw appropriate boundaries for juvenile court jurisdiction. Effective intervention for some youths involved in certain career paths may require extending the age of juvenile court jurisdiction for purposes of treatment and supervision. Other career patterns could help clarify when youths cannot be helped by juvenile court and should be held more accountable for their behavior through certification to criminal court. To assure public safety, for example, violent chronic offenders who have not benefited from their juvenile justice treatment and who are likely to continue their offending for many years, may be suitable targets for imprisonment via mandatory sentencing in criminal justice. In these situations, criminal court access to juvenile records for sentencing would be necessary. Given the potential gravity of the outcome, it is important that sound criteria guide these decisions.

Other changes in juvenile justice that appear to "criminalize" the delinquent might be reconsidered or implemented more selectively and narrowly in view of evidence from criminal career research. Prehearing detention, for example, is one stage of juvenile justice which could benefit from the information. Despite a nationwide movement to reduce rates of detention, the use of detention has actually escalated, particularly for minority youths (OJJDP, 1993; Snyder, 1990). One reason for this may be that, in its 1984 *Schall v. Martin* decision, the Supreme Court conceded that preventive detention based on a potential threat to public safety is an appropriate objective of prehearing detention; whereas, only the best interests of the youth have traditionally guided this decision. The prediction of which youths are at risk of preadjudicatory crime remains a subjective and discretionary decision. Research might provide better information on which to base this type of judgment. Moreover, detention often is identified as the best predictor of adjudication and more restrictive dispositions, so there should be concerns for how these decisions are made.

As some juvenile courts take on a punishment orientation, concern has increased over the due process rights of juveniles. This has led to more formalized roles for attorneys and more of an adversarial proceeding. Prosecutors now tend to screen juvenile cases for legal sufficiency and probable cause, rather than rely solely on the needs and best interests of the child. Both the American Bar Association and the National District Attorney's Association advocate even more influence by attorneys in a trial setting for youths and throughout juvenile justice (American Bar Association, 1977; Shine and Price, 1992). The quality of representation and the stage at which legal counsel is acquired are important issues in juvenile justice because youths with counsel tend to receive harsher outcomes (Feld, 1988). The ability of some youths to understand the consequences of waiving their right to counsel or providing counsel with direction on how best to proceed also are questioned (Feld, 1988; Guggenheim, 1984).

The growing prominence of attorneys and the formal juvenile court processing of more cases means heavier caseloads, more protracted proceedings, and greater use of restrictive placements. Rather than continue to expand the net and dilute the entire system, it may be that only a minority of the more serious cases warrant the additional efforts. Youthful offender statutes, which dictate more restrictive facilities and intensive treatment for serious older adolescents and young adults with juvenile records, typify this modification. Information on juvenile careers could be used to target those cases more effectively.

The Criminal Justice Policy Arena

Criminal career development, beginning with delinquency and including the progression to adult crime, engenders a need for decision makers to consider the total career when designing and implementing criminal justice policy. However, differences in court organizational structures, record keeping, and general philosophy, traditionally have precluded criminal court access to juvenile records. Boland and Wilson (1978) and Langan and Farrington (1983) have argued that current systems which separate juvenile and adult procedures, what has come to be called a "two-track system of justice," are unfair. Recent policy changes in some states and in the federal system do make access to the total criminal career somewhat more likely now. For example, federal regulations were recently changed to allow the FBI to accept juvenile court records regarding all "serious and/or significant" offenses (Criminal Law Reporter, 1992). Of course, the informality of juvenile records in many states, particularly in rural jurisdictions, leaves them woefully ill-equipped to provide the information, and the program is voluntary, so total coverage is not assured.

Others argue that it is unwise to adopt uniformity in criminal justice policies. Feld (1988, 1992) has concerns that procedural parity between cases involving juveniles and adults can never be achieved without making special provisions for youths. Cline contends, "the capacity to respond fairly and appropriately to individuals at different points in their lives should remain an important component of the criminal justice system" (1980: 670). Bernard (1992: 154–182) reinforces this view with his outline of sequential juvenile justice consequences distinct from criminal justice. In addition, Fagan, Forst, and Vivona (1987) report that prior records accumulate differently based on race. Further, concerns of racial bias have prompted a federal mandate to examine differential treatment throughout the juvenile justice system (Juvenile Justice and Delinquency Prevention Act of 1974, as amended [Public Law 93-415, Section 223 [a][23]]).

As the issues of separate systems for juveniles and uniformity in criminal records continue to be debated and as policies change based on sentiment more often than research-based knowledge, many opportunities exist for criminal career research. Evidence of differential criminal career patterns could show the extent to which criminal justice administrators might benefit from access to official records covering the life span, as well as identify specific juvenile careers for which the shared information would be most important. It could also underscore the value of differential treatment based on age, such as providing youth discounts at sentencing for some situations or maintaining private records when offending patterns indicate desistance.

Amidst growing concern for enhanced equity through uniform, and sometimes mandatory sentencing models, evidence of criminal career patterns might enable the criminal justice system and individual branches of it to develop more effective intervention programs targeted at offenders in one or more career patterns. Periodic efforts concentrated on criminal careers, or "crackdowns," could be developed and used to thwart crime. In addition, offenders could be routinely handled differently in accord with a priority scheme designed to focus on certain crimes or offenders considered most dangerous to society. One example of this is the development of special "career criminal" prosecution units whose task it is to concentrate on the identification and successful conviction of career criminals (Petersilia, 1980).

Similarly focused strategies could also be justifiable for law enforcement (Blumstein et al. 1986; Boland and Wilson, 1978) and correctional administrators. For example, Gibbons (1975: 151) concluded that crime typologies offered some encouragement for the development of differential treatment programs centered around diagnostic types. The imposition of harsher treatment for those persons who persist in crime throughout their lives might reflect their inability to learn from prior lessons provided by the criminal justice system. Others might exhibit patterns of changing behavior, such as "cafeteria style" offending, or offending between long crime-free intervals. Or perhaps differential treatment is needed for offenders in some criminal careers who might encounter the certainty and severity elements, among others, of deterrence in a manner apart from other offenders. Thus, identification of unique career patterns may provide support for individualized treatment for offenders with different criminal careers or at different stages in their careers.

It has been more than a decade since Petersilia advised us that, "a better understanding of the characteristics of the criminal career should enable criminal justice policies to be designed to intervene in the career at an effective point, whether for crime control or rehabilitative purposes" (1980: 322). In the interim, public fear of crime has escalated and confidence in the criminal justice system has declined. Rehabilitative objectives have been replaced by interest in punishment and just deserts. Judicial authority has been reduced through mandatory and presumptive sentencing and automatic certification policies. Prosecutors and legislators have gained power as a result of these changes, and populations under correctional supervision have skyrocketed. Administrators have been too busy building facilities, providing supervision, fund-raising, and generally trying to cope with the huge number of offenders to reflect on the objectives of policies or how research might help them.

Criminal career research has not fared much better. Most efforts have been merely descriptive. Emphasis has been on disseminating findings on chronic offending, without attendant recommendations for policy. Given this, it is little wonder that public support for "three-strikes and you're out" and other mandatory confinement policies became so strong. When policy ideas have accompanied the research, preventive detention, or selective incapacitation, have been the most popular.

Evaluations of the implications of adopting such a policy have revealed the low levels of predictive accuracy currently achieved by the incapacitation models and the corresponding ethical dilemma posed by the error in detention of future nonoffenders (Blumstein, Cohen, and Nagin, 1978; Blumstein and Cohen, 1979; Chaiken and Rolph, 1978; Ehrlich, 1973; Forst, 1983; Gottfredson and Gottfredson, 1985; Greenberg, 1975; Greenwood with Abrahamse, 1982; McCord, 1981; Shinnar and Shinnar, 1975).

Of course, the development of selective incapacitation models has concentrated on general recidivism, and if attention were directed at a more precise offender subgroup, such as those exhibiting unique career patterns, an improved level of predictive accuracy might be attainable. But, the very fact that extralegal criteria are now necessary in order to distinguish future offenders from nonoffenders makes this idea at odds with provisions in the Bill of Rights for equity and justice, and currently is not a viable policy reform.

Clearly, studies of criminal career development can and should do better. Criminal justice policies need to be rejuvenated with creative and ethical ideas. Public demand for increased safety requires that criminal justice interventions become more effective. They also must become more efficient as resources are more constrained. Information on different patterns of offending, and changes that occur between adolescence and young adulthood, should provide a sound foundation on which policy debate can become better informed.

3

Review of Related Research

In the previous two chapters we demonstrated that research on criminal careers, despite some unfavorable criticism, has been a viable part of the research enterprise of criminology since the early days of the Chicago School and it has continued until the present. We also showed how longitudinal approaches to the study of delinquent and criminal careers, in which subjects are followed over a substantial portion of the life course, have come to dominate the criminal career agenda. Moreover, we have also demonstrated that there are significant issues concerning theory development and criminal justice policy formulation that attend research on criminal careers. In particular, we have argued that one of the most significant areas of inquiry concerns the life course perspective, in which interest centers on the transition from the status of youth to that of adult, and the accompanying transition from the venue of delinquent behaviors to that of adult criminality.

Another valuable way to view this transition from delinquency to crime along a continuum of illegal conduct has been termed "developmental criminology" by Loeber and Le Blanc (1990). They write:

> There are several reasons why the study of the continuity of antisocial behavior is useful. First, such studies elucidate the degree of individuals' continuity in antisocial acts and demonstrate that continuity is much higher for some individuals than for others. Second, such studies help to establish the extent to which continuity between conduct problems and offending reflects the continuity of a more general deviance. Third, such studies may aid in the identification of early markers that distinguish between those whose deviance is more persistent and those whose deviance is occasional and temporary. (1990: 384)

We would necessarily adopt the position that investigating the concept of continuity, and by association, discontinuity in offending, offered by Loeber and Le Blanc would be highly desirable within any particular segment of an offender's career (i.e., either juvenile or adult). This continuity takes on even more crucial significance when it is measured *across* these two time segments, as various transitions are affected and perhaps even reinforced. That is, some delinquents desist and never commit an adult crime; these delinquents mature, they burn out, etc. Other delinquents continue their illegal conduct as adults. Still other persons who were never processed as delinquents begin their violations of the law only as adults. Last, most persons never commit illegal acts, either as juveniles or as adults. We argue here that investigating these various transitions is crucial to both theory and policy.

It would thus be expected, given the central importance of the delinquency-to-crime transition, in both its developmental and legal contexts, that there would be a plethora of studies that have investigated this transition. One would expect that by now they would have provided volumes of important data on the likelihood that delinquents will continue their careers into adulthood. More important, it would also be expected that such research would have analyzed the specific aspects of a youth's delinquent history that are associated with a greater likelihood of continuing illegal conduct into adult life. However, these expectations have not been fulfilled. The delinquency-to-crime transition has not been investigated to the extent that its importance would suggest. In fact, there have been comparatively few studies on this topic. Wolfgang has recently noted that, "The transition from juvenile delinquency to adult crime is one of the least researched territories in criminology" (1995: 141).

As a consequence of this lack of investigation, the literature reviewed in this chapter has necessarily included studies bearing directly on the continuation of criminal careers, especially the longitudinal studies, but it also includes other research which has addressed goals other than that of the criminal career. For example, we have included etiological investigations, prediction studies, and evaluations of segments of the criminal justice process (especially offender treatment programs), because these particular studies have also addressed issues which are critical to the present endeavor.

The principal tasks are to identify youths who are most apt to commit crimes as adults, and the differentiation of the factors affecting their continuity between delinquency status and adult status. To accomplish these goals and the complementary task of predicting which youths will become adult offenders, categories of youths based on criteria pertaining to the criminal career must be selected. The literature identifies five relevant categories, which fit into the following typology of youths:

1. Persistent (and especially chronic) delinquents
2. Confirmed nondelinquents
3. Career of diminishing delinquency

4. Delinquents who commit offenses of certain types, or who may even specialize in certain forms of delinquent conduct
5. Delinquents who achieve a certain level of severity in delinquent conduct

After a brief overview of the major career continuity studies that have arisen from criminal career/career criminal investigations, this chapter will proceed, in accord with the classification frame identified herein, with discussion of the important empirical findings from earlier research.

Career Continuity Research

In 1926, Healy, a physician, together with his wife, Augusta Bronner, a psychologist, were among the first to examine criminal career patterns. The goal of their research was to develop better methods of treatment for juvenile delinquency in an effort to prevent adult crime. The subjects in their studies were obtained through referral from juvenile court to the Judge Baker Guidance Centers in Chicago and Boston. The Judge Baker Guidance Centers were designed to function as a resource to the first juvenile courts. Drs. Healy and Bronner, who helped direct the facilities, were thus able to pursue their longitudinal interests in crime. Their etiological investigations emphasized the role of the family and included the study of numerous pairs of delinquent and nondelinquent siblings. The evaluations Healy and Bronner made of the effectiveness of the court and correctional process, based on the subsequent careers of people who experienced it in Chicago and Boston between 1909 and 1923, was foremost among the research on this issue.

The results of their investigations provided prevalence measures for continuity in criminal careers. Among 400 males from the Boston Juvenile Court who were followed until age 25, 21% were subsequently convicted for nonminor offenses and 6% were committed to a penal institution. Among the Chicago court sample of 420 males, 50% were convicted as adults and 37% were sentenced to a penal institution (Healy and Bronner, 1926).

In their investigations of the etiology of crime, Sheldon and Eleanor Glueck became well known for their perspective on life stage development. Data used in their studies included information from many sources on subjects from as young as age 5 through adolescence and into adulthood. Their initial research sample included 1,000 boys adjudicated as delinquents who were followed into adulthood. This sample of

1,000, or subsamples taken from it, served as the basis for many of the investigations made by Glueck and Glueck. The second sample from which important findings were made was a group of 510 adjudicated delinquents released from a Massachusetts reformatory between 1917 and 1918 with a matched control group of 500 nondelinquents. At the time of selection, two-thirds of the second sample was less than 20 years old. The careers of the offender subjects were traced through three 5-year follow-up periods, concluding 20 years after their release from the reformatory.

The Gluecks found that, among the 1,000 males who had appeared in Boston Juvenile Court between 1917 and 1922 and who had been referred to the Judge Baker Guidance Center, 66% were arrested for felonies or misdemeanors and 34% had been committed to a jail or prison up to the age of 24 (Glueck and Glueck, 1940).

Shaw's (1947; as cited in Langan and Farrington, 1983) later work on the progression of delinquent careers involved two follow-up studies of youths who had appeared in Chicago Juvenile Court. In one study, Shaw followed to age 41 a sample of 1,178 males who had appeared in juvenile court in 1920. He found that as adults 60% had been arrested, 43% had been convicted, and 22% had been committed to jail or prison for felonies or misdemeanors. In another follow-up, Shaw looked at 1,336 males who had appeared in juvenile court in 1930. He similarly discovered that up to age 31, 66% had been arrested, 52% had been convicted, and 36% had been committed to jail or prison.

Robins and O'Neal (1958) and Robins (1966) retrospectively studied child guidance clinic patients at the St. Louis Municipal Psychiatric Clinic who were treated between 1924 and 1929 and 100 nonpatient public school children matched by age, sex, race, I.Q., and neighborhood residence. A 30-year follow-up, through police records and interviews of 82% of the subjects, was conducted. The goal of this longitudinal study was to describe the life histories of persons afflicted with various psychological disorders.

Robins and O'Neal have reported that, among 176 males and females who had appeared in St. Louis Juvenile Court and who had been referred to the St. Louis Psychiatric Clinic, 60% had been arrested for nontraffic offenses (23% multiple times) and 17% had been committed to prison up to the age of 43.

Robins (1966) also found that 75% of the male juveniles who had been referred to the clinic for antisocial behavior later suffered at least one arrest between the ages of 31 and 43, and 49% of this group had at least three arrests as adults. This relationship was even more pronounced among those subjects who had been officially labeled as delinquent by the court prior to their referral to the St. Louis Municipal Psychiatric Clinic. Robins (1966) also identified persistent criminal careers by finding arrest records both between age 18 and 20 and from 30 to 43 for 133 males among her follow-up sample of 419 former patients and matched controls. Robins concluded that childhood behavior disturbance was a forerunner of a general social inadequacy in adulthood (1966: 112).

In an effort to evaluate the effectiveness of a delinquency prevention program designed in 1935 by Richard C. Cabot and subsequently implemented in 1939, the Cambridge-Somerville Youth Study (Powers and Witmer, 1951), McCord and McCord (1959) and McCord (1978, 1979) obtained 10-year and 30-year follow-up data on the 253 study pairs (out of the original 325 pairs) involved in the Massachusetts program when it concluded in 1945. Boys had been randomly assigned to the treatment program from a pool of both "difficult" and average youth recommended by school, welfare, church, and police officials. Subjects in the treatment group and members of their families were each given physical examinations and interviewed by social workers who then assigned them delinquency prediction scores. The treatment program included bi-weekly home visitation by family counselors, academic tutoring, medical and psychiatric attention, exposure to Boy Scouts, the YMCA, and other community programs; in addition, one-fourth of the boys in the experimental group were sent to summer camps. The matched control group of difficult and average referrals was asked only to provide information about themselves.

The 506 men were traced in 1975 and 1976 through court, mental hospital, and alcohol treatment center records. The vital statistics of Massachusetts, city directories, motor vehicle registrations, and marriage and death certificates were also used. Four hundred thirty-two men were located. Questionnaires were mailed to 410 subjects and 235 responses were received. Court conviction records from the states in which the men resided were used to assess criminal behavior. McCord found that 46% of the men who had a juvenile record went on to an adult arrest as compared to 18% of the men who had not been delinquent.

Two data collection efforts in Wayne County, Michigan, facilitated a prediction study by Dunham and Knauer (1954) and the subsequent criminal career investigation by Chaitin and Dunham (1966). The first procedure involved the random selection of 100 juvenile court cases which involved males between the ages of 10 and 17 who had been adjudicated as delinquent for the first time during the first year of each 5-year period between 1920 and 1940 (i.e., 1920, 1925, 1930, 1935, 1940). This information was used to predict the percentage of the total number

of boys who pass through the juvenile court and who would later become adult criminals. Dunham and Knauer (1954) reported that 31% of
the combined samples had experienced an adult arrest for a nonminor
offense up to the age of 21.

The second effort to gather information was a duplication of the
first method, with samples of 100 youthful offenders drawn from 1941,
1944, 1946, 1948, 1950, and 1952. These subsequent data were used to
evaluate the predictions made in the original study. For this second
study, Chaitin and Dunham (1966) have reported that 40% of the combined samples experienced an adult arrest up to age 21 for a nonminor
offense.

Stott and Wilson (1977) joined two independent samples of subjects
from previous studies of delinquency in Glasgow, Scotland, and a new
culturally matched control group for their follow-up study of crime
from youth into adulthood. The original samples included 414 boys who
had been placed on probation for the first time in Glasgow during 1957,
and 292 boys and 20 girls who had been found guilty of an offense in
Glasgow between January and May, 1959. Twenty-six of the subjects
from the original studies were excluded from the follow-up study for
various reasons. Information on offending through December 31, 1968,
was obtained from the Scottish Criminal Records Office for the 700 former delinquents, including 19 females, and 615 control subjects. The
control group was matched according to information obtained from
records held by the Registrar of Births, Marriages and Deaths for age
and childhood neighborhood location. Information to age 24 was obtained for these persons.

The purpose of the investigation was to determine whether personal instability, identified as behavior disturbance, could account for
the continuation of criminality from adolescence into adulthood. Stott
and Wilson's follow-up study of the 700 former delinquents and 600
matched control subjects revealed a distribution of adult convictions
among the former juvenile delinquents that showed the incidence of recidivism greater than that expected by chance. The authors offered the
following explanation of the results, "If those former delinquents who
were convicted as adults were only the unlucky ones among a general
population of casual offenders, it would have been virtually impossible,
by chance alone, for the majority (140 out of 260) to have been unlucky
twice and for 59 of them to have been unlucky three or more times"
(Stott and Wilson, 1977: 54).

During the years 1964 to 1980, four data collection efforts were conducted by Polk and researchers at the University of Oregon. The initial
sample of 1,227 male high school sophomores was selected in 1964 from

responses to a large survey administered for another purpose. In 1967, three subsamples were selected. The first subsample was a 25% random sample of the 1,227 (n = 309) of which 284 were interviewed during their senior year of high school. A second group (n = 303) was identified through juvenile delinquency records and interviewed. Records of one or more contacts with police after reaching adulthood through 1980 were used to identify the final group of 379 adult offenders. Polk et al. (1981) have reported that, in follow-ups from age 18 to 30, 49% of the delinquents had adult arrests as compared to 22% of the nondelinquents.

Information on three birth cohorts was collected through 1974 and later examined by Shannon and his colleagues at the Iowa Urban Community Research Center in Iowa City, Iowa. There were 1,352 males and females in the 1942 cohort; 2,099 members in the 1949 cohort; and 2,676 in the 1955 cohort. Subjects were identified from police, private school, and parochial school records. Continuous residence in Racine, Wisconsin (measured from age 6 to 1974 and excluding no more than 3 years absence from Racine) restricted the research populations to 633 persons from the 1942 cohort; 1,297 from the 1949 cohort; 2,149 from the 1955 cohort. Information on offending was obtained from official records held by the Racine Police department; these data included Part I and II offenses of the Uniform Crime Reports and juvenile status offenses. In addition, social and demographic information and self-reported criminality were obtained in lengthy personal interviews with 333 members of the 1942 cohort and 556 members of the 1949 cohort.

Shannon (1978, 1980, 1988) has provided a range of important findings concerning career continuity. Among the 356 males in the 1942 cohort, follow-up data were reported for the ages of 21 to 32 and show that 54% of the delinquents compared to 36% of the nondelinquents achieved adult arrests. For the remaining two cohorts (i.e., 1949 and 1955), the discrepancy becomes even wider. Among the 740 males in the 1949 cohort, 44% of the delinquents and 15% of the nondelinquents were arrested between the ages of 21 to 26. In the 1955 cohort, the 1,114 males experienced adult arrests for 31% of the delinquents as compared to just 3% of the nondelinquents to age 21.

The Cambridge Study in Delinquent Development is a prospective longitudinal survey begun in 1961 under the direction of West, who was later joined by Farrington and others. The study sample of 411 males was selected when the boys were ages 8 and 9 from the registers of six state primary schools located near the research office and one local school for the educationally subnormal. The sample was predominantly British, white, and from working class families. Psychological tests were administered to the boys at school when they were ages 8, 10, and 14.

They were interviewed at the research office when they were ages 16, 18, and 21. Parents of the boys were interviewed in their homes annually by female social workers while the boys were between the ages 8 and 14. Questionnaires about the boys' behavior were given to their teachers when the boys were ages 8, 10, 12, and 14. Official records of conviction in London before age 17 and in all of England and Wales after age 17 were obtained from repeated searches of files in the central Criminal Record office in London.

Farrington (1983), like Shannon, has provided valuable evidence of career continuity from the Cambridge Study in Delinquent Development. He has reported that to age 24, the chronic offenders constituted just 6% of the sample and 17% of the convicted youths, yet these chronics were responsible for one-half of the convictions. As adults, 71% of the delinquents as compared to just 16% of the nondelinquents experienced adult arrests between the ages of 18 to 25.

Langan and Farrington (1983) have not only provided one of the most comprehensive reviews of research concerning juvenile to adult continuity, but they have also reported additional findings from the Cambridge Study in Delinquent Development. Using a subsample of 395 youths thought to be at risk of a known conviction for the period from age 10 to the 25th birthday, Langan and Farrington found the following continuity results. Of the 78 youths convicted as juveniles, 70.5% were also convicted as adults as compared to 16.4% of the 317 youths who had not experienced a juvenile conviction.

Concerning the frequency of juvenile convictions and its association with adult convictions, Langan and Farrington found that the more juvenile convictions a boy had, the more adult convictions he was likely to experience. They reported that 10 of the 13 boys who had four or more juvenile convictions also had four or more adult convictions. These 10 boys, 76.9% of the total, is in very sharp contrast to the 2.2% of the 317 males with no juvenile convictions who were recorded as having four or more adult convictions.

The Bureau of Justice Statistics sponsored a national study of criminal career patterns and considered the findings significant enough to make the report the first issue of the Bureau's Special Report publication series. The research objective was to describe criminal career patterns and distinguish between long and short career offenders. Langan and Greenfeld (1983) used a sample of 827 male inmates, who were at least age 40 when they entered prison, that was drawn from a 1979 survey administered in 215 State correctional facilities. Langan and Greenfeld found that nearly 92% of the inmates with incarcerations during adolescence continued their criminal careers into young adulthood. They also found that 46.6% of the sample had no record of incarceration during either adolescence or young adulthood.

In an effort to learn more about violent crime, Hamparian et al. (1978) conducted a longitudinal investigation of a cohort of violent juveniles in Columbus, Ohio. The cohort consisted of 1,222 youths born between 1956 and 1960 who had been arrested for at least one violent offense as juveniles. These individuals had collectively experienced 4,841 juvenile arrests. A subsample of 811 members of the cohort whose delinquency career period had concluded by 1976 was analyzed separately. The objective of the project was to describe juveniles who commit violent crime and determine the degree to which characteristics of the offenses, offenders, and criminal justice responses might be interrelated.

Hamparian, Davis, Jacobson, and McGraw (1985) conducted a follow-up investigation of the cohort and collected adult criminal history data that covered the cohort through about their mid-twenties. They have reported several results that have direct bearing on juvenile-to-adult continuity for the violent juvenile cohort.

First, 59% of the cohort were arrested as adults. The data revealed a pronounced sex effect—60% of males as compared to less than one-third of the females were arrested as adults. Second, concerning age at onset, about 66% of cohort members first arrested before age 12 were arrested as adults, compared to 56% with an onset age after age 12. Third, concerning chronic offender status, 77.5% of juvenile chronics were arrested as adults as compared with 36.1% of one-time juvenile offenders. Fourth, concerning apparent desistance as juveniles, 70.4% of violent juveniles who had remained active at ages 16 and 17 were arrested as adults as compared to just 38.4% who had committed their delinquencies at age 15 or younger.

Under the direction of Marvin Wolfgang, researchers at the Sellin Center for Studies in Criminology and Criminal Law at the University of Pennsylvania have investigated, using a longitudinal birth cohort design, the onset, duration, persistence, and severity of the delinquency careers in the 1945 birth cohort (Wolfgang et al., 1972). The 9,945-member cohort was identified from public, private, and parochial school records and tracked by police, court, and selective service records. Official police records were obtained for 3,475 (35%) of the cohort subjects who were thereby identified as delinquent.

When the cohort was age 26, a 10% sample of the birth cohort was selected for self-reported delinquency interviews and local, state, and national records of arrest, conviction, and incarceration through 1975, when the cohort was age 30. These data are surpassed in magnitude only by the 1958 Philadelphia Birth Cohort study, of which our investigation is a component. This retrospective longitudinal cohort study of 1945 is the most extensive investigation of criminal career patterns to date.

The Wolfgang, Thornberry, and Figlio (1987) follow-up data of 975 members of the cohort indicated that 15% were chronic offenders. These chronics or career criminals committed 74% of all the official crime noted to age 30, including 84% of the personal injury offenses and 82% of the property offenses. Wolfgang et al. (1987: 22) also reported that among the 459 offenders in the follow-up sample, 170 (37%) were juvenile delinquents only, 111 (24.2%) were adult offenders only, and 178 (38.8%) were offenders during both time periods. This large research project has thus found that males who were delinquent in adolescence were more likely to be criminal in young adulthood (44%) than were males who were noncriminal in adolescence (12%).

Career Continuity Issues in Previous Research

At this point it is desirable to highlight the previous research concerning career continuity by summarizing the studies in terms of the particular focus or issue related to the juvenile-to-adult transition.

The Delinquency Career Continues

Naturally, the most fundamental question in prior research has concerned whether a history of delinquency is associated with continuing a life of crime as an adult. The earliest studies adopted this "delinquency only" focus. Studies such as those by Chaitin and Dunham (1966), Dunham and Knauer (1954), Glueck and Glueck (1940), Healy and Bronner (1926), Robins and O'Neal (1958), and Shaw (1947) have all confirmed that criminal involvement during adulthood is likely for former juvenile offenders. These research results have been interpreted as an indication that a transitionary career pattern exists from delinquency to adult crime.

However, because these studies did not involve comparative analyses between delinquents and nondelinquents and the relative prevalence of their subsequent adult criminality, these studies represent only a starting point in continuity research. It is not sufficient to know that delinquents continue on to adult crime, we also need to know whether delinquents continue at a greater rate than nondelinquents who begin their careers in crime only after reaching adulthood. Further, we also need to examine the specific mechanisms of delinquent conduct that may be associated with the delinquency-to-adult continuity. Finally, there is an urgent need to elaborate on the official interventions during the juvenile career to determine their efficacy in reducing the risk of subsequent adult crime.

Delinquents versus Nondelinquents

After the early investigations, other researchers began to include samples of nondelinquents along with delinquents and have thus investigated delinquency status and its relationship to adult crime. These studies, Robins (1966), McCord (1978, 1979), Stott and Wilson (1977), Polk et al. (1981), Shannon (1982, 1988), Farrington (1983, 1994), Langan and Farrington (1983), Hamparian et al. (1985), and Wolfgang et al. (1987), have all indicated that youths with a history of juvenile delinquency are much more likely to continue their careers in crime when they become adults as compared to the likelihood that youths who have no such delinquency involvement will begin to commit crimes only in the adult stage of their lives.

For example, the continuity pattern of the nondelinquent was strongly supported in the 1945 Philadelphia Birth Cohort Study. Wolfgang et al. (1987) have reported that of the nondelinquent subjects 81.9% were also classified as nonoffenders during adulthood. Moreover Wolfgang and his colleagues also found that only 3% of the nondelinquents were arrested five or more times after age 18.

The Chronic Juvenile Offender

While the comparative studies have provided useful data concerning the continuity of delinquents versus the discontinuity of the "virgin" adult offenders, there is also concern to differentiate further and investigate the various types of delinquency careers and their association with a career as an adult criminal. Surely, if delinquents have a much greater probability than nondelinquents of engaging in adult crime, then various subgroups of very frequent and/or very serious delinquents may differ from occasional or trivial offenders in the likelihood of career continuity. In this regard, concern thus emerges about particular delinquency career patterns and the transition to adult criminality. Quite reasonably, the argument proposed is that individuals with the greatest number of juvenile offenses are more likely to commit crimes as adults; hence, habitual or chronic offenders merit greater scrutiny by the criminal justice system.

In investigating career differences among juvenile offenders, Dunham and Knauer (1954) found that juvenile delinquent recidivists proceed to adult crime more often than one-time juvenile offenders. A follow-up study by Chaitin and Dunham (1966) found that only 31.9% of all one-time offenders were subsequently registered with the police as adults, whereas 54.3% of all young recidivists became adult offenders. Similarly, Langan and Farrington (1983) have concluded that youths who were relatively frequent offenders during their juvenile years tended to continue to be frequent offenders during their early adult years. This chronic offender effect has also been reported by Hamparian et al. (1985), Shannon (1980, 1988), and Wolfgang et al. (1987).

The results of Stott and Wilson's (1977) study in Glasgow indicated significant career pattern differences between former delinquents and 615 culturally matched nondelinquent control subjects. However, they did not find such differences within the former delinquent group. That is, individuals with one delinquency were as likely to commit adult crime as were chronic delinquents. Within the group of delinquent offenders there is little difference in the mean adult arrest scores between those having one, two, or three convictions, and those having four or more convictions.

We now know that chronic delinquents are more likely to continue into adult crime. Prior research, however, has not identified particular aspects of delinquency, other than frequency, that seem to be driving career continuity. There are three candidates for the role of this driving force: (1) persistence versus desistance; (2) seriousness; and (3) offense specialization. These aspects of a chronic delinquency career may be associated with the career progression from delinquency to adult crime which differentiates the chronic delinquent from his nondelinquent and trivial delinquent counterparts.

The Diminishing Delinquency Career

Most of the studies of criminal career patterns, which have examined frequency of criminal violations, have been concerned with persistent criminality. Yet, the proposition of change exhibited by diminishing criminal involvement has also received attention. Sheldon and Eleanor Glueck (1943) examined 1,000 adjudicated males in their longitudinal study and found 1,333 total arrests, or 1.33 arrests per boy during adolescence, while as adults, the 730 men were responsible for 2,195 arrests by the age of 30, or 2.92 arrests per man. But, 27% of these adjudicated males had apparently desisted from crime by the age of 30. After tracing the careers of their subjects, the Gluecks concluded that a "burning out" process from serious crime to minor crime to desistance exists as delinquents mature.

Similarly, Robins and O'Neal (1958) identified a pattern of desistance in their follow-up study of former psychiatric patients and a matched control group. They noted that, even the former juvenile delinquents, who ranked first in the proportion of adults with criminal offenses, included 38% who had reached a median age of 43 years without an adult police record.

The 1945 Philadelphia Birth Cohort Study (Wolfgang et al., 1987) has found this same pattern of desistance across delinquency status categories: 62% of the one-time delinquents, 55% of the two-time delinquents, 45% of the three-time delinquents, 32% of the four-time delinquents, and 22% of the chronic delinquents experienced no reported crime involvement during adulthood.

Likewise, in the Racine cohorts, Shannon (1978) found that 24.1% of the 1942 cohort males and 34.7% of the 1949 cohort males had police contacts at either or both the juvenile period or young adult period (i.e., ages 18 and 21), but no arrests after the age of 21. Polk and his associates (1981) described it as a process of "maturational reform," after they found that 51% of their sample had been involved in crime during early adulthood, but only 13% committed violations after age 27. In the Dangerous Offender Project, 59% of the youths who began their delinquent careers at ages 13 to 14 had desisted by age 16 (Dinitz and Conrad, 1984; Hamparian et al., 1978).

Stott and Wilson (1977: 52) also reported on an abating criminal career pattern in their follow-up of two Glasgow samples of delinquents and a matched control group. They found that 38% of the juvenile delinquents in the combined sample of 700 subjects had at least one conviction between the ages of 18 and 21, but only 15% experienced the same between the ages of 21 and 24. When examined separately, none of the 19 females who had been delinquents committed offenses after the age of 21. While a culturally matched comparison group of 615 subjects exhibited far less criminality than the test samples during the entire research period, the number of their convictions also dropped to less than half (from 4.5% to 2.1%) in the second age period. Stott and Wilson found this to be evidence of a general trend of diminishing delinquency.

Blumstein and Moitra (1980) have shown that the probability of desistance must be viewed as distinct from the number of prior criminal violations and the probability of continuing these violations. That is, they found that individuals with lengthy criminal records were just as likely as the shorter-record "amateurs" to have made their current arrest their last. Blumstein et al. (1982) have also shown that age varies inversely with criminality—that most persons who begin their criminal career at age 18 drop out of crime by the time they reach age 30.

Thus, whether it is referred to as "burning out," "maturational reform," or "desistance" from criminality, the notion of a diminishing criminal career suggests a transitionary pattern of development distinct from the persistent criminal career. Research on the development, progression, and continuation of criminal careers needs, therefore, to be concerned with desisting of offensive behavior in an effort to identify whether constancy or change is the dominant career pattern and under what circumstances each is likely to occur. The degree to which cessation during youth continues throughout adulthood is of specific interest. That is, do youths who discontinue juvenile delinquency later commit adult crime, even after years of such desistance?

Serious Juvenile Crime

Offense seriousness is a matter of concern in the investigation of criminal career development, in view of the widely held beliefs that individuals who engage in serious crime at an early age are likely to continue offending, and that the gravity of their ensuing behavior may even escalate. These views of a career pattern with continued criminality or incremental severity are rivaled not only by findings of waning crime severity during the criminal career but also by indications that the level of seriousness achieved by an offense is unrelated to subsequent behavior.

Support for the notion that criminality continues as a result of serious initial offending was found in three studies. In the St. Louis Follow-Up Study of psychiatric patients and matched controls, Robins (1966) found that her dichotomous measure of crime severity was a strong predictor of subsequent behavior—no child without frequent or serious antisocial behavior became a sociopathic adult. Next, Wolfgang et al. (1972) reported a relationship between seriousness and crime continuation in the 1945 Philadelphia Birth Cohort Study—boys who committed nonindex first offenses were somewhat more likely to stop after the first offense than were boys who inflicted some bodily or property harm. Finally, the Rand Corporation survey of 624 California inmates found that, "Respondents who committed a serious crime before age 16 tended to report more adult crime, commit more types of crime, commit violent crimes at a higher rate, and hold professional criminal attitudes" (Petersilia, 1980: 347).

In addition to patterns of continued crime following serious initial offending, the contention of escalating crime severity was also supported in survey findings from the Rand Corporation Habitual Offenders Program. Joan Petersilia (1980) reported that most criminal careers begin with minor misconduct, sometimes even status offenses. Self-report studies indicate that the most frequent pattern begins with truancy and incorrigibility, followed first by petty theft and auto theft and then by more serious property crimes. Similarly, according to Langan and Farrington (1983), based on their research using the Cambridge Study in Delinquent Development, it seemed clear that the average amount stolen increased with age.

These results which suggest career patterns of progression in seriousness are called into question not only by the plausible career of diminishing delinquency discussed previously, but also by empirical evidence of a pivotal career stage after which offending behavior decreases in seriousness (Cline, 1980).

In the St. Louis study, of the 105 former child guidance clinic patients who had at least three arrests, at least one of which was for a major crime, the most recent crime for 50% of the former patients was a minor offense (Robins, 1966). The combined results of the St. Louis study suggest that while serious behavior may precede continued offending, the behavior does not necessarily escalate in severity.

The absence of any orderly career scheme involving crime seriousness was also found in the 1945 Philadelphia Birth Cohort Study. In fact, Wolfgang et al. (1972) found relatively stable delinquency careers. They noted that, although each offense tended to be somewhat more serious than a preceding offense, the observed increase in seriousness scores was quite small. Generally, with the exception of injury offenses, for which there was a tendency of increasing seriousness, the offenses committed by the cohort did not become increasingly serious as their delinquent careers developed (Wolfgang et al., 1972).

Neither the 1945 Philadelphia Birth Cohort Study (Wolfgang et al., 1972: 282), nor the Racine, Wisconsin, birth cohorts (Shannon, 1978: 135; 1982) found evidence of a systematic progression in severity among offenders. After testing the notion of career escalation and achieving nonsignificant results, studies by Bursik (1980), Hamparian et al. (1978: 129–130), Klein (1979), and Rojek and Erickson (1982) arrived at essentially the same conclusion found in the Philadelphia and Racine cohort investigations.

The results of previous research concerning the effect of crime severity, and changes in severity across the juvenile career on subsequent delinquent or criminal behavior, attests to the need for a study that can determine whether youth who commit offenses of a serious nature are more likely than others to commit crimes upon reaching adulthood. Many investigations, including several longitudinal studies, utilizing various research designs and with data drawn from numerous sources have been attempted. A review of this literature revealed that some of the issues have received considerable attention by researchers, while others were given only casual mention in a few studies. The review has shown that none of these important research issues has been rigorously examined to the degree sufficient to achieve resolution.

The Offense Specialists

The issue of offense specialization is an important consideration for the determination of whether criminal patterns are more likely to remain invariable or fluctuate across many crime categories, and whether they move from law violation and law abidance. Despite the importance of the issue, research efforts concentrating on specialization and its effects on continuity have been few and limited in their success.

The early work of Healy and Bronner (1926) reported that continued offending or desistance from crime rarely had any relation to the offense type committed. Although the methodology of the study lacked sophistication and the offense categories examined were broad, the absence of specialization reported by Healy and Bronner was generally accepted and the issue was not carefully investigated again for several decades.

Conceptual efforts to establish offender typologies to characterize different career patterns and specialties (Clinard and Quinney, 1973; Cloward and Ohlin, 1960; Gibbons, 1965), as well as numerous offender subtypes (Conklin, 1972; Gottfredson, 1967; Guttmacher, 1960; McCaghy, 1967; Neustatter, 1967; Roebuck and Cadwallader, 1961; and Wright and Decker, 1994), and classification schemes for institutionalized offenders (Roebuck, 1966; Schrag, 1944, 1961; and Sykes, 1958) were each designed to overcome the behavioral exceptions found in an individual all-encompassing theory and to provide for differential treatment according to offender and offense type.

Following his comprehensive review of offender typologies, Gibbons (1975) conceded that these classification schemes generally have been deficient in clarity and objectivity, have often failed to develop mutually exclusive and comprehensive categories, and seldom have been examined empirically. He further concluded: "After two decades of work in this tradition, relatively little progress in typological directions can be discerned" (1975: 153).

Interest in specialization was renewed when empirical investigations of criminal careers increased in popularity. The issue, though, was typically of secondary importance and interest was restricted to looking at patterns of specialization versus versatility (Klein, 1984) or generalization (Farrington, 1986).

By using stochastic (probability) techniques with longitudinal data to age 18, the 1945 Philadelphia Birth Cohort Study (Wolfgang et al.,

1972) has been considered among the studies better able to address the issue of specialization. In an analysis unmatched up to 1972, the delinquency careers of the cohort were followed to the ninth offense. The results showed that regardless of previous offense type, an offender was most likely to have subsequent involvement in a nonindex event. If a nonindex event did not occur next, the state of desistance was likely. Among the index crimes, each category was more likely to follow itself than to change.

Thus, the 1945 cohort study uncovered conditional probabilities of like offense transitions for the index offense categories. Despite this indication of specialization, the overall conclusion was to reject specialization, because the estimates failed to achieve satisfactory probability levels for like offense repeats (Wolfgang et al., 1972: 166–188). Klein (1979) cited the apparent lack of juvenile specialization in the 1945 Philadelphia Birth Cohort Study to explain the failure of diversion programs for status offenders. More recently, Petersilia (1980) used the Philadelphia findings to challenge specially designated career criminal prosecution units.

Of course, while the 1945 Philadelphia Birth Cohort study offered many advantages due to the quality of the data and the level of sophistication of the analyses, some of its inherent limitations require that the results be viewed cautiously.

First, the crime categories in the Philadelphia study were devised to measure severity (Wolfgang et al., 1972: 46; Sellin and Wolfgang, 1964) and were not ideally suited for offense specialization. The requirement of mutually exclusive categories, for example, was not met because the separate classification of nonindex crimes and events involving combinations from other categories allowed similar types of behavior to be contained in different crime groups.

Second, less active youth with delinquency careers that ended prior to the ninth offense, who might have been less likely to develop patterns of specialization, were included in the same analyses as the very active delinquents. This undifferentiated inclusion may have confounded the results.

Finally, while specialization was traced to the ninth offense before cell frequencies became too small for analysis, and no other study has progressed to even this rank offense number, the total careers of many delinquents were not captured within this data-imposed boundary.

In addition to the 1945 Philadelphia Cohort Study, several other studies have examined the issue of crime specialization (Blumstein and Greene, 1979; Buikhuisen and Jongman, 1970; Bursik, 1980; Chaiken and Chaiken, 1982a; 1982b; Christensen, Elers-Nielsen, Le Maire, and Sturup, 1965; Farrington, 1979; Heuser, 1978; Hindelang, 1971; Klein, 1971, 1979, 1984; Kobrin, Hellum, and Peterson, 1980; McClintock, 1963; Petersilia, Greenwood, and Lavin, 1977; Peterson, 1980; Peterson, Pittman, and O'Neal, 1962; Rojek and Erickson, 1982; Shannon, 1968; Smith and Smith, 1984; Soothill and Pope, 1973; West and Farrington, 1977; and Wright and Decker, 1994).

These studies obtained their subjects from a variety of sources, including birth cohorts, cohorts of violent offenders, institutionalized offenders, gang members, and students. They used multiple methods of investigation including transition matrix analysis, factor analysis, scaling techniques, and simple comparisons of crime category involvement. As with the 1945 Philadelphia Birth Cohort Study, each of these independent investigations failed to support the specialist career pattern.

While research on offense specialization has failed to support the predicted career pattern, there have been results indicating that the phenomenon is more likely to be observed within unique crime categories, during certain career stages, or among some demographic subgroups. When broad offense definitions were used, repeated involvement was shown in the categories of property crime (Bursik, 1980; Peterson et al., 1962; Peterson et al., 1980; Petersilia, 1980; Rojek and Erickson, 1982; Wallerstedt, 1984) and personal crime (Farrington, 1979; Peterson et al., 1980; Peterson et al., 1962; and Petersilia, 1980). Several studies (Clarke, 1975; Kobrin et al., 1980; Rojek and Erickson, 1982; Tielman and Peterson, 1981) have also shown a tendency for delinquency specialization among status offenders.

The results of three studies (Bursik, 1980; Quay and Blumen, 1968; and Farrington, 1986) suggest that specialization may be more evident as criminal careers become more established. Unique age and period involvement in certain crime categories were reported in several studies (Glueck and Glueck, 1943; Havighurst, Bowman, Liddle, Matthews, and Pierce, 1966; Langan and Farrington, 1983; McCord and McCord, 1959; Robins, 1966; and Wolfgang, 1977). Following his analysis of national UCR data for 1977, Cline (1980) conceded that the degree to which crime specialization occurs remains unknown and inadequately investigated.

The results of previous investigations of specialization must be interpreted with caution and should not be viewed as conclusive, because problems exist particularly in the areas of crime category specification, the portion of career examined, and the method of measurement.

Ideally, the classification scheme for offenses should involve mutually exclusive crime categories. Using the 1945 Philadelphia Birth Cohort as an example, this requirement has not always been satisfied. In this study, crime categories that were designed to measure seriousness (Wolfgang et al., 1972; Sellin and Wolfgang, 1964), included separate identification of index crimes (an observed severity component) versus nonindex crimes (no severity component). However, index crimes are further divided into injury, theft, damage, and combinations of these. These combinations are not mutually exclusive and can lead to misclassifications.

The difficulty in developing a typology is further evident in Klein's (1984) report of factor analysis undertaken with 40 types of offenses, which produced five factors with no identifiable conceptual basis. This finding led Klein and his colleagues to conclude that there is "cafeteria-style" delinquency. Finally, in their rational choice theory of crime Clarke and Cornish (1985) have proposed crime-specific models. They argue that no classification scheme which groups offenses can adequately identify offender involvement.

The proportion of the criminal career investigated is an important issue, because the definition of criminal career provides for the designation of subsequences, such as that which rational choice theory identifies as separate stages of crime involvement. Unless the entire criminal career is followed, research results cannot be generalized beyond their respective domains.

Hirschi's (1985) rejection of specialization appears to be based on results from surveys of the Rand Habitual Offenders Program. These surveys restrict the recall period to 3 years, a period from which generalization to the entire criminal career is likely to be problematic. A further limitation exists because, while it is plausible that a self-report study of offenders could reveal patterns of undetected, or "successful" criminal careers, the reliance on institutionalized inmates in the Rand surveys (Chaiken and Chaiken, 1982a, 1982b; Petersilia et al., 1977; Peterson et al., 1980) limited the findings to unique convicted offenders, who were less likely to have been truly representative of the criminal population. Consequently, the potential benefit of self-reported data was less fruitful in these investigations.

Authors of two substantial and independent reviews of prior investigations of offense specialization (Farrington, 1979; and Klein, 1985) each concluded that future efforts should focus on improvement in measurement of specialization, which could enhance validity and better allow comparison of results. The relevance to rational choice and social control theories in Klein's proposal is self-evident; "research for offense patterns may best be served now by analytic techniques which are most sensitive to offense/offender interactions, especially among the highest frequency offenders" (1985: 192).

According to Farrington, "Most importantly, there is a need for a standard summary measure of specialization versus generalization" (1986: 43). Farrington's proposal is for a "coefficient of specialization" for each diagonal cell in a transition matrix. Farrington explained that, "This coefficient seems useful because it is zero when there is complete generalization (and hence the observed figure equals the expected one) and 1 when there is perfect specialization (and hence every conviction offense becomes the same type of reconviction offense)" (1986: 44).

The review of research on the pattern of specialization has found that the issue has not nearly achieved resolution. Prior research is weak in the areas of: (1) conceptualization of crime categories; (2) generalization beyond certain career stages; and (3) methods of measurement. Each of these concerns undoubtedly is associated with the inadequacy of earlier research findings and the subsequent widespread dismissal of specialization as a significant research area.

In the context of the numerous studies reviewed above, the objective of the current study of criminal career continuity is to confirm whether juvenile delinquents are more likely than nondelinquents to proceed to adult crime. If this is indeed the case, subsequent inquiry will be devoted to whether certain patterns of delinquency are more closely associated with such continuity than are other delinquency patterns. It is clear that prior research has not sufficiently investigated these topics using a large enough set of subjects in the first instance to permit generalizability and, in the second instance, to provide sufficient cases for sophisticated analyses (whether conceptually or statistically).

Drawing from the issues examined critically in this chapter, we describe in Chapter 4 the design and measurement aspects of this investigation, which will permit us to focus on the career paths exhibited by both nondelinquents and delinquents as they move to adulthood. This design will also permit us to examine the critical delinquency issues of persistence, inactivity, seriousness, severity, and chronic offending, and their association with continuity versus discontinuity in criminal careers.

Owing to the longitudinal nature of the 1958 birth cohort study, with continuous criminal history data from the point of onset of delinquency through the age of 26, and the size and representativeness of the study (27,160 subjects, with both gender and racial balance), this research effort proceeds with the anticipation that this study will provide data and statistical analyses sufficient for a meaningful examination of these important issues.

4

Research Design and Methodology

In this chapter we discuss the design and methodology required to identify and analyze patterns of offending across the most crime-prone years. The benefits of such procedures will be highlighted and compared to the procedures followed in prior research. Following this, we present the technique of investigation adopted in this study and its advantages and limitations will be fully noted and elaborated.

Research Design

Investigation of the possible continuity in offending between adolescence and delinquency on the one hand and adulthood and criminality on the other is a research focus that necessarily involves the resolution of a number of important research requirements. These requirements range from issues concerning the size and diversity of the study population, to the extent of the data available, to the length of the time frames under scrutiny (i.e., the baseline period of delinquency and the criterion period of adult crime). These issues are discussed below.

First, career continuity research must start with a group of subjects with particular attributes so as to avoid external validity problems and thereby ensure that any results and conclusions may be generalized to a meaningful population. Thus, the race, gender, and social class characteristics of the study group must be sufficiently diverse so as not to exclude substantively relevant and theoretically significant demographic groups.

Second, career continuity research must also ensure that a sufficiently large number of subjects are investigated to permit reliable analysis of quantitatively or qualitatively different dimensions of both delinquency and adult crime. The number and variability surrounding the cases are crucial to the rigorous statistical analyses and predictions necessary in examining the juvenile-to-adult transition over time and across the various characteristics of offenders and offenses. Simply, an insufficient number of cases, or an insufficient number of cases that reflect the fullest possible range of the phenomena under investigation, forestalls the identification of statistically significant and substantively meaningful results.

Third, career continuity research requires collection of criminal history data that are not only complete, but also reflect a certain data specificity that is requisite for measuring and classifying various typologies of offenders and the extent, quality, and sequencing of their offending behavior.

We believe the research design best suited to accomplish this series of difficult tasks necessarily involves a longitudinal procedure. Longitudinal investigations can follow the behavior of research subjects prospectively as it occurs, or the offenses can be reconstructed through retrospective data collection. The time period under scrutiny should cover as much of the career as possible. Ideally, the entire juvenile career, from onset of delinquency through the transition to adult status, should be covered, and a meaningful component of the adult time period must also be included. That is, covering only the juvenile period from age 14 or 15 onward, for example, would necessarily exclude the early delinquents who start their careers before age 14, and who, by virtue of this early onset, may be qualitatively different than the average or late starters. Likewise, truncating the adult period at age 21 or 22 or 23, etc., ignores that many offenders continue to commit offenses well into their late twenties.

This substantial time requirement of criminal career investigations makes prospective longitudinal designs almost cost-prohibitive. The number of years required to capture the dynamics of criminal career development adequately has not yet been established. But surely, employing only a cross-section of an offender's career is insufficient to represent the full dynamics of such a career. Obviously, a complete career is the best possible basis for investigation. The data collection efforts in earlier works ranged between 3 years and the subjects' lifetime and included a number of different research designs.

Population versus Sampling

The 1958 birth cohort study employs a cohort of subjects with two eligibility requirements for inclusion in the cohort. First, the subjects had to have been born in the same year. The particular year that was chosen (i.e., 1958) was based upon the need for a second cohort that could facilitate the investigation of cohort effects. That is, the 1945 birth cohort was born the year World War II ended. Its delinquency years essentially span the period from 1955 through 1962. In many ways the rates, types, and severity of delinquency exhibited by the 1945 cohort reflect the social milieu of that period, a period that may be very different from other more contemporary times, such as the 1960s or 1970s. Thus, a primary requirement for the second cohort study was a birth cohort born sufficiently later than its predecessor. Its span of delinquency years thus reflected a different social milieu and perhaps a different push to or pull away from delinquency.

The 1958 cohort seems to meet this requirement. It was born 13 years after its predecessor, which puts its delinquency-prone years (i.e., from 1968 to 1975) in a potentially very different milieu. This period coincides with America's involvement in the Vietnam War, the rise in drug use, social protest, and the like, and thus represents a time of great social change compared to the more tranquil adolescence of the 1945 cohort. Because of this differential social atmosphere, distinct cohort effects were theoretically quite possible. This suggested that their detection and measurement should constitute the primary focus of our analyses.

In addition to birth in the year 1958, the other eligibility requirement for membership in the present cohort is identical to that of the 1945 cohort—continued residence in Philadelphia at least from the age of 10 until the 18th birthday. The upper bound simply reflects the statutory age limit of delinquency. The lower bound is, of course, arbitrary but does reflect the age at which delinquency onset is ordinarily most likely to occur. We would thus argue that the ages of 10 through 17 reflect the most likely period for the vast majority of youths to begin their delinquency careers. In fact, we found for the males in the 1958 birth cohort that cumulatively, only 6.7% of the delinquents began their delinquency careers prior to age 10 (Tracy et al., 1990). Therefore, the 8-year period from 10 through 17 is a sufficiently long period at risk with which to establish a valid cohort rate of delinquency.

The 1958 birth cohort arguably represents a population, not a sample. It is true that persons born in a particular year, thus constituting a particular birth cohort, are but a sample of many possible birth cohorts. Yet, a birth cohort still represents a complete enumeration of all the subjects similarly situated and similarly at risk for offending. The most important consequence of this complete enumeration is that any data pertaining to the prevalence of offending, the proportion of the cohort that is recorded as delinquent or criminal, are not affected by sample selection issues and the potential biases that can affect the generalizability of samples.

The use of a birth cohort design in this research is in contrast to research using samples from a population. Several issues inherent in the sampling process are of concern. First, there is always the potential for sampling error. Second, accidental samples selected according to ready availability are likely to reflect sampling bias by their very nature, because exclusive criteria were used to define sample membership. These restrictions limited the sphere of eligible participants in most previous studies and consequently, threaten the generalizability of the results.

The quality of samples can affect the overall value of the research findings, and the extent to which conclusions can be drawn from them and generalized to meaningful segments of the population. The selection procedure, the size of the sample population, the characteristics of subjects included in the sample, and the effects of attrition can either promote or hinder the validity of the findings, as well as the degree to which the results can be generalized to other populations, geographic locations, and time periods. The obstacle of assuring adequate representation may be overcome only when the entire population is included in the study and this complete enumeration is the goal of cohort investigations (Ryder, 1965).

When the population of interest is unavailable in its entirety for study, as is most often the situation, random selection procedures that afford each member of the population an equivalent opportunity to be included in the sample are, of course, available. Random sampling procedures were adhered to in seven of the 27 studies reviewed. The original populations from which research samples were randomly selected in these studies included: the 1945 Philadelphia Birth Cohort (Collins, 1977a; 1977b), high school students from one Oregon county (Polk et al., 1981), delinquents adjudicated in various juvenile courts (Bursik, 1980; Chaitin and Dunham, 1966; Dunham and Knauer, 1954; Rojek and Erickson, 1982) former psychiatric patients (Robins, 1966), and inmates from five California institutions (Peterson et al., 1980). Most studies avoided random selection in drawing the research sample, however, and chose instead convenience samples from previously defined groups, such as students, and arrested or incarcerated individuals.

Although random sampling was not used, random assignment to either the treatment or control group was used in the Cambridge-Somerville Youth Study (McCord, 1978; 1979; 1981; 1984; McCord and McCord, 1959; and McCord, McCord, and Zola, 1969) as were attempts without random assignment to match delinquents with nondelinquents (Glueck and Glueck, 1950; Sampson and Laub, 1993), and patients with nonpatients (Robins, 1966). These studies used comparison groups to minimize error in sample distributions by including similar proportions of subjects with given characteristics.

While these attempts to achieve comparable research groups are commendable, the combined test–control groups failed to provide representative samples except in the study by Robins (1966) in which the sample was initially selected randomly. The remaining studies from which empirical findings relevant to the development of criminal careers were obtained were based on research samples obtained without random selection from accommodating courts and correctional facilities (Chaiken and Chaiken, 1982a, 1982b; Glueck and Glueck, 1930, 1934, 1937, 1940, 1943, 1957, 1968; Healy and Bronner, 1926, 1936; Langan and Greenfeld, 1983; Petersilia et al., 1977; Sampson and Laub, 1993; Stott and Wilson, 1977) or from conveniently located public school classrooms (Farrington, 1982a; Farrington and West, 1981; West, 1969, 1982; West and Farrington, 1973, 1977).

The social and demographic composition of the research sample can also affect the quality of research results. If only male subjects are analyzed, as was done in many studies (Chaiken and Chaiken, 1982a, 1982b; Chaitin and Dunham, 1966; Dunham and Knauer, 1954; Farrington, 1982a, 1982b, 1983; Farrington and West, 1981; Glueck and Glueck, 1930, 1934, 1937, 1940, 1943, 1957; Healy and Bronner, 1926, 1936; Langan and Greenfeld, 1983; McCord, 1978; Petersilia et al., 1977; Peterson et al., 1980; Polk et al., 1981; Rojek and Erickson, 1982; Sampson and Laub, 1993; West, 1982), then the extent to which females behave in a comparable manner remains unknown, thus greatly limiting the generalizability of these studies. A similar void exists for the measurement or estimation of a phenomenon when the race and socioeconomic status of the population is not properly reflected in the sample distribution.

Investigations of crime involvement also should not be restricted to just individuals who have received official sanctions from the criminal justice system (Bursik, 1980; Chaiken and Chaiken, 1982; Chaitin and Dunham, 1966; Dunham and Knauer, 1954; Glueck and Glueck, 1930, 1934, 1937, 1940, 1943, 1957; Healy and Bronner, 1926; Langan and Greenfeld, 1983; Petersilia et al., 1977; Peterson et al., 1981; Rojek and Erickson, 1982; Stott and Wilson, 1977). Clearly, restricting a sample to just official offenders is problematic, owing to the possibility of very plausible and unique characteristics of offenders who are able to avoid apprehension, conviction, or incarceration, and thus, are not captured in such samples.

Although a small group of individuals who were randomly selected is better able to support the generalization of research findings to the larger population than is a large sample selected according to specific criteria or availability, investigations of life span development and criminal careers require samples large enough to sustain the necessary statistical analysis. Small samples can prove ineffectual in revealing sufficient variability in the criteria for which an explanation is desired. This potential problem is magnified among low base-rate, or infrequently occurring, phenomena, such as crime and especially repeated crime involvement. In addition to their weakness in handling low base-rate phenomena, small samples are of minimal value when the simultaneous examination of several factors is required.

The number of subjects selected for study in the research reviewed ranged from 49 armed robbery inmates (Petersilia et al., 1977) to 11,004 residents of Aberdeen, Scotland (May, 1981). The sample of 49 inmates would be unable to provide support for analysis of the important criminal career issues, such as persistent involvement, desistance, crime specialization, and serious juvenile delinquency, in addition to controlling for concerns of age, race, sex, and socioeconomic status. The sample size sufficient in magnitude to satisfy the analytical requirements, however, remains unknown. While no such analysis has been reported for the Aberdeen Cohort, even the 9,945 members of the 1945 Philadelphia Birth Cohort did not produce enough cell frequencies to analyze offense specialization for lengthy delinquency careers.

The issue of sample mortality is also a significant research concern for investigations of behavior over the life course because the careers of subjects must be traced for many years. The dilemmas presented by individuals who move to inconvenient or unknown locations, refuse to participate in the study, or die during the research period must be minimized, because the design requires enormous sample size. A serious threat to validity is posed by those subjects who drop out of the sample, because they likely are qualitatively distinct from the remaining subjects. Sample attrition to different degrees afflicted several earlier studies related to criminal career development (Bursik, 1980; Collins, 1977a, 1977b; Farrington, 1981; West, 1982; Glueck and Glueck, 1940; Healy and Bronner, 1926; May, 1981; McCord, 1978; Robins, 1966; Rojek and Erickson, 1982; Sampson and Laub, 1993; Shannon, 1982; Stott and Wilson, 1977; West, 1982; and Wolfgang, 1977).

An illustration of the dangers associated with all of the preceding sampling problems is the recent award-winning book by Sampson and Laub (1993). This work is an impressive and ambitious attempt to reanalyze the Gluecks' (1950) Unraveling Juvenile Delinquency data. The stature of the Gluecks' study is well known in criminology, as are the methodological and statistical criticisms of the research (see, for example, Hirschi and Selvin, 1967; Kamin, 1986; Reiss, 1951; Robins and Hill, 1969; Short, 1969; Wilkins, 1969). In light of the authors' claims that many of the historical criticisms of the Gluecks' data and statistical analyses were resolved in the reanalysis, it is important to highlight a few salient aspects of the Glueck's original study that concern sampling. There is also the question of the representativeness of the Gluecks' data.

First, it must be remembered that the Gluecks did not use probability sampling methods in the Unraveling Juvenile Delinquency study. The sample of 500 delinquents was purposefully chosen from two Massachusetts correctional schools, to maximize offense differences with the nondelinquent sample. Likewise, the sample of nondelinquents was not a probability sample, but rather was matched, on a case by case basis, to the delinquent group on the factors of age, ethnicity, neighborhood (low income), and intelligence. Nonprobability samples naturally suffer from generalizability problems and selection biases (Campbell and Stanley, 1963; Spector, 1981). This can lead to confounded measures, because sample estimators are likely to be inefficient, if not biased, as sample size increases (Kalton, 1983).

Sampson and Laub suggest that, "although clearly not a random selection, the samples thus appear representative of the population of persistent official delinquents and generally nondelinquent youth in Boston at the time" (1993: 26). The authors' conclusion is interesting, because the authors themselves noted that Long and Vaillant have found that the nondelinquent sample "did not represent a particularly law-abiding group" (1984: 345).

Thus, in the absence of evidence that the nondelinquent sample reasonably reflected a meaningful population of nondelinquents, the external validity problems of the Gluecks' sampling design remain problematic. The findings of the research, then, whether the original results reported by the Gluecks, or the reanalyses offered by Sampson and Laub must be viewed advisedly.

Second, the Gluecks' data suffer from mortality problems, particularly the delinquent sample, owing to the attrition of the samples during the follow-up. That is, of the original 1,000 subjects at the start of the study, 12% were not available for follow-up. Further, among the approximately 880 cases that were followed up, respondents were subsequently lost owing to unavailability problems. For example, 150 of the delinquents were excluded from subsequent waves of data collection because of criminal justice imprisonment or military service, and 50 nondelinquents were similarly lost because of extended military service. Concerning the sample attrition issue, Sampson and Laub have commented that:

> Unfortunately, the excluded cases do not represent a random sample of the men. Those with lengthy incarceration time had longer criminal records and were thus presumably more prone to crime. We also cannot assume that those who served in the military for long periods reflect the characteristics of the rest of the men. For these reasons, results may be biased because of systematic selection bias, undermining both external and internal validity (1993: 150).

Third, in addition to the original samples, which were unrepresentative at the outset, and which both suffered from selectivity in case attrition—and therefore, most likely constituted biased samples at the point of follow-up—it must also be noted that the Gluecks' samples consisted only of men who came from low-income neighborhoods, and who were of only a single race (whites, although of varying ethnicity). The fact that only high-risk white males are included in the samples is extremely important substantively.

Clearly, the race factor is crucial in criminological research. From all available research evidence, we know that blacks have higher rates of violent crime and also commit certain drug offenses. These and other factors have resulted in a disproportionate percentage of blacks incarcerated or under the supervision of the criminal justice system in some other way. Of course, there is strong speculation that these data may be affected by differential, if not biased, law enforcement practices that target offenders on the basis of race. Further, minorities may also suffer a cumulative disadvantage in criminal court processing and subsequent sentencing.

Beyond the criminal justice system, we know that a disproportionate percentage of blacks compared to whites grow up below the poverty line or are raised in female-headed households, or both. Black males have by far the highest unemployment rates. Blacks also face institutional and individual racism, which greatly disadvantages them and places them at much higher risk compared to whites for a host of social problems, including crime. Thus, the problems of the black underclass are exacerbated by racism in society and racism in the criminal justice system. It is this dual racism that sharply differentiates the risk of blacks from whites in suffering disproportionately from "underclass" status.

Sampson and Laub seem to discount the inherent problems in an all-white, all-male sample. They suggest instead that the Gluecks' samples provide an important comparative statement on current concerns with race, crime, and the underclass. Because race is not available as an explanatory factor, this fact undermines some of the prominent conceptions about crime (1993: 254). In particular, Sampson and Laub argue that:

> Simply, the Glueck data allow us to discuss crime in a "deracialized" and, we hope, depoliticized context. In this regard we believe that the causes of crime across the life course are rooted not in race, and not simply in drugs, gangs, and guns—today's policy obsessions—but rather in structural disadvantage, weakened informal social bonds to family, school, and work, and the disruption of social relations between individuals and institutions that provide social capital (1993: 255).

It is difficult to comprehend an argument that the racial context— and all the social, and economic disadvantages that it represents to blacks in America—is not a highly important factor in studying the causes of crime and society's response to it. Suffice it to say that, while Sampson and Laub claim that, "Our findings based on the Glueck data thus become a window from which to view contemporary research and begin a dialogue on crime and crime policy, especially in a non-race specific context" (1993: 254), we believe the window is clouded and will permit only a distorted perception of the reality of crime and the role of race. We suspect a similar difficulty owing to the omission of females in the Gluecks' samples.

While the investigation of cohort groups potentially displaces many of these concerns about sampling and the generalizability of findings raised above, caution must be exercised to ensure that overzealous conclusions are not offered. Effects due to unique experiences of members of a cohort, such as their generation, particular life events for a particular cohort, and residential location, preclude the adaptation of conclusions based on analysis from one cohort to different aged populations from other geographic locations and from other historical periods. Yet, a birth cohort is still one of the best possible designs in which to reduce, if not eliminate, many of the concerns that usually surround sampling and the generalizability of results.

Data

This study incorporates the data files from the 1958 Philadelphia Birth Cohort Study. These data include officially based school information on 27,160 males and females born in 1958 who resided in Philadelphia at least from ages 10 through 17. Together with the criminal history data that were collected for the cohort through age 26, these data allow unprecedented depth and sophistication of investigations. The present data permit the systematic structuring of the longitudinal sequence of police contacts and thereby help to facilitate the identification of youths—both delinquents and nondelinquents—most likely to proceed to adult crime.

The 1958 Philadelphia birth cohort comprises a population and, as such, is not vulnerable to the usual threats of external validity posed by sampling procedures. Every available subject is included, regardless of his or her delinquency or adult crime status. This cohort of 27,160 individuals is the largest of its kind and includes detailed information drawn from several sources able to identify characteristics of its members. The cohort includes 13,160 males and 14,000 females. Representation of both race and level of socioeconomic status are sufficiently well distributed to allow meaningful analysis and statistical controls for these important social and demographic characteristics. Table 4.1 displays the layout of the 1958 birth cohort.

The requirement of Philadelphia residence between ages 10 and 18 for defining the cohort provides a uniform time frame and setting within which cohort members were at risk of offending. Sample mortality is not problematic in this longitudinal investigation, because the retrospective data collection involved unobtrusive archival examination of records which are maintained routinely by the Philadelphia Police Department and area schools.

TABLE 4.1
Layout of 1958 Cohort by Gender, Race, and Socioeconomic Status

Socioeconomic status	White	Black	Hispanic	Other	Total
	Males				
Low	1318	4779	305	12	6414
	10.0%	36.3%	2.3%	.1	48.7%
High	4898	1782	50	16	6746
	37.2%	13.5%	.4%	.1%	51.3%
Total	6216	6561	355	28	13160
	47.2%	49.9%	2.7%	.2%	100%
	Females				
Low	1478	5153	304	13	6948
	10.6%	36.8%	2.2%	.1%	49.6%
High	5159	1815	66	12	7052
	36.9%	13.0%	.5%	.1%	50.4%
Total	6637	6968	370	25	14000
	47.4%	49.8%	2.6%	.2%	100%

Several data sources contributed to the 1958 Philadelphia Birth Cohort Study and provided information that is required for this investigation of dynamics of the criminal career. Cohort members were identified from school records obtained from all public and private schools in Philadelphia. Identification information on race, sex, date of birth, and residence also was obtained from the school records.

Police rap sheets and investigation reports were provided by the Juvenile Aid Division of the Philadelphia Police Department to characterize police encounters experienced by the cohort before age 18. In addition to official arrests, the rap sheet data also contain "police contact" information. The police maintain records of these contacts which result in "remedial," or informal, handling of the youth by an officer whereby youth are generally remanded to the custody of their parents. Thus, the juvenile delinquency data contain both official arrests and informal contacts that did not result in an arrest thus representing a total record of official delinquency, and further, representing a much better record of delinquency than data that were based solely on arrest information. The police investigation reports were used to supplement information provided in the rap sheets with detailed descriptions of the criminal event in which the subject was involved.

The Municipal and Court of Common Pleas of Philadelphia served as data sources for offenses committed by the cohort after reaching the legislatively imposed adult status of age 18. Court files included police reports, so data on adult crime are comparable to that for delinquency. The exception, of course, is that no official "remedial" report exists for adults who encountered police, but who were not arrested. Adult criminal history data are available through December 31, 1984, or through age 26 for all cohort members. The 1958 Philadelphia Birth Cohort Study is rich in the criminal history and offense data available to assess important criminological issues. Further description of the 1958 Philadelphia Birth Cohort Study data collection procedures and the results of a comparison study of the juvenile delinquency careers for males in the 1958 and 1945 Philadelphia cohorts may be found in Tracy et al. (1985; 1990).

Specification of Variables

Juvenile Delinquency

Juvenile delinquency is defined as any official police contact before age 18. This is a comprehensive and all inclusive measure of delinquency because crimes, whether trivial or serious, and status offenses are all included and received no censoring. This measurement is also much less vulnerable to selection bias on the part of individual police officers because, in addition to delinquent acts that resulted in official arrest and subsequent juvenile court processing, the data also include police encounters which resulted in informal or "remedial" actions by the officer. However, traffic violations are excluded from consideration.

Delinquency status is measured as both a dichotomous variable (official contact versus no official contact), as a discrete variable with four categories (no offenses, 1 offense, 2 to 4 offenses, 5 or more offenses), a further discrete category which includes five categories designed to differentiate the chronic delinquent (5–9 offenses) from the very chronic delinquent (10 or more offenses) as well as the nonoffender, the one-time offender, and the nonchronic recidivist (2–4 offenses), and as a continuous variable ranging from zero delinquencies to 53 offenses.

We previously reported that, of those 1958 cohort members identified as delinquent, 42% of the males had only one offense, 35% were nonchronic recidivists with 2 to 4 offenses, and 23% had experienced five or more police encounters and were classified as chronic delinquents. Among females, the distribution across the three categories was 60% one-time, 33% nonchronic, and 7% chronic. These distributions of delinquency status categories confirm that these classifications will serve as meaningful delinquency dimensions and will facilitate the comparison of findings herein with related studies which defined chronicity in the same manner (Hamparian et al., 1978; Shannon, 1978; Wolfgang et al., 1972; 1987).

Adult Offender Status

Adult offender status is operationalized primarily as a dichotomous variable signifying the presence or absence of at least one adult arrest between 1976 and 1984. The measurement of adult criminality thus spans age 18 through age 26 inclusive, or a period covering the first 8 years of adult crime. Given the declining age curve that has repeatedly been reported in the literature, this period should cover the vast majority of persons who will ever initiate any criminal behavior as an adult. Offenses committed outside the Philadelphia jurisdiction are also not identified. Like the delinquency data, we use three measures of adult crime: (1) a dichotomy; (2) a four-level measure; and (3) a continuous variable.

The use of police arrests prior to court disposition to define crime raises concerns because the legal determination of guilt has not been established at this stage. This measure of adult crime, however, is comparable to the police-based indicator of delinquency that we used for the juvenile period, except that no adult-equivalent exists for the juvenile remedial policy. Moreover, most criminal career research utilizes arrest rather than conviction data.

Offense Seriousness

Offense seriousness of the delinquent events and adult crimes is measured through multiple indicators designed to capture alternative dimensions of offense severity. By distinguishing the gravity or seriousness of offenses, we simultaneously classify offenders and their careers. In turn, this permits the investigation of differential delinquency pathways that may be associated with the transition to adult criminality.

Sellin–Wolfgang Scale

The first indicator concerns the Sellin-Wolfgang scale of offense severity. Their pioneering work, *The Measurement of Delinquency* (1964), produced a seriousness scoring scale which typifies the severity of crime in a quantitative fashion and avoids the often misleading nature of legal labels. The scale was used in the original cohort study. Since then, the Sellin Center has continued to investigate the perceived severity of crime and has developed an updated version of the scale. These data come from a national survey that was conducted as part of the National Crime Panel Surveys (Wolfgang et al., 1985). The revised severity scale was used in the juvenile component of the 1958 birth cohort study (Tracy et al., 1990).

The Sellin–Wolfgang scale maintains that a crime severity index must be based on certain kinds of offensive conduct. However, instead of selecting these kinds of conduct on the basis of the title given them by the criminal code, the Sellin-Wolfgang scale measures the nature of the harm actually inflicted in a criminal event. The components of this scale concern violations of the criminal law that inflict *bodily harm* on one or more victims and/or cause property loss by *theft* or *damage/destruction*.

The Sellin–Wolfgang system for selecting events for a crime index differs in two major respects from the one used in the UCR system. First, it does not allow the inclusion of offenses that produce none of the effects described. Thus, the offenses incorporated into our scale all share one very important feature—some degree of measurable social harm to the community. Second, the Sellin–Wolfgang system includes many offenses that are not counted among the index crimes category of the UCR.

Thus, by employing the Sellin–Wolfgang system in this investigation, one of our severity measures represents discernable consequences over that of an ordered set of legal categories which may or may not appropriately reflect the seriousness of criminal behavior. Third, the UCR system of designating as an index offense a crime that represents an unsuccessful attempted index offense is rejected.

The application of the Sellin–Wolfgang system to our data produces several measures of seriousness. First, each offense is categorized as either "index" or "nonindex" based upon the presence or absence of a seriousness component. Second, each index offense can be further divided into three categories in order to indicate the major effect associated with the offense. The first category includes those events that produce bodily harm to one or more victims even though property theft or damage may also be involved. The second class of events consists of those offenses that do not involve injury but have a property theft component even when accompanied by damage. The last category consists of those offenses that involve only damage to property. Third, each offense (whether index or not) receives a quantitative severity score based upon the crime severity component and associated weights given in Table 4.2.

Table 4.2 lists the seriousness scoring components and the associated weights used in the scale. The seriousness score for an event is com-

TABLE 4.2
Seriousness Scoring Components and Weights

Component	Weight
1. Physical injury	
a. Minor harm	1.474
b. Treated and discharged	8.525
c. Hospitalized	11.980
d. Fatal	35.669
2. Forcible sex acts	25.920
3. Intimidation	
a. Verbal or physical	4.900
b. By weapon	5.600
4. Premises forcibly entered	1.500
5. Motor vehicles stolen	
a. Recovered	4.460
b. Unrecovered	8.070
6. Amount of theft/damage = $\log_{10} Y = .26776656 \log_{10} X$, (where Y = seriousness weight and X = dollar value of theft/damage)	

puted as follows. The weight for components 1 through 5 is multiplied by the number of victims who were so affected and the various scores are summed. In addition, the total dollar loss to the victim(s) in terms of both theft and damage is inserted into the formula for component 6. The severity score for monetary loss is then added to that for the other components.

Legal Category Severity

The second seriousness measure concerns the categorization of offenses according to the legal labels used in statutory crime codes to reflect the relative severity of crime. While it may be true that the component-based severity scale of Sellin-Wolfgang may be superior to seriousness based upon legal labels, we nonetheless include these latter measures of severity to enhance our classification of crimes and thereby maximize our prediction and discrimination efforts.

Our data include the Philadelphia crime code classifications for the juvenile and adult offenses. We used these crimes codes to construct seven categories of offense seriousness. These categories are: (1) no seriousness; (2) minor property; (3) minor violence; (4) drugs; (5) weapons; (6) major property; and (7) major violence. Each offense is scored for each of these seven dummy variables, and in addition, we also conceived of these categories as an ordinal severity scale and assigned a score from 0 to 6.

Delinquency Specialization

The issue of offense specialization, like that of offense severity, was also measured through two methods. First, the Sellin–Wolfgang scale classifies offenses as either injury, theft, damage, or nonindex. An alternative typology for testing delinquency specialization involved grouping offenses based upon the Philadelphia crime codes into the following six categories: (1) person; (2) robbery; (3) property; (4) drugs; (5) status; and (6) other. We again scored each event across these dummy variables and aggregated across offenders so that we can typify the career by the total of such crimes, as well as by the percentage of an offender's career represented by each offense type.

Juvenile Court Dispositions

Our data include for each offense that was referred to court the final juvenile court disposition in the case. These dispositions are: adjustment (i.e., a disposition which represents a warning from the court), probation, juvenile facility (i.e., a commitment to a juvenile training school), and waiver (i.e., transfer of the case to adult court).

Demographic Variables

We have available the race–ethnicity (white, black, Hispanic, and Asian/American Indian) and gender classification of the entire cohort. In addition, we measured the socioeconomic status of the subjects using a composite indicator which includes the following 10 dimensions:

1. Median family income
2. Percentage of families below median income
3. Families below poverty line
4. Percentage ages 18–24 with less than high school education
5. Population on welfare
6. Percentage age 25 and older with less than high school education
7. Percentage age 16 and older out of school and unemployed
8. Percentage ages 16 to 21, out of school and unemployed
9. Percentage employed in unskilled labor
10. Percentage female headed families.

The final socioeconomic status index is the result of a previous effort (Tracy, 1981 and Tracy et al. 1990; also reported in Kempf, 1983) in which the subset of highly correlated variables was factor analyzed in an effort to explain variation in aggregate rates of delinquency across Philadelphia census tracts. The first principle component was ultimately retained as the composite index. This variable includes numerous socioeconomic status dimensions and is better able to measure the multidimensional concept than a single indicator could achieve.

Technique of Investigation

This study will seek to contribute to the knowledge base of criminal career development and progression by the identification of youth most likely to offend upon reaching adulthood. There will also be an effort to predict adult offending based on specified categories of delinquency. The typology of delinquency careers revealed earlier in the review of related research—the persistent (and especially chronic) delinquency career, the confirmed nondelinquent, the career of diminishing delinquency, the offense specialists, and the career of those youth who commit offenses of a serious nature—is adopted herein. This typology invites the following research questions:

1. *Confirmed Noncriminal Career:* Whether adult crime is less likely to occur among juveniles who experienced no police contacts as juveniles compared to delinquents.
2. *Persistent Criminal Career:* Whether the probability of adult crime increases as the number of juvenile delinquencies increase.
3. *Diminishing Criminal Career:* Whether the probability of adult crime decreases with desisting from juvenile delinquency.
4. *Serious Delinquency:* Whether the probability of adult offending increases as the severity of juvenile delinquencies increase.
5. *Delinquency Specialization:* Whether the probability of adult crime increases with offense specialization in juvenile delinquency.

Analysis Strategy

Chapter 5 addresses the issue of the "confirmed noncriminal career" by examining differences between delinquents and nondelinquents in the likelihood of committing adult crimes. Our interest here focuses on the proportion of the 1958 cohort that affected a sequence of continuity versus discontinuity in the transition to adult hood. Simply, continuity is possible for both delinquents and nondelinquents as they continue the same behavior pattern as adults that they began and reinforced as juveniles. We examine the likelihood of continuity separately for males and females, and within categories of race and socioeconomic status. Specifically, both the ratio of delinquents to nondelinquents who became adult offenders, and the ratio of adult offenders to nonoffenders who had previously been delinquents, are identified.

Chapter 5 also pursues the second (persistence of delinquency) and third (desisting from delinquency) possible transitions between delinquency and adult crime. We first investigate the persistent career of delinquency through the total number of police encounters experienced by each cohort delinquent during the juvenile period. The total number of police contacts during the juvenile period is collapsed to identify the four dimensions of delinquency prevalence: (1) no police contacts; (2) one-time offenders; (3) nonchronic recidivists (i.e., 2–4 contacts); and (4) chronic delinquents (i.e., 5 or more contacts. Adult offenders who had experienced many contacts with police as juveniles are compared to those who followed the same persistent delinquency career pattern yet did not continue with offensivity after age 18.

However, because the frequency of delinquent offending belies a number of important collateral issues, we also investigate in Chapter 6 a series of time-related dimensions of the delinquency career. Thus, in addition to number of police contacts, we examine age at onset, age at last offense, length of career, and periods of inactivity or interruption in offending (especially the time from last juvenile offense until reaching adult age (i.e., eighteen) and the time between last juvenile offense and first adult offense). We test whether these temporal dimensions of delinquent careers, and any apparent desistance from delinquency (as measured by the period of inactivity), augment the sheer frequency of delinquent events as predictors of adult crime. Finally, in addition to the timing of delinquent acts, Chapter 6 also investigates the nature and timing of the juvenile court dispositions that were applied to the 1958 cohort.

Chapter 7 turns to the issues of whether delinquents who committed certain offenses are more likely to continue their illegal conduct after reaching adulthood. Similarly, Chapter 7 also examines whether delinquents who exhibit some measure of offense specialization are more likely to move on to adult crime than are nonspecialists. In order to determine whether juvenile specialists were more likely than other juveniles to commit crime as adults, we restricted the analysis to delinquents who had committed at least three offenses.

Clearly, one-time offenders cannot have exhibited specialization since they committed but one offense. Similarly, two-time delinquents are constrained to fall into one of only two categories—no specialization because the two offenses were of different types or complete specialization because both offenses were the same. Thus, it is inappropriate from both a conceptual and empirical stance to consider two-time delinquents as specialists.

The literature contains several different measurements of offense specialization. It was noted in Chapter 3 that some researchers have used transition matrix analyses (Figlio, 1981; Wolfgang et al., 1972; and Tracy et al., 1990), while others have used the coefficient of specialization suggested by Farrington (1986). In none of the research reviewed were definitive results reported confirming that specialization could be detected at all, let alone by any particular method versus another.

In this research we have decided to adopt a commonsense conceptualization of specialization, and one that is empirical rather than theoretical. That is, we have classified events according to the Sellin–Wolfgang index categories of injury, theft, damage, and nonindex, and we have also used crime code categories to group each offense into crimes against persons, robbery, property, status, drugs, and other. We aggregated these types across all offenses in a delinquent's career and calculated the percentage of the career attributable to particular types. Thus, offense concentrations range from 0% up to 100%. We use these concentration distributions to determine whether particular levels of concentration reflect offense specialization (50, 60, 75%, etc.) and whether such degrees of specialization are related to adult crime.

Chapter 8 turns to the analysis of the quality of delinquent conduct as a predictor of adult crime. We specified above that a variety of measures of offense severity are available including: the *Sellin-Wolfgang Scale* ("index" vs. "nonindex" offenses, injury, theft, and damage offenses, and a quantitative severity score based upon the crime severity component and associated weights) and the *Legal Category Scale* (no seriousness, minor property, minor violence, drugs, weapons, major property, and major violence and a seven point severity scale).

Our concern is whether seriousness of delinquent events permits discrimination between delinquents likely to go on to adult crime and delinquents who desist from criminal conduct. We use the following four measures of seriousness: (1) ever committing particular offenses; (2) the percentage of a career represented by such offenses; (3) the frequency of commission of such offenses, or (4) the average severity across all offenses, Further, by conducting such analyses by gender, race, and socioeconomic status, we can specify the particular delinquent subgroups for whom such continuity is more probable.

Range of Statistical Analysis

The identification of youth who are more likely than others to commit crime as adults, and the explanation of such subsequent adult offending, requires extensive statistical analyses. Statistical models must be able to distinguish simultaneously the relevant offense dynamics, such as age parameters, levels of offense gravity, and frequencies of criminal behavior for the various career paths of interest, while controlling concurrently for the likely related characteristics of age, sex, race, and socioeconomic status. Analyses capable of accomplishing these interrelated tasks necessarily involve the class of multivariate techniques that have come to characterize recent criminological research.

However, such multivariate analyses were used only infrequently in prior research. Whether due to data or measurement constraints, sample size, or the unavailability of certain multivariate techniques, prior research often remained within the confines of descriptive statistics. Typical results provided comparisons of the mean scores and the proportions of the samples exhibiting a single characteristic. When used, the statistical control of multiple factors was seldom more rigorous than the few variables that can be controlled through contingency table analyses. In fact, measures of statistical significance and association, such as chi-square, gamma, and phi statistics, were reported in not quite half of the studies.

When the interrelationships of variables were examined with multivariate procedures, the models tested were developed for purposes other than the objective of determining which youth are more apt to proceed to adult crime. Many of the previous studies were concerned with etiological explanations for or descriptions of delinquency (Farrington, 1982a, 1982b; McCord, 1979; Polk et al., 1981; Shannon, 1980; and Wolfgang et al., 1972), although other work has focused on the prediction of policy outcomes (Chaiken and Chaiken, 1982a, b; Collins, 1977; and Greenwood with Abrahamse, 1982).

In the Cambridge–Somerville Follow-Up Study, Joan McCord (1979: 1481–1482) explained 24 to 26% of the variation in property, personal and total crimes committed by 201 convicted men by child-rearing practices. She reported no multivariate analyses for criminal career investigations of the entire sample.

A multiple regression model with five causal indicators representing school achievement, peer and delinquency involvement was able to explain 19% of the variation in offense seriousness committed by the 379 subjects (124 former delinquents and 205 nondelinquents) in the Marion County Youth Study who had an adult police record (Polk et al., 1981: 359). Unfortunately, similar procedures were not used to identify the types of careers experienced by these 379 subjects, nor to distinguish the adult offenders from the nonoffenders.

The Cambridge Study in Delinquent Development is a notable exception and has reported the results from sophisticated statistical analyses. For example, Farrington (1982) reported a logit analysis to predict court convictions between ages 21 and 24 and five dichotomous correlates measuring prior conviction, family income, employment, and attitude. Farrington and associates have also reported probabilistic models of: youthful criminal careers (Barnett et al., 1987); criminal potential stability between childhood and adulthood (Nagin and Farrington, 1992); and the onset and persistence of offending (Nagin and Farrington, 1992).

Thus, few previous investigations of criminal career development, progression, and continuity to adulthood have used rigorous multivariate statistical analyses to examine the categories of youth that are most likely to proceed to adult crime and to specify the effect parameters that are associated with this transition. In this volume, we provide the usual contingency tables and other descriptive results where appropriate. We also use multivariate regression and logistic regression models to disentangle the effects that are not discernable with the more basic techniques.

Data Limitations and Constraints

We realize the data used in this research are not without limitations and accompanying constraints. By highlighting the limitations of our data here, we hope to place our subsequent findings, conclusions, and implications in a proper context.

Criminal History Data

The first concern pertains to the specific measures of delinquency and crime that we use in this research. Our criminal history data are based on official police contacts for the juvenile delinquency in the cohort and on official arrests for the adult venue of the cohort. These data cover the entire juvenile career from beginning to end, and the adult career from its initiation through age 26. Thus, only offenders who were officially processed by the police are classified as offenders and thereby, only their known offenses are included in the sequencing of their careers.

We are well aware that multiple methods of crime measurement are preferred to single methods because they provide the opportunity for cross-validation of information. We have addressed the correspondence between official crime data and self-reported measures elsewhere (Tracy et al., 1990; Tracy, 1987) as have others (Elliott and Ageton, 1980, Weis, 1986). Moreover, it is valuable to point out here that resources are not often available to allow multiple indicators of criminality. It would be next to impossible to collect self-reported delinquency and crime data on the entire birth cohort. Interviews with 27,160 people, even if possible, would involve investments of time and money that are unwarranted given the focus of this study. Self-reported data were collected in a follow-up interview of a sample of the 1958 cohort, and we reserve the issues of hidden offending and the congruence between self-report and official measures for future study.

This is a study of the official delinquent and criminal careers of the cohort. We use only a single measure of crime (i.e., official contacts for juveniles and official arrests for adults). We subscribe to the early admonition of Sellin and Wolfgang (1964) that a crime measure should be chosen as close to the actual event as is feasible. This thwarts information that may be lost in the progression through the criminal justice system and thus avoids possible bias that may be introduced. The law enforcement contact is, therefore, the first unobtrusive point in which the most information about the criminal event is available.

We acknowledge the contrary view expressed by Bernard and Ritti (1990), which raises the important issue that police contacts are not necessarily equivalent to "offenses." We further acknowledge their warning that citizen contacts with police are affected by a number of nonlegal characteristics besides offending (Bernard and Ritti, 1990: 35). However, we maintain that a more inclusive definition of delinquency is preferable for our purposes.

As we noted earlier, our juvenile delinquency data contain both events for which the offender was officially arrested and events for which the police responded informally with a remedial contact that did not result in an arrest. We suggest that police contacts represent a better record of delinquency than data that were based solely on arrest information. With our data we can differentiate between the remedials and the arrests, and investigate whether there are correlates, or even biases, of the contact decision made by the police officer.

We are also satisfied with official data in the present context because, as we discussed in Chapter 2, we are concerned with the policy implications of our research as they pertain to juvenile court handling of delinquents before they make the transition to adult crime. Courts generally have available and, perhaps arguably, should only use records of official offenses in determining preferred dispositions for delinquents. The use of extralegal factors (e.g., family context, I.Q. or achievement scores, teacher reports, and so on), insofar as they may be correlated with a delinquent's race, social class, or gender, would introduce an unacceptable risk that the offender would be penalized unfairly and given a more severe disposition because of the presumed association between the factor and further recidivism.

Socioeconomic Status

However sophisticated our efforts to measure socioeconomic status—to capture the many relevant dimensions and express them statistically, our measure of socioeconomic status is based on aggregate census tract data. Equivalent status was attributed to each cohort member who resided in the same census tract. We would have preferred an individual measure of socioeconomic status, but such a measure was not possible. As in a previous volume (Tracy et al., 1990), we intend to interpret socioeconomic status findings cautiously.

Migratory Cases

The last meaningful caveat is that our adult crime measure includes offenses committed and officially processed in Philadelphia only. While we knew for certain that all cohort members were residents in Philadelphia when they were age 17, we had to assume that the same was true for the adult period as well. We did collect FBI rap sheet data, but we did not include these data in this research because it was difficult to ensure that the FBI rap sheets actually belonged to our particular cohort member. This identity problem was especially acute for the females, many of whom married and changed their surnames.

The Prevalence of Adult Criminality

The first issue that properly concerns us in our analysis is to establish the proportion of the 1958 cohort population that occupy the status of adult criminal, that is, the proportion that had at least one official arrest in Philadelphia after the age of 17 (i.e., adult criminality). In keeping with prior work with the 1958 cohort, and with the majority of the extant literature, this measure of the proportion of a group that is officially recorded as criminal will be referred to as *prevalence*. The prevalence data reported here are a necessary first step in our analysis of continuity and discontinuity in the 1958 birth cohort.

The prevalence data provide valuable descriptive information on the relative size of the adult criminal population by our prime measure, delinquency status, and across the various demographic groups (i.e., race, socioeconomic status, and gender). These basic prevalence data are necessary to establish the boundaries of continuity and discontinuity between the juvenile and adult criminal career venues and to specify any differential effects of race, socioeconomic status, and gender on the transition between the prior period of delinquency and the follow-up period of adult crime.

Delinquency Status and Adult Status

Table 5.1 reports basic descriptive data concerning the number and percentage of adult offenders across the four main predictor variables— delinquency status, race, socioeconomic status, and gender. In all instances, the prevalence of adult criminality differs substantially across the various subgroups examined, thus indicating observable relationships with adult crime that will subsequently be analyzed.

First, with respect to delinquency status, the data indicate quite prominently that continuity in offending is more likely than discontinuity. That is, among cohort subjects who had previously been recorded as delinquent, almost one-third (32.5%) were also arrested as adults compared to just 7.6% of the cohort subjects who were arrested as adults but had not been officially processed for delinquency as juveniles. The prevalence ratio thus indicates that continuing a criminal career occurs 4.2 times more often than beginning a criminal career as an adult only. Looking at the data in reverse, we note that if we start with adult offender status, 2,041 of the 3,617 adult arrestees, or 56% were previously delinquent.

However, the delinquency status data also indicate another extremely important finding—offending is a very rare event, even among persons who had a prior career of juvenile delinquency. About two-thirds (67.5%) of the cohort delinquents, or a total of 4,246 cohort subjects, did not continue their offending behavior as adults, and over 90% of the nondelinquents continued lives free from official criminal behavior (at least through age 26).

When we express the relative percentages as a function of the overall cohort population, the differing concentration of the cohort across the four categories stands out distinctly. The vast majority of cohort members, 19,297, or 71%, remained free of both official delinquency and adult crime throughout the period of their lives through age 26. These

TABLE 5.1
Number and Percentage of Adult Offender Status by Delinquency Status, Race,
Socioeconomic Status, and Gender

| | Adult Status | | | |
| | Nonoffender | | Offender | |
	N	%	N	%
Nondelinquent	19297	92.4	1576	7.6
Delinquent	4246	67.5	2041	32.5
White	11681	90.9	1172	9.1
Black	11180	82.6	2349	17.4
Hispanic	630	86.9	95	13.1
Other	52	98.1	1	1.9
Low socioeconomic status	11083	76.6	2279	17.1
High socioeconomic status	12460	90.3	1338	9.7
Female	1340	96.1	540	3.9
Male	10083	76.6	3077	23.4

nonoffenders are followed by the 4,246 subjects, or 15.6%, who had an official record of delinquency but who desisted as juveniles and did not go on to adult crime. We have 2,041 cohort members, or 7.5%, who committed criminal acts during both time frames and we have 1,576, or 5.8%, who committed crimes only as adults.

Second, when we examine the adult prevalence data across the three demographic groups we also find very discernable differences. Across race categories we note that blacks (17.4%) are the most likely to have an adult arrest followed by Hispanics (13.1%), and then by whites (9.1%). The residual category of 52 Asians/American Indians contained only one adult arrestee. By socioeconomic status, the data show that low socioeconomic status subjects (17.1%) are about two times more likely to have an adult arrest than high socioeconomic status subjects (9.7%). Finally, the gender data present the highest differential as males (23.4%) were six times more likely than females to have a record of adult crime.

The data in Table 5.1 are useful to describe the layout of the relative frequencies and percentages of adult crime status. But, cross-tabular data alone do not have sufficient capacity to show the strength of the various effects, especially the strength of the effects while other factors are controlled. Because the dependent measure (adult offender status) is dichotomous, we employed logistic regression analysis, a statistical technique that is designed to accommodate a binary dependent variable and to permit the estimation of multivariate coefficients for the independent variables.

Table 5.2 reports the logistic regression of adult offender status on the four main independent variables shown in Table 5.1. Logistic regression results contain a number of different statistics. These are: (1) the regression coefficient, which represents a log-odds ratio; (2) the s.e., which is the standard error of the coefficient; (3) an indication whether the coefficient is significant (the *p*-value is determined by the square of the ratio of the regression coefficient to its standard error, which follows a chi-square distribution thus permitting a test of whether the coefficient is significantly different from 0, given the degrees of freedom); and (4) the Exp(B), which is the antilog of the coefficient and thus represents the conditional odds-ratio between the independent variable and the dependent variable adjusting for the other independent variables.[1]

---

[1]There are other statistics produced by logistic regression routines, such as the model chi-square and classification results which we have not reported. Our interest concerns neither the overall fit of the models nor the classification results. Our interest centers on particular explanatory variables and whether such variables have significant effects on the dependent variable and the conditional odds ratios across the specific categories of these variables.

TABLE 5.2
Logistic Regression of Adult Offender Status On Delinquency Status, Race,
Socioeconomic Status, and Gender

	Coeff.	s.e.	Exp(B)
Delinquency status	1.3666**	.0400	3.9219
Socioeconomic status	−.3162**	.0461	.7289
Gender	1.8291**	.0499	6.2284
Race			
White	.4034	.2585	1.4968
Black	.8186**	.2577	2.2674
Hispanic	.4682	.2708	1.5972
Constant	−4.0648**	.2614	

$**p < .01$

Table 5.2 indicates that gender, delinquency status, and socioeconomic status have significant main effects (interaction effects models did not produce significant effects for any of the interactions) on the likelihood of adult offender status (all coefficients have significant p-values), net of the effects of the other factors. The strongest effect (1.8291) is due to gender, which has associated odds of being an adult offender that are 6.2 times greater for males than is the case for females. Delinquency status is the second strongest effect (1.3666) with an odds-ratio of 3.9 for delinquents vs. nondelinquents. The socioeconomic status dichotomy is the next strongest and indicates that as socioeconomic status increases, the odds of being an adult offender decline. Among the race categories, the results indicate that when compared to the overall race effect on the likelihood of adult offender status, only blacks have significantly higher odds of being an adult criminal.[2]

Because the data in Tables 5.1 and 5.2 report the familiar criminological result that the prevalence of offending varies most appreciably by gender, the effects of delinquency status, race, and socioeconomic status may also differ within gender categories, what may be operative for males may not hold for females and vice versa. Thus, in order to elaborate any such conditional effects, especially within a context in which

---

[2]In the Windows version of the SPSS (Statistical Package for the Social Sciences) software, the dummy variable routine allows effect parameters to be generated for (a) the included categories compared to the excluded category; or (b) the included categories compared to the overall effect of a variable. In all the logistic regression models, we excluded the "other" race category, but we used the latter procedure for estimating the race effects. Thus, whites are compared to everyone else, and so on.

TABLE 5.3

Number and Percentage of Adult Offender Status by Race and Delinquency Status

	Females				Males			
	Nonoffender		Offender		Nonoffender		Offender	
	N	%	N	%	N	%	N	%
White								
Nondelinquent	5954	98.8	73	1.2	4280	89.1	524	10.9
Delinquent	557	91.3	53	8.7	890	63.0	522	37.0
Black								
Nondelinquent	5448	96.1	224	3.9	3085	81.3	708	18.7
Delinquent	1116	86.1	180	13.9	1531	55.3	1237	44.7
Hispanic								
Nondelinquent	301	97.7	7	2.3	190	82.6	40	17.4
Delinquent	59	95.2	3	4.8	80	64.0	45	36.0
Other								
Nondelinquent	21	100.0	—	—	18	100.0	—	—
Delinquent	4	100.0	—	—	9	90.0	1	10.0

only 3.9% of females were arrested as adults, compared to almost 25% of males, all of the remaining analyses will be reported separately by gender.

Table 5.3 presents adult prevalence data by race and delinquency status for males and females. Regardless of race, males who had been official delinquents were much more likely to experience arrests as adults compared to nondelinquents. Black males had the highest percentages of adult criminals (44.7% of delinquents and 18.7% of nondelinquents). White males, however, had the highest differential as 3.4 times as many delinquents (37.0%) as compared to nondelinquents (10.9%) were arrested as adults. Among Hispanic males, the delinquency effect was clear but less striking (36.0% of delinquents vs. 17.4% of nondelinquents). Only one of the 27 Asians/American Indians had an adult arrest, and he was a prior delinquent.

In Table 5.3 we also report the parallel data for females. Again we note that regardless of race, delinquents are more likely than nondelinquents to have an adult arrest. The biggest percentage difference occurs among black cohort females, for whom 13.9% of delinquents compared to 3.9% of nondelinquents were adult offenders. The largest ratio, however, occurs for white females, for whom delinquents (8.7%) are 7.3 times more likely to be adult offenders than are nondelinquents (1.2%).

TABLE 5.4

Number and Percentage of Adult Offender Status by Socioeconomic Status and Delinquency Status

	Females				Males			
	Nonoffender		Offender		Nonoffender		Offender	
	N	%	N	%	N	%	N	%
Low socioeconomic status								
Nondelinquent	5449	96.6	194	3.4	3007	81.0	704	19.0
Delinquent	1127	86.4	178	13.6	1500	55.5	1203	44.5
High socioeconomic status								
Nondelinquent	6275	98.3	110	1.7	4566	88.9	568	11.1
Delinquent	609	91.3	58	8.7	1010	62.7	602	37.3

Hispanic females are last with a much smaller difference between delinquents (4.8%) and nondelinquents (2.3%). There were no adult female offenders among the 25 persons in the "other" race category.

In Table 5.4 we report the adult prevalence data for males by socioeconomic status and delinquency status. Like the case for race, the introduction of socioeconomic status does nothing to affect the delinquency status influence on adult criminality for males. It is interesting to note that while delinquency status produces observable differences at both the low and high socioeconomic status levels, it seems to be strongest at the high level of socioeconomic status. That is, high socioeconomic status male delinquents (37.3%) were 3.4 times more likely to be adult offenders as compared to high socioeconomic status nondelinquents (11.1%). At the low level of socioeconomic status, the delinquency status comparison produced a ratio of 2.3 between delinquents (44.5%) and nondelinquents (19.0%). Thus, a prior delinquency status among high socioeconomic status males reduces the usual insulating effect of social class.

The data reported in Table 5.4 for females indicates the same findings as for males. The ratio of adult offenders among delinquents vs. nondelinquents was 5.1 among high socioeconomic status subjects and 4.0 at the low socioeconomic status level.

As with the overall data reported in Table 5.1, we used logistic regression models to estimate the multivariate effects on adult offender status of the three demographic measures. Table 5.5 reports the gender-specific logistic regression results for adult offender status on delinquency status, dichotomous socioeconomic status, and three race dum-

TABLE 5.5

Logistic Regression of Adult Offender Status On Delinquency Status, Socioeconomic Status, and Race

	Coeff.	s.e.	Exp(B)
Males			
Delinquency status	1.3390**	.0442	3.8153
Socioeconomic status	−.3239**	.0509	.7233
Race			
White	.4041	.2596	1.4980
Black	.7346**	.2587	2.0846
Hispanic	.4783	.2740	1.6134
Constant	−2.1697**	.2598	
Females			
Delinquency status	1.4891**	.0922	4.4331
Socioeconomic status	−.2785**	.1081	.7569
Race			
White	.6486	1.7896	1.9128
Black	1.4739	1.7885	4.3661
Hispanic	.6820	1.8028	1.9777
Constant	−4.6562**	1.7890	

**p<.01

mies. The results in Table 5.5 for males show that there are significant delinquency status, socioeconomic status, and black effects, indicating greater odds of being an adult criminal. Delinquency status has the strongest effect with a conditional odds-ratio of 3.8 for the likelihood that a delinquent compared to a nondelinquent will go on to adult crime. The socioeconomic status effect is much weaker, as evidenced by the odds-ratio of .7233. When compared with the overall race effect, only blacks have significantly greater odds (2.0846) of adult offender status.

Table 5.5 indicates for females that delinquency status and socioeconomic status again have significant main effects. Delinquents have a significant and substantially higher odds-ratio (4.43) of becoming adult offenders compared to nondelinquents. Socioeconomic status has about the same effect for females (.7569) as it did for males (.7233). However, there are no significant race effects. Although the conditional odds-ratios are high, they are associated with high standard errors owing to the comparatively lower frequencies of adult criminals among females thus producing insignificant coefficients.

With respect to delinquency status, all of the previous data support the observation that being a delinquent is clearly associated with a significantly higher odds of making a consistent transition to adult crime. This indicates that continuity is the more likely pattern compared to discontinuity. We found that this continuity was true for the 1958 cohort overall, and for males and females separately. Further, we found a distinct delinquency effect regardless of the effects of two other important factors, socioeconomic status and race, that are very often related to the prevalence of criminality.

Delinquency Groups and Adult Status

While both interesting and important, the preceding analyses treated juvenile delinquency status as a dichotomous attribute (i.e., delinquent vs. nondelinquent). A dichotomy treats all delinquents alike and necessarily ignores the levels of prevalence by which delinquents can be further classified into meaningful categories. Some delinquents

TABLE 5.6
Number and Percentage of Adult Offender Status by Juvenile Offender Groups and Race

	Nonoffender		Offender	
	N	%	N	%
Males				
White				
Nonoffender	4280	89.1	524	10.9
One-time	550	75.0	183	25.0
Recidivist	266	56.6	204	43.4
Chronic	74	35.4	135	64.6
Black				
Nonoffender	3085	81.3	708	18.7
One-time	702	69.4	310	30.6
Recidivist	550	54.5	459	45.5
Chronic	279	37.3	468	62.7
Hispanic				
Nonoffender	190	82.6	40	17.4
One-time	43	76.8	13	23.2
Recidivist	28	63.6	16	36.4
Chronic	9	36.0	16	64.0
Other				
Nonoffender	18	100.0	—	—
One-time	2	66.7	1	33.3
Recidivist	6	100.0	—	—
Chronic	1	100.0	—	—

TABLE 5.6 (continued)

	Nonoffender		Offender	
	N	%	N	%
Females				
White				
Nonoffender	5954	98.8	73	1.2
One-time	369	94.9	20	5.1
Recidivist	163	87.2	24	12.8
Chronic	25	73.5	9	26.5
Black				
Nonoffender	5448	96.1	224	3.9
One-time	669	89.4	79	10.6
Recidivist	369	84.2	69	15.8
Chronic	78	70.9	32	29.1
Hispanic				
Nonoffender	301	97.7	7	2.3
One-time	41	97.6	1	2.4
Recidivist	16	94.1	1	5.9
Chronic	2	66.7	1	33.3
Other				
Nonoffender	21	100.0	—	—
One-time	3	100.0	—	—
Recidivist	1	100.0	—	—
Chronic	—	—	—	—

commit only one offense then desist, while other delinquents commit two, three, four, or more offenses. We needed to confirm whether the dichotomous attribute of delinquency was related to adult crime status, but having done so, we need to investigate the same issue in terms of levels of delinquency.

Thus, we now expand our measure of delinquency prevalence to include categories of various frequencies of offending—one-time, recidivist (2–4 offenses), and chronic (5 or more offenses) in addition to the nonoffender category. Table 5.6 presents the number and percentage of adult offenders and adult nonoffenders for males, by race and the four possible levels of delinquency prevalence. The results show that as the frequency of delinquency increases, there is a substantial increase in the percentage of adult offenders, regardless of race group. The smallest percentage of adult offenders always occurs among nondelinquents, and the highest percentage occurs for chronic recidivists. The percentages of chronic offenders who continue their criminal careers as adults are consistently similar across the race categories (white = 64.6%; black =

TABLE 5.7

Number and Percentage of Adult Offender Status by Juvenile Offender Groups and Socioeconomic Status

	Nonoffender		Offender	
	N	%	N	%
Females				
Low socioeconomic status				
Nonoffender	5449	96.6	194	3.49
One-time	669	89.8	76	10.2
Recidivist	385	84.6	70	15.4
Chronic	73	69.5	32	30.5
High socioeconomic status				
Nonoffender	6275	98.3	110	1.7
One-time	413	94.5	24	5.5
Recidivist	164	87.2	24	12.8
Chronic	32	76.2	10	23.8
Males				
Low socioeconomic status				
Nonoffender	3007	81.0	704	19.0
One-time	694	69.7	301	30.3
Recidivist	550	55.7	437	44.3
Chronic	256	35.5	465	64.5
High socioeconomic status				
Nonoffender	4566	88.90	568	11.1
One-time	603	74.5	206	25.5
Recidivist	300	55.4	242	44.6
Chronic	107	41.0	154	59.0

62.7%; and Hispanic = 64.0%), thus indicating a pronounced chronic offender effect that is independent of race.

For females, the results are again consistent, but the percentages are of a different magnitude (shown in Table 5.6). These differences occur because of the lower overall prevalence of adult criminality among females. The prevalence of adult offenders increases monotonically as the level of delinquency increases, as it did for males. However, the range among females is smaller because they are less likely to commit adult crime than are males, even when chronic delinquency is considered.

Table 5.7 displays the effect of delinquency prevalence categories by the two socioeconomic status levels for males. As was the case of race reported above, the particular delinquency category produces higher per-

TABLE 5.8

Logistic Regression of Adult Offender Status On Juvenile Offender Groups, Race, and Socioeconomic Status

	Coeff.	s.e.	Exp(B)
	Males		
Delinquency group			
One-time	.7780**	.0611	2.1771
Recidivist	1.4511**	.0608	4.2679
Chronic	2.1610**	.0742	8.6797
Socioeconomic status	−.2849**	.0518	.7521
Race			
White	.4318	.2605	1.5400
Black	.7093	.2597	2.0325
Hispanic	.5070	.2754	1.6602
Constant	−2.1900**	.2608	
	Females		
Delinquency group			
One-time	1.1258**	.1209	3.0827
Recidivist	1.6989**	.1280	5.4679
Chronic	2.5160**	.1948	12.3789
Socioeconomic status	−.2625**	.1088	.7692
Race			
White	.6285	1.7980	1.8749
Black	1.4451	1.7970	4.2424
Hispanic	.6942	1.8112	2.0021
Constant	−4.6368**	1.7974	

**p < .01

centages of adult offenders for males, and at both socioeconomic status levels. The most interesting result is that chronic delinquency status is practically as strong among high socioeconomic status males, 59.0%, as among low socioeconomic status males, 64.5%.

For females, there also is a distinct delinquency prevalence effect that clearly increases the percentage of adult offenders regardless of socioeconomic status level (shown in Table 5.7). But again, these data do not show the same magnitude of the effect because of the lower prevalence of adult crime among females.

In Table 5.8 we move to the logistic regression results from regressing adult offender status on delinquency group, socioeconomic status level, and race. The findings for both males and females show quite demonstratively the significant effect of the three delinquency group categories. Among males, one-time offenders (2.17) have twice the odds of becoming an adult offender compared to nondelinquents. For recidivists, the odds increase to 4.26, while for chronic delinquents, the odds increase to 8.67. Thus, as one moves from nondelinquent to one-time to recidivist to chronic recidivist, the odds of an adult crime status double each time. For females, the same progression occurs, but with even greater increases each time. The odds increase to 3.08 from nondelinquent to one-time, then to 5.46 for recidivists, and finally to 12.37 for chronic female recidivists.

Table 5.8 also displays important results by socioeconomic status and race. For both males and females, socioeconomic status has a significant effect on the likelihood of adult crime, regardless of delinquency group, the higher the socioeconomic status, the lower the odds of adult criminality. By race, however, the data for both males and females indicate the important result that none of the race categories has a significant effect on adult offender status, thereby suggesting that the delinquency group and socioeconomic status effects are independent of the usual contamination from race. Thus, a history of prior delinquency and a disadvantaged social context operate as significant risk factors for the genesis of adult criminality for both males and females.

Delinquency Groups and Adult Offender Groups

We have established that the basic delinquency status dichotomy is predictive of adult criminality and that the level of prior delinquency is even more predictive of adult offender status, regardless of the effects of usually important factors like race and socioeconomic status. We now present two tables in which adult offender status is also expanded to include the same four levels as delinquency status (i.e., nonoffender, one-time, recidivist, and chronic). In this way, we can examine whether levels of delinquency status are further associated with levels of adult offending rather than just the status of adult offending. Thus, we address the issue of whether delinquency recidivism is associated with adult recidivism.

Table 5.9 reports data for males showing the relationship between juvenile and adult offender groups by race. These data present an unmistakable pattern—as level of delinquency increases, there is generally a concomitant increase in the level of adult criminality.

Among white males, chronic delinquents are substantially less likely than anyone else to be a nonoffender (35.4%), have a low prevalence of one-time adult offender status (16.3%), and have the highest percentages of adult recidivist (24.9%) and adult chronic statuses (23.4%). Among black males, we again find that chronic delinquents are comparatively unlikely to be nonoffenders (37.3%) as adults and are less likely than recidivists to commit just one (12.4% vs. 17.3%) adult offense. Similarly, chronic black delinquents are more likely to commit from two to four adult crimes (27.0% vs. 21.1%) and are substantially more likely to commit five or more adult crimes (23.2% vs. 7.0%) than are black recidivists. The data for Hispanic males repeat these findings consistently. The data for the "other" race category are not relevant as only one adult offender existed for this group.

Table 5.9 also reports the data for females. Although the relative prevalence of both delinquency and adult crime are lower for females, the pattern of increasing delinquency and increasing adult criminality is nonetheless maintained. Among white females, delinquent recidivists

TABLE 5.9
Number and Percentage of Adult Offender Groups by Race and
Juvenile Offender Groups

	Adult offender group							
	Nonoffender		One-time		Recidivist		Chronic	
	N	%	N	%	N	%	N	%
	Males							
White								
Nonoffender	4280	89.1	343	7.1	149	3.1	32	0.7
One-time	550	75.0	112	15.3	58	7.9	13	1.8
Recidivist	266	56.6	93	19.8	87	18.5	24	5.1
Chronic	74	35.4	34	16.3	52	24.9	49	23.4
Black								
Nonoffender	3085	81.3	401	10.6	237	6.2	70	1.8
One-time	702	69.4	161	15.9	111	11.0	38	3.8
Recidivist	550	54.5	175	17.3	213	21.1	71	7.0
Chronic	279	37.3	93	12.4	202	27.0	173	23.2
Hispanic								
Nonoffender	190	82.6	21	9.1	16	7.0	3	1.3
One-time	43	76.8	8	14.3	4	7.1	1	1.8
Recidivist	28	63.6	6	13.6	6	13.6	4	9.1
Chronic	9	36.0	4	16.0	5	20.0	7	28.0
Other								
Nonoffender	18	100.0	—	—	—	—	—	—
One-time	2	66.70	—	—	1	33.3	—	—
Recidivist	6	100.0	—	—	—	—	—	—
Chronic	1	100.0	—	—	—	—	—	—

(continued)

TABLE 5.9 (continued)

	Adult offender group							
	Nonoffender		One-time		Recidivist		Chronic	
	N	%	N	%	N	%	N	%
	Females							
White								
Nonoffender	5954	98.8	55	0.9	17	0.3	1	0.0
One-time	369	94.9	16	4.1	4	1.0	—	—
Recidivist	163	87.2	12	6.4	10	5.3	2	1.1
Chronic	25	73.5	5	14.7	3	8.8	1	2.9
Black								
Nonoffender	5448	96.1	171	3.0	48	0.8	5	0.1
One-time	669	89.4	63	8.4	13	1.7	3	0.4
Recidivist	369	84.2	42	9.6	24	5.5	3	0.7
Chronic	78	70.9	13	11.8	13	11.8	6	5.5
Hispanic								
Nonoffender	301	97.7	5	1.6	2	0.6	—	—
One-time	41	97.6	1	2.4	—	—	—	—
Recidivist	16	94.1	1	—	—	—	—	—
Chronic	2	66.7	1	33.3	—	—	—	—
Other								
Nonoffender	21	100.0	—	—	—	—	—	—
One-time	3	100.0	—	—	—	—	—	—
Recidivist	1	100.0	—	—	—	—	—	—
Chronic	—	—	—	—	—	—	—	—

are less likely to be adult nonoffenders (87.2% vs. 94.9%) and more likely to be adult one-time offenders (14.7% vs. 6.4%), adult recidivists (5.3% vs. 1.0%), and adult chronic recidivists (1.1% vs. 0.0%) than are females who committed only one delinquency. Similarly, if the white female was a chronic delinquent, then compared to her juvenile recidivist counterpart, she is much more likely to be any level of adult offender. The data for Hispanic and "other" females are constrained by the small number of such subjects and the relative absence of adult criminals.

Table 5.10 introduces socioeconomic status into the juvenile and adult offender groups relationship. These data confirm that regardless of socioeconomic status level, the relationship between juvenile group and adult group still holds. Among low socioeconomic status males, chronic delinquency is highly predictive of adult crime, as 65% of juvenile chronics commit at least one adult crime, and of these, 80% commit

TABLE 5.10

Number and Percentage of Adult Offender Groups by Socioeconomic Status and Juvenile Offender Groups

	Adult offender group							
	Nonoffender		One-time		Recidivist		Chronic	
	N	%	N	%	N	%	N	%
Females								
Low socioeconomic status								
Nonoffender	5954	96.6	149	2.6	41	0.7	4	0.1
One-time	669	89.8	60	8.1	13	1.7	3	0.4
Recidivist	385	84.6	42	9.2	25	5.5	3	0.7
Chronic	73	69.5	15	14.3	12	11.4	5	4.8
High socioeconomic status								
Nonoffender	6275	98.3	82	1.3	26	0.4	2	0.0
One-time	413	94.5	20	4.6	43	0.9	—	—
Recidivist	164	87.2	13	6.9	9	4.8	2	1.1
Chronic	32	76.2	4	9.5	4	9.5	2	4.8
Males								
Low socioeconomic status								
Nonoffender	3007	81.0	395	10.6	239	6.4	70	1.9
One-time	694	69.7	157	15.8	108	10.9	36	3.6
Recidivist	550	55.7	173	17.5	197	20.0	67	6.8
Chronic	256	35.5	93	12.9	192	26.6	180	25.0
High socioeconomic status								
Nonoffender	4566	88.9	370	7.2	163	3.2	35	0.7
One-time	603	74.5	124	15.3	66	8.2	16	2.0
Recidivist	300	55.4	101	18.6	109	20.1	32	5.9
Chronic	107	41.0	38	14.6	67	25.7	49	18.8

adult crimes as recidivists or as chronic recidivists. Table 5.10 also shows that even among high socioeconomic status males, the chronic offender effect is pronounced, as 59% of high socioeconomic status juvenile chronics go on to adult crime and 75% of these juvenile chronics, who go on to commit adult crime, do so at the adult recidivist and chronic levels. Neither low socioeconomic status nor high socioeconomic status juvenile recidivists produce such a striking pattern, and juvenile one-time offenders have only scarce representation at the adult recidivist or chronic recidivist levels.

The socioeconomic status data for females shown in Table 5.10 present the now familiar finding that the pattern observed for males is replicated with females, but the level of the effects is diminished. That is, regardless of socioeconomic status, an increasing level of female delinquency is associated with increasing levels of adult crime but within a smaller range of prevalence.

Discontinuity: Nondelinquent Adult Criminals

There is one remaining stage of this initial chapter reporting the results of the analyses. When we began our basic analysis of the relationship between prior delinquency status and subsequent adult status, we had the possibility of two categories of continuity and two categories of discontinuity which produce the following four categories of cohort members. The first continuity group concerns cohort members who were never recorded as delinquent and who continued this nonoffender life-style as adults. There were 19,297 subjects, or 71% of the 1958 cohort, who could be so classified. The second continuity group concerns cohort members who had been officially processed as juvenile delinquents and who continued their careers by committing adult crimes. There were 2,041, or 7.5% of the cohort and 32.5% of the delinquent subset who made a transition from delinquency to crime. Thus, about 78% of the 1958 cohort behaved as adults in the same fashion as they had previously behaved as juveniles.

On the other hand, there were two groups that behaved quite differently between their juvenile and adult life contexts. The first discontinuity group concerns cohort delinquents who desisted from crime and were not recorded as adult offenders. There were 4,246 cohort delinquents who represent about 16% of the cohort and two-thirds of the delinquent subset who did not continue their criminal careers as adults. The second discontinuity group involves cohort members whose first involvement with official criminal behavior occurred as adults; they were not previously recorded as delinquents. There were 1,576 such "virgin" adult criminals who represent about 6% of the cohort and about 44% of the adult criminals.

The nature of our data, juvenile and adult criminal history records, and the topics that we will subsequently investigate, exclusively concern analyses of the possible differences in the delinquency careers of juvenile offenders who continue to commit crime as adults vs. those delinquents who desist and do not make the transition to adult criminality. These prior delinquency careers may be differentiated in terms of the age at which the delinquent begins his or her career, the pace of subsequent delinquency, the type of offenses committed, the severity of such offenses and so on.

We will necessarily leave behind two kinds of cases. First, for obvious reasons we will no longer be examining the nondelinquent—noncriminal adult. These persons committed neither delinquency nor crime and are beyond the scope of our analysis here. In our follow-up study, which consisted of personal interviews with a sample of the cohort, we can pursue this type of cases further and investigate the possible factors that insulated these persons from official criminality, or examine whether these persons did commit either hidden delinquent or criminal acts but escaped detection.

Second, we are also unable to include the "virgin" adult offenders in our subsequent investigation for an equally obvious reason—they have no prior record of delinquency that we can analyze as predictive of adult crime. Again, in our follow-up study we can investigate the situational factors in the adult lives of these "virgin" offenders to pursue explanations of why these cohort members began adult criminal careers without having had a prior delinquency career.

Because we must leave behind these adult only offenders, it is important to examine these particular cases before we move on to our analyses of the delinquency careers of the delinquent subset. Although these adult only offenders committed no acts of official delinquency, we can compare the adult only offender to the offender with both delinquent acts and adult crimes in terms of their adult careers. In this way, we can provide evidence, rather than speculation, that such "virgin" adult offenders are possibly different in some meaningful fashion from the delinquents who maintain a consistent criminal life-style. We provide such evidence below in Tables 5.11 through 5.13.

Table 5.11 compares the distribution of adult offender groups by race and continuity status (i.e., both juvenile and adult crime vs. adult crime only), as well as separately for males and females. These data are useful to indicate whether adult crime level differs by continuity status. Among males with an adult arrest record, the data clearly indicate significant differences, regardless of either race or socioeconomic status level, between the two continuity statuses.

Looking first at the data by race, we find that among whites, the adult only offender (65.5%) is more likely than his juvenile-to-adult continuity counterpart (45.8%) to commit just one adult crime; he is also less likely than his counterpart to be an adult recidivist (28.4% vs. 37.7%) and much less likely to be a chronic adult criminal (6.1% vs. 16.5%). The data for black males are also significant. They show that the delinquent who continues his offending career as an adult, compared to the adult only offender, is much less likely to be a one-time offender (34.7% vs. 56.6%), is more likely to be a recidivist (42.5% vs. 33.3%), and substantially more likely to be a chronic adult criminal (22.8% vs. 9.9%). The data for Hispanic males were also significant, but as evidenced by the higher p-value (.05 vs. .01), the differences were less striking, except at the level of chronic adult crime for which the juvenile-to-adult offender is substantially more likely to commit his adult crimes as a chronic recidivist compared to the adult only offender (26.7% vs. 7.5%).

The data for males by socioeconomic status present the same pattern shown by race. Whether looking at the low or high level of socioeconomic status, the juvenile who continues his career in crime as an adult is significantly different from the adult only offender. The delinquent

TABLE 5.11
Number and Percentage of Adult Offender Groups by Continuity Status, Race, and Socioeconomic Status

Race and continuity status	One-time		Recidivist		Chronic	
	N	%	N	%	N	%
Males						
White						
Juvenile and adult	239	45.8	197	37.7	86	16.5
Adult only	343	65.5	149	28.4	32	6.1
	(*p* value < .01)					
Black						
Juvenile and adult	429	34.7	526	42.5	282	22.8
Adult only	401	56.6	237	33.3	70	9.9
	(*p* value < .01)					
Hispanic						
Juvenile and adult	18	40.0	15	33.3	12	26.7
Adult only	21	52.5	16	40.0	3	7.5
	(*p* value < .05)					
Socioeconomic status and continuity status						
Low socioeconomic status						
Juvenile and adult	423	35.2	497	41.3	283	23.5
Adult only	395	56.1	239	33.9	70	9.9
	(*p* value < .01)					
High socioeconomic status						
Juvenile and adult	263	43.7	242	40.2	97	16.1
Adult only	370	65.1	163	28.7	36	6.2
	(*p* value < .01)					

TABLE 5.11 (continued)

Race and continuity status	One-time		Recidivist		Chronic	
	N	%	N	%	N	%
Females						
White						
Juvenile and adult	33	62.3	17	32.1	3	5.7
Adult only	55	75.3	17	23.3	1	1.4
		(*p* value n.s.)				
Black						
Juvenile and adult	118	65.6	50	27.8	12	6.7
Adult only	171	76.3	48	21.4	5	2.2
		(*p* value < .05)				
Hispanic						
Juvenile and adult	3	100.0	—	—	—	—
Adult only	5	71.4	2	28.6	—	—
		(*p* value n.s.)				
Socioeconomic status and continuity status						
Low socioeconomic status						
Juvenile and adult	117	65.7	50	28.1	11	6.2
Adult only	149	76.8	41	21.1	4	2.1
		(*p* value < .05)				
High socioeconomic status						
Juvenile and adult	37	63.8	17	29.3	4	6.9
Adult only	82	74.5	26	23.6	2	1.8
		(*p* value n.s.)				

who continues in crime is *less* likely to commit only one adult offense, and is *more* likely to be labeled as either a recidivist or a chronic recidivist, than his counterpart who begins to commit illegal acts only after the age of 17.

The data for females show results that also are in the expected direction, but only reach statistical significance for black females (shown in Table 5.11). For black females, the juvenile-to-adult career is less likely to involve a one-time adult crime and more likely to involve either adult recidivism or chronic adult recidivism than the "virgin" adult career. The data for white females replicate this pattern perfectly, but were not significant because of small cell frequencies. The data for Hispanic females are inconclusive because of the very small number of cases.

The socioeconomic status data for females were significant at the low level of socioeconomic status. They show that career continuity is associated with a greater chance of adult recidivism and chronic adult recidivism compared to the adult only career. At the high socioeconomic status level, the results were in the expected direction but were again nonsignificant in light of small frequencies at the level of chronic adult crime.

In Table 5.12 we compare the mean differences between the juvenile-to-adult offender and his or her adult only counterpart across 12 measures of adult criminality, age dimensions, the frequency, and the severity of adult crime. These data permit us to determine whether there are any significant differences by continuity status in the onset, nature, and extent of adult crime.

Among males the results were significant for 11 of the 12 measures of adult criminality. As Table 5.12 shows, delinquents who also offend as adults are different from those in the cohort who began offending only as adults. In terms of age, the juvenile-to-adult group, on average, begins an adult career earlier (20.45 yr vs. 20.94 yr), and concludes its career later (22.82 yr vs. 22.26 yr) than the adult only group of criminals. The juvenile-to-adult criminal achieves, on average, about one more official adult crime than the adult only offender (3.09 vs. 2.02 offenses).

TABLE 5.12
Mean Number of Select Adult Offenses by Continuity Status for Males

1. *Age at First Adult Offense*	Mean	Standard deviation	Sum of squares	Cases
Juvenile and adult	20.4563	2.3055	9589.0011	1805
Adult offender only	20.9382	2.3489	7012.8188	1272
Within groups total	20.6555	2.3236	16601.8198	3077

Source	Sum of squares	d.f.	Mean square	F	prob
Between groups	173.3109	1	173.3109	32.1008	<.01
Within groups	16601.8198	3075	5.3990		

2. *Age at Last Adult Offense*	Mean	Standard deviation	Sum of squares	Cases
Juvenile and adult	22.8215	2.5158	11417.8501	1805
Adult offender only	22.2562	2.5215	8081.0768	1272
Within groups total	22.5878	2.5182	19498.9268	3077

Source	Sum of squares	d.f.	Mean square	F	prob
Between groups	238.4569	1	238.4569	37.6049	<.01
Within groups	19498.9268	3075	6.3411		

TABLE 5.12 (continued)

3. *Adult Offenses*		Mean	Standard deviation	Sum of squares	Cases
Juvenile and adult		3.0892	2.8719	14878.6393	1805
Adult offender only		2.0228	1.9823	4994.3388	1272
Within groups total		2.6484	2.5422	19872.9782	3077

Source	Sum of squares	d.f.	Mean square	F	prob
Between groups	848.5460	1	848.5460	131.2978	<.01
Within groups	19872.9782	3075	6.4628		

4. *Adult Person Offenses*		Mean	Standard deviation	Sum of squares	Cases
Juvenile and adult		.7501	1.0708	2068.3125	1805
Adult offender only		.4921	7743	761.9214	1272
Within groups total		.6435	.9594	2830.2338	3077

Source	Sum of squares	d.f.	Mean square	F	prob
Between groups	49.6680	1	49.6680	53.9634	<.01
Within groups	2830.2338	3075	.9204		

5. *Adult Injury Offenses*		Mean	Standard deviation	Sum of squares	Cases
Juvenile and adult		.8737	1.2268	2715.2000	1805
Adult offender only		.5228	.8832	991.3388	1272
Within groups total		.7286	1.0979	3706.5388	3077

Source	Sum of squares	d.f.	Mean square	F	prob
Between groups	91.8687	1	91.8687	76.2156	<.01
Within groups	3706.5388	3075	1.2054		

6. *Adult Robbery Offenses*		Mean	Standard deviation	Sum of squares	Cases
Juvenile and adult		.4681	.9915	1773.4183	1805
Adult only offender		.2280	.6530	541.8836	1272
Within groups total		.3689	.8677	2315.3019	3077

Source	Sum of squares	d.f.	Mean square	F	prob
Between groups	43.0354	1	43.0354	57.1562	<.01
Within groups	2315.3019	3075	.7529		

(continued)

TABLE 5.12 (continued)

7. *Adult Index Offenses*		Mean	Standard deviation	Sum of squares	Cases
Juvenile and adult		1.8554	2.1376	8243.2598	1805
Adult offender only		1.0959	1.4928	2832.2987	1272
Within groups total		1.5414	1.8978	11075.5586	3077

Source	Sum of squares	d.f.	Mean square	F	prob
Between groups	430.4083	1	430.4083	119.4979	<.01
Within groups	11075.5586	3075	3.6018		

8. *Adult Weapon Offenses*		Mean	Standard deviation	Sum of squares	Cases
Juvenile and adult		.5806	.9988	1799.5213	1805
Adult offender only		.3184	.6543	544.0495	1272
Within groups total		.4722	.8730	2343.5709	3077

Source	Sum of squares	d.f.	Mean square	F	prob
Between groups	51.3034	1	51.3034	67.3152	<.01
Within groups	2343.5709	3075	.7621		

9. *Adult Handgun Offenses*		Mean	Standard deviation	Sum of squares	Cases
Juvenile and adult		.2676	.6863	849.7540	1805
Adult offender only		.1399	.4246	229.0912	1272
Within groups total		.2148	.5923	1078.8452	3077

Source	Sum of squares	d.f.	Mean square	F	prob
Between groups	12.1590	1	12.1590	34.6565	<.01
Within groups	1078.8452	3075	.3508		

10. *Adult Offenses with any Gun*		Mean	Standard deviation	Sum of squares	Cases
Juvenile and adult		.3030	.7154	923.2332	1805
Adult offender only		.1612	.4505	257.9615	1272
Within groups total		.2444	.6198	1181.1947	3077

Source	Sum of squares	d.f.	Mean square	F	prob
Between groups	15.0211	1	15.0211	39.1043	<.01
Within groups	1181.1947	3075	.3841		

TABLE 5.12 (continued)

11. *Adult Drug Offenses*		Mean	Standard deviation	Sum of squares	Cases
Juvenile and adult		.4150	.8325	1250.1961	1805
Adult offender only		.3349	.6786	585.3302	1272
Within groups total		.3819	.7726	1835.5263	3077

Source	Sum of squares	d.f.	Mean square	F	prob
Between groups	4.7818	1	4.7818	8.0108	<.01
Within groups	1835.5263	3075	.5969		

12. *Adult Liquor Offenses*		Mean	Standard deviation	Sum of squares	Cases
Juvenile and adult		.1568	.4783	412.6294	1805
Adult offender only		.1855	.5051	324.2138	1272
Within groups total		.1687	.4895	736.8432	3077

Source	Sum of squares	d.f.	Mean square	F	prob
Between groups	.6167	1	.6167	2.5735	n.s.
Within groups	736.8432	3075	.2396		

When we move to offense types, we find that the juvenile-to-adult offender commits significantly more offenses than his adult only counterpart in terms of offenses against the person (.75 vs. .49), offenses that involve personal injury to a victim (.87 vs. .52), robberies (.46 vs. .22), and index offenses (1.86 vs. 1.09). The group of juvenile-to-adult offenders is also significantly different from its adult only counterpart in terms of weapon use: any weapon (.58 vs. .31), handguns (.26 vs. .13), or any type of gun (.30 vs. .16). The delinquent-to-criminal commits significantly more drug offenses (.41 vs. .33) than the "virgin" adult criminal, but the groups not only differ with respect to offenses involving liquor law violations, but also the "virgin" adult offender has the higher mean number of such offenses (.18 vs. .15).

The data for females (shown in Table 5.13) are consistent with the pattern of results obtained for males, and 8 of the 12 comparisons reached the level of statistical significance. The "virgin" female begins adult crime at a later age (21.6 yr vs. 21.3 yr) and ends her criminal earlier (22.2 yr vs. 22.3 yr) than her delinquent-to-criminal counterpart, but these differences are not significant. However, like her male counterparts in the cohort, the "virgin" female criminal accumulates far fewer total offenses than the female who was both delinquent and criminal (1.4 offenses vs. 2.0 offenses).

The examination of type of adult crimes similarly produces the expected differences, most of which were significant. The "virgin" female offender accumulates significantly fewer offenses against the person (.30 vs. .55) and injury offenses (.29 vs. .50). She is significantly less likely to be involved in index crimes than the delinquent criminal (.69 vs. 1.1). Further, her offenses are significantly less likely to involve a weapon (.18 vs. .31), a handgun (.05 vs. .10), or any gun (.05 vs. .12).

TABLE 5.13
Mean Number of Select Adult Offenses by Continuity Status for Females

1. *Age At First Adult Offense*	Mean	Standard deviation	Sum of squares	Cases
Juvenile and adult	21.3351	2.3325	1278.4784	236
Adult offender only	21.6469	2.3273	1641.2010	304
Within groups total	21.5106	2.3296	2919.6795	540

Source	Sum of squares	d.f.	Mean square	F	prob
Between groups	12.9190	1	12.9190	2.3806	n.s.
Within groups	2919.6795	538	5.4296		

2. *Age At Last Adult Offense*	Mean	Standard deviation	Sum of squares	Cases
Juvenile and adult	22.3729	2.4601	1422.2837	236
Adult offender only	22.1680	2.4456	1812.2008	304
Within groups total	22.2576	2.4519	3234.4845	540

Source	Sum of squares	d.f.	Mean square	F	prob
Between groups	5.5749	1	5.5749	.9273	n.s.
Within groups	3234.4845	538	6.0121		

3. *Adult offenses*	Mean	Standard deviation	Sum of squares	Cases
Juvenile and adult	2.0424	3.2325	2455.5763	236
Adult offender only	1.4013	1.0640	343.0395	304
Within groups total	1.6815	2.2808	2798.6157	540

Source	Sum of squares	d.f.	Mean square	F	prob
Between groups	54.5991	1	54.5991	10.4960	<.01
Within groups	2798.6157	538	5.2019		

TABLE 5.13 (continued)

4. *Adult Person Offenses*		Mean	Standard deviation	Sum of squares	Cases
Juvenile and adult		.5593	.9457	210.1695	236
Adult offender only		.3026	.5332	86.1579	304
Within groups total		.4148	.7422	296.3274	540

Source	Sum of squares	d.f.	Mean square	F	prob
Between groups	8.7541	1	8.7541	15.8936	<.01
Within groups	296.3274	538	.5508		

5. *Adult Injury Offenses*		Mean	Standard deviation	Sum of squares	Cases
Juvenile and adult		.5085	.8920	186.9831	236
Adult offender only		.2961	.5182	81.3553	304
Within groups total		.3889	.7062	268.3383	540

Source	Sum of squares	d.f.	Mean square	F	prob
Between groups	5.9950	1	5.9950	12.0196	<.01
Within groups	268.3383	538	.4988		

6. *Adult Robbery Offenses*		Mean	Standard deviation	Sum of squares	Cases
Juvenile and adult		.1144	.4515	47.9110	236
Adult only offender		.0658	.2613	20.6842	304
Within groups total		.0870	.3571	68.5952	540

Source	Sum of squares	d.f.	Mean square	F	prob
Between groups	.3140	1	.3140	2.4630	n.s.
Within groups	68.5952	538	.1275		

7. *Adult Index Offenses*		Mean	Standard deviation	Sum of squares	Cases
Juvenile and adult		1.0636	1.8382	794.0466	236
Adult offender only		.6941	.8136	200.5493	304
Within groups total		.8556	1.3597	994.5960	540

Source	Sum of squares	d.f.	Mean square	F	prob
Between groups	18.1374	1	18.1374	9.8109	<.01
Within groups	994.5960	538	1.8487		

(continued)

TABLE 5.13 (continued)

8. *Adult Weapon Offenses*		Mean	Standard deviation	Sum of squares	Cases
Juvenile and adult		.3178	.6939	113.1653	236
Adult offender only		.1842	.4130	51.6842	304
Within groups total		.2426	.5535	164.8495	540

Source	Sum of squares	d.f.	Mean square	F	prob
Between groups	2.3709	1	2.3709	7.7376	<.01
Within groups	164.8495	538	.3064		

9. *Adult Handgun Offenses*		Mean	Standard deviation	Sum of squares	Cases
Juvenile and adult		.1059	.3710	32.3517	236
Adult offender only		.0559	.2301	16.0493	304
Within groups total		.0778	.2999	48.4010	540

Source	Sum of squares	d.f.	Mean square	F	prob
Between groups	.3323	1	.3323	3.6936	<.05
Within groups	48.4010	538	.0900		

10. *Adult Offenses with any Gun*		Mean	Standard deviation	Sum of squares	Cases
Juvenile and adult		.1229	.3991	37.4364	236
Adult offender only		.0592	.2364	16.9342	304
Within groups total		.0870	.3179	54.3707	540

Source	Sum of squares	d.f.	Mean square	F	prob
Between groups	.5386	1	.5386	5.3296	<.05
Within groups	54.3707	538	.1011		

11. *Adult Drug Offenses*		Mean	Standard deviation	Sum of squares	Cases
Juvenile and adult		.1822	.4574	49.1653	236
Adult offender only		.2664	.4989	75.4178	304
Within groups total		.2296	.4812	124.5830	540

Source	Sum of squares	d.f.	Mean square	F	prob
Between groups	.9429	1	.9429	4.0719	<.05
Within groups	124.5830	538	.2316		

TABLE 5.13 (continued)

12. *Adult Liquor Offenses*		Mean	Standard deviation	Sum of squares	Cases
Juvenile and adult		.0551	.2286	12.2839	236
Adult offender only		.0625	.2683	21.8125	304
Within groups total		.0593	.2517	34.0964	540

Source	Sum of squares	d.f.	Mean square	F	prob
Between groups	.0073	1	.0073	.1153	n.s.
Within groups	34.0964	538	.0634		

Two of the offense comparisons did not show significant differences. Prior delinquency status does produce the expected higher number of adult robberies (.11 vs. .06), but does not show significant differences between the delinquent-to-criminals and the "virgin" adult offenders. Concerning liquor offenses, the adult only female had a higher number of such crimes than her delinquent-to-criminal counterpart (.06 vs. .05). Finally, for drug offenses, it is the "virgin" female who had the significantly greater number of such crimes compared to the adult criminal with a prior history of delinquency (.26 vs. .18).

The findings that adult criminals with prior delinquency are different from offenders who committed crimes only as adults are definitive in two major respects. First, among males, the "virgin" adult offender is significantly more likely to be a one-time offender, and less likely to be a recidivist or a chronic recidivist. Simply, offenders who initiate their criminal careers only after reaching adulthood predominate at the lower end of the frequency continuum. This result holds for socioeconomic status and race. Among females, the results are in the same direction as for males, but are statistically significant only for the subgroups of black and low socioeconomic status females.

Second, among males, the nature and extent of adult crime are significantly different between delinquents-to-criminals and the "virgin" adult offenders. The former delinquents begin committing adult crimes earlier, stop later, and accumulate more offenses. These offenses are significantly more likely to be serious offenses against the person, involve injury, Sellin-Wolfgang index components, and weapon use. For females, the results also were in the expected direction for 11 of the 12 measures, and were significant in 8 of the comparisons between "virgin" adult offenders and female criminals with prior delinquency.

In light of these comparisons between the delinquents who continue as adults vs. the offenders who begin only as adults, we can move on to our subsequent analyses of the possible factors in delinquency careers that may increase the chances that particular delinquents will continue their careers in crime as adults. We can move on without any major concern that the group of "virgin" adult offenders we are leaving behind represents a disproportionately frequent or serious group of adult criminals whose absence might bias our results or reduce their substantive significance in an appreciable manner. To the contrary, it is the group of adult criminals who have a prior record of delinquency that represents the *most* serious and *most* frequent and *most* dangerous offenders, who are the *most* worthy of further study.

Prevalence Summary

This chapter sought to establish that the proportion of the 1958 cohort population with at least one official arrest in Philadelphia after the age of 17 (i.e., adult criminality) differs by the prior delinquency history of the cohort members. We presented results from a series of analyses that establish this connection conclusively. We found that knowledge of delinquency status (nondelinquent vs. delinquent) effectively differentiates the prevalence of adult crime. That is, about one-third of delinquents become adult criminals, compared to just 7.6% of nondelinquents. Further, if we start with adult status and look backward, we found that 56% of adult criminals come from the ranks of persons with a prior history of delinquency. We also found that gender and socioeconomic status were consistently associated with adult offender status, thereby requiring that we estimate separate models for males and females.

The separate analyses for males and females not only confirm the importance of prior delinquency status, but also highlight the differential effects for males who were far more likely to be both delinquent and criminal. The most important of these results are discussed next.

Among males, delinquency status was significantly associated with adult status for all three race groups, white, black, and Hispanic (there were only 27 Asian/American Indians with only 1 adult criminal). Overall, 59% of adult criminals had been delinquent. By race the percentage was 50% for whites, 53% for Hispanics, and 64% for blacks. Delinquency status also was associated with adult status for both levels of socioeconomic status. Delinquents were more than three times as likely as nondelinquents (37.3% vs. 11.1%) among high socioeconomic status males, and over twice as likely among low socioeconomic status subjects (44.5%

vs. 19.0%), to be adult criminals. Looking in reverse, among adult criminals, 51.4% of the high socioeconomic status criminals and 63% of the low socioeconomic status criminals had been delinquent. We estimated multivariate logistic regression models and found that delinquents, low socioeconomic status subjects, and blacks had significantly higher odds of making a transition to adult crime.

After examining the effect of the delinquency status dichotomy, we expanded the delinquency measure to include prevalance. We found that as prevalence of delinquency increased, from none to one-time, to two to four offenses, to five or more offenses, there was a consistent and substantial increase in the likelihood that the cohort member became an adult criminal. We observed this trend for whites, blacks, Hispanics, and at both levels of socioeconomic status. The multivariate logistic regression models confirmed these results and revealed significantly increasing odds ratios as level of delinquency increased. We also found that this delinquency prevalence effect was independent of both race and socioeconomic status.

Last, we expanded adult offender status to include the fourfold classification of nonoffender, one-time, recidivist, and chronic recidivist, as we had done for delinquency prevalence. This fourfold comparison of both delinquency and adult prevalence revealed that as delinquency level increased, there was a substantial and consistent increase in the level of adult criminality. This was true for all race categories and both socioeconomic status levels.

The results for females were generally consistent with the findings uncovered for males. Because females had such lower prevalence of adult criminality than males, however, the strength of the effects sometimes were diminished. Of course, that the effects were observed and often achieved statistical significance may make them all the more important because we have a more narrow range of adult criminality among females.

First, female delinquents exhibited a higher prevalence of adult crime than female nondelinquents for whites, blacks, and Hispanics and at both socioeconomic status levels. Like the case for males, female delinquents had a significant odds ratio (4.43) of adult crime, compared to nondelinquents, and independent of the effects of race and socioeconomic status.

Second, the prevalence measure of delinquency revealed the same increasing trend, that the higher the level of delinquency, the higher the likelihood of adult crime, regardless of race or socioeconomic status level. The logistic regression again produced significant and increasing odds of adult crime as one-time (2.1), recidivists (4.3), and chronic recidivists (8.7) were compared to nonoffenders.

Third, we found among females that the level of delinquency was associated with the level of adult crime. It was especially clear that only females who had been recidivists or chronic recidivists experienced the higher levels of adult criminality. This was so for black females, and to a lesser extent white females. There were too few Hispanics and "others" to generate any meaningful comparisons. The increasing delinquency effect on increasing prevalence of adult crime was also observed at both socioeconomic status levels.

The last stage in this analysis was to determine differences in adult crime between the adult only criminals—who will not be subsequently examined further in this volume—and the adult criminals who were previously recorded as juvenile delinquents. Our results for both males and females showed that the "virgin" adult offenders are: (1) considerably more likely than their delinquent counterparts to be less frequent adult offenders; and (2) very likely to be adult criminals with but one adult crime. Also, the seriousness and offense type differences observed between these two groups, would support argument that the most frequent and most serious adult criminals are those who also were juvenile delinquents.

While it may be fruitful to examine the juvenile lives and then the adult life-styles of persons who escape delinquency and then make a transition to crime status only as adults, they are beyond the scope of this investigation. We are concerned here with any observable differences in delinquency careers that may be related to a delinquent stopping, rather than continuing his or her career in crime. By focusing hereafter only on delinquents, those who offend as adults represent more frequent and more serious adult criminals. It is this group who were previously known to juvenile justice officials, and thus, it is the future adult criminality of this group that could have been averted by particular intervention strategies during their adolescence.

In the next three chapters we will investigate select aspects of the delinquency career to determine whether subsequent adult crime can be predicted from these particular aspects of delinquency history, including the manner in which the delinquents were handled by the juvenile authorities.

6

Predicting Adult Crime Status from Delinquency, Age, Frequency, and Court Dispositions

The previous chapter established the basic parameters surrounding the prevalence of adult criminality in the 1958 birth cohort. Generally, we found that continuity rather than discontinuity was the more likely type of transition from childhood to adulthood. The prevalence data also clearly established that, as the frequency of delinquency increases, there is a discernible and substantial increase in the percentage of adult offenders, for both males and females and regardless of either race or socioeconomic status level. Further, it was also even more clearly established that, as the frequency of delinquency increases, there is generally a concomitant increase in the level of adult criminality, again regardless of the usual confounding effects of race and socioeconomic status.

These results concerning the effect of delinquency prevalence on adult criminality suggest the need for analyses of various delinquency career factors that may influence the likelihood that some delinquents will continue their illegal behaviors as adults, while other delinquents will desist and end their criminal careers as juveniles. In this chapter, therefore, we have restricted our analyses to the delinquent subset of the 1958 cohort and will report on three of these possible delinquency career dimensions as they relate to the prevalence of adult criminality.

There are three dimensions of delinquency that we have isolated for investigation here. First, we pursue measures of the age factors surrounding delinquency careers. Second, we explore the frequency of delinquent acts by looking at overall frequency and the frequency of select subsets of offenses. Last, we analyze whether the juvenile court dispositions received by the offenders have a discernible influence on the transition between delinquency and adult crime.

Age, Timing of Delinquency, and Adult Status

The point at which a juvenile begins his or her delinquent career, from the point of view of research on delinquent recidivism and later adult criminality, may be highly significant in one crucial respect. Age at onset, given the fact that delinquency is limited to some maximum age by statute (age 17 in Pennsylvania for the 1958 birth cohort), forever establishes the maximum length of the juvenile career that an offender can attain. Because the juvenile period at risk is thus permanently set, the extent of subsequent delinquent behavior, or even the character and severity of the subsequent offenses, may be influenced by the offender's particular age at onset.

Simply, a delinquent who begins his or her delinquent activities early will have a greater opportunity to commit offenses, may accumulate more offenses, and perhaps consequently, might engage in the commission of a higher percentage of serious offenses because he or she has had a longer developmental period in which to establish a career. In turn, a delinquent who indeed began his or her criminal career early, and who thus accumulated a higher frequency and/or severity of delinquency, may be more likely to continue this career as an adult compared to other delinquents who began later, accumulated fewer offenses, and consequently, did not establish as strong a commitment to a deviant lifestyle, and did not become an adult criminal.

In the first set of analyses in this chapter, we investigate three interrelated aspects of age and delinquency. We analyze the relationship between adult criminality and the age at onset and age at last offense for the delinquency career. Age at onset refers to the age at which a child designated as delinquent was first taken into custody by the Philadelphia police, and thereby marks the beginning of the exposure period of official delinquency. The age at last offense pertains to the age of the delinquent's last recorded offense on his or her juvenile rap sheet. Of course, an early age at onset does not guarantee a lengthy juvenile career, it merely sets the maximum that such career length can attain. Therefore, we have used the two age measures to calculate a third measure—juvenile career length.

Table 6.1 provides descriptive delinquency data by adult offender status for the three timing measures for males. Among male delinquents, we note that the results are significant for all three measures. Adult criminals began their delinquency careers an average of about 3 months earlier than delinquents who did not become adult offenders. Similarly, the adult offenders committed their last juvenile offense an average of about 8 months later than the adult non-offenders. Taken together, the age measures indicate that the delinquency career of adult criminals was approximately one year longer than that of delinquents who did not go on to commit adult crimes (2.4 years vs. 1.3 years).

In Table 6.2 we report the results, for males, of logistic regression analyses in which adult crime status is predicted from the alternate age measures of delinquency. In the upper half of Table 6.2, the logistic regression results indicate that the age at which a delinquent begins his delinquency activities and the age at which he commits his last offense are both significant predictors of adult status. The later the age at onset (−.1364), the less likely a delinquent is to make a transition to adult crime. However, the later the age at which the delinquent commits his last offense (.3543), the delinquent is even more likely to become an adult offender. In addition to these age effects, Table 6.2 indicates that black (.6284) male delinquents and low socioeconomic status (-.1424) male delinquents are significantly more likely than their counterparts to commit crimes as adults.

TABLE 6.1
Mean Number of Select Delinquency Age Measures by Adult Offender Status for Males

	Mean	Standard deviation	Sum of squares	Cases
Age at onset				
Nonoffender	14.4940	2.4365	14895.3435	2510
Adult offender	14.1872	2.4960	11239.0641	1805
Within groups total	14.3656	2.4616	26134.4076	4315
	$F = 16.3088; p < .01$			
Age at last offense				
Nonoffender	15.8741	1.9805	9841.7071	2510
Adult offender	16.6307	1.4449	3766.2353	1805
Within groups total	16.1906	1.7763	13607.9424	4315
	$F = 190.5128; p < .01$			
Juvenile career length				
Nonoffender	1.3801	2.1107	11177.7199	2510
Adult offender	2.4436	2.5608	11830.0754	1805
Within groups total	1.8250	2.3097	23007.7953	4315
	$F = 222.5792; p < .01$			

The bottom portion of Table 6.2 uses alternate measures of age to reflect two other dimensions of delinquency timing. We used the previous two age measures, onset and last offense, to compute the total time of the offender's delinquency *career length*. Similarly, we used the age at last offense subtracted from the delinquent's 18th birthday to reflect the amount of *transition time remaining* between the end of the juvenile career and the point at which delinquents statutorily become at risk for adult crime. The career length variable is a straightforward measure designed to capture the differential effects of delinquency careers of varying lengths. However, the time remaining measure was envisioned as a way to estimate whether there are differential risks of adult crime associated with a continuation of delinquent activity closer and closer to the point at which the juvenile "graduates" from the delinquency venue.

As with the individual age measures, these new measures of delinquency career length and transition time were significant predictors of adult crime status. The longer the delinquency career (.1364), the greater the chance the delinquent will become an adult criminal. Interestingly, after controlling for the effect of career length, we found that the less

TABLE 6.2

Logistic Regression of Adult Offender Status on Delinquency Timing Measures, Race, and Socioeconomic Status for Males

		Coeff.	s.e.	Exp(B)
Age at				
First juvenile offense		−.1364**	.0147	.8725
Last juvenile offense		.3543**	.0230	1.4252
White	(1412)	.4648	.2729	1.5917
Black	(2768)	.6284*	.2708	1.8747
Hispanic	(125)	.3654	.3024	1.4411
Socioeconomic status		−.1424*	.0753	.8673
Constant		−4.6488**	.4568	
Juvenile career length		.1364**	.0147	1.1462
Transition time		−.2179**	.0227	.8042
White	(1412)	.4648	.2729	1.5917
Black	(2768)	.6284*	.2708	1.8747
Hispanic	(125)	.3654	.3024	1.4411
Socioeconomic status		−.1424*	.0753	.8673
Constant		−.7269**	.2754	

*p<.05   **p<.01

time remaining (−.2179) between the last juvenile offense and the delinquent's 18th birthday, the greater the likelihood of the delinquent exhibiting continuity in offending. Again, the effects of black (.6284) males and low socioeconomic status males (−.1424) were also significant.

In the analyses reported in Table 6.2, all the age and time measures were included as continuous measures. Although the effects appear to be linear, we developed discrete measures for the age and time variables in an effort to distinguish, if possible, any specific points along the age and time dimensions that might stand out and have differential effects predictive of adult crime. Table 6.3 reports these results. The transition time measure is a discrete categorization of the time between the last juvenile offense and the 18th birthday. The categories were purposefully selected to reflect an increasing amount of time as the subject moves away from the 18th birthday (i.e., 1 month, then 2 to 3 months, then 4 to 6 months, and so on). The age at onset measure treats the ages at onset from age 11 and under as a single category, while all others (i.e., ages 12 through 17) have their own category. Lastly, career length was included as a covariate.

Table 6.3 displays these discrete career timing measures and the usual controls for race and socioeconomic status. Looking first at the seven transition time categories, the results for six of the categories are significant and are very important in the particular trend that is observed. That is, when a particular transition time category is compared to the omitted category (three or more years between the date of the last offense and the 18th birthday, all categories are significantly more likely to make a transition to adult crime except the 25 to 36 month category. Thus, when a delinquent commits his last offense anywhere from one month before his 18th birthday up to and including age 15, he is significantly more likely than delinquents who did not have any official acts of delinquency recorded during ages 15, 16, or 17 to commit an adult crime.

Moreover, the results in Table 6.3 indicate a strong trend that as the time remaining until adulthood decreases, the conditional odds of adult crime status increase, and increase consistently. These odds range from 1.58 for delinquents with a 1 1/2- to a 2-year time gap, to 2.28 for delinquents with a gap of 7 to 12 months, to 2.90 for delinquents with one month or less remaining until their 18th birthday.

In order to ensure that these "time remaining" results are genuine, we also included age-at-onset categories to make sure that we were not picking up late starters who, by virtue of beginning their delinquency careers late, must have a comparatively short time period remaining. These data show that compared to males who began their careers at age

TABLE 6.3

Logistic Regression of Adult Offender Status on Discrete Delinquency Timing Measures, Career Length, Race, and Socioeconomic Status for Males

Transition time (mos)		Coeff.	s.e.	Exp(B)
1	(182)	1.0666**	.2044	2.9055
2–3	(313)	1.0306**	.1774	2.8028
4–6	(441)	.8593**	.1613	2.3615
7–12	(716)	.8254**	.1429	2.2827
13–18	(639)	.6117**	.1393	1.8435
19–24	(491)	.4603**	.1439	1.5846
25–36	(613)	.0567	.1358	1.0583
Age at onset				
11	(581)	.3899*	.1527	1.4768
12	(443)	.3672*	.1575	1.4062
13	(599)	.5418**	.1699	1.7192
14	(658)	.5126**	.1966	1.6697
15	(777)	.2183	.2210	1.2440
16	(730)	.2920	.2413	1.3391
Career length		.1623**	.0303	1.1762
White	(1412)	.4641	.2744	1.5906
Black	(2768)	.6388*	.2722	1.8943
Hispanic	(125)	.3890	.3042	1.4754
Socioeconomic status		−.1404	.0759	.8690
Constant		−1.9899**	.3154	

*p<.05   **p<.01

17 (the omitted category), males who began their careers at ages 11 and under, 12, 13, and 14 are significantly more likely to become adult criminals. Delinquents who started at ages 15 or 16 were not significantly different from age 17 starters in the propensity for adult crime. The results also indicate that two particular ages, 13 and 14, had the strongest conditional odds of becoming adult criminals.

In addition to including age at onset, we also included the career length measure, race, and socioeconomic status as control variables. The results indicate that career length is significant, as it was in Table 6.2, which shows that the longer the career the greater likelihood of adult crime status. The results for socioeconomic status were not significant, but the effect of being a black male in the cohort was significant.

Lastly, Table 6.3 reports the results of only the main effects model. We also tested models with interaction effects to determine whether any of the significant main effects depended on or were conditional to other factors. None of these interaction models produced significant interaction effects so they are not shown.

Thus, delinquents who began engaging in delinquency from age 14 or younger are more likely to have comparatively longer careers and remain active in delinquency to age 17. As a consequence of these factors, especially the delinquent activity being committed closer and closer to age 18, these delinquents have significantly greater odds of following a pattern of continued criminality as they become adults at age 18. Moreover, black delinquents are significantly more likely to make a transition to adult crime.

When we turn to the data for females, Table 6.4 indicates that there was no difference in the ages at which adult offenders and nonoffenders began their delinquency careers. However, like males, the adult offender group committed delinquencies significantly later in the juvenile period and had juvenile careers that were almost twice as long as those of adult nonoffenders (1.4 years vs. .79 years).

TABLE 6.4
Mean Number of Select Delinquency Age Measures by Adult Offender Status for Females

	Mean	Standard deviation	Sum of squares	Cases
Age at onset				
Nonoffender	14.5836	2.1631	8117.7559	1736
Adult offender	14.4368	1.8974	846.0363	236
Within groups total	14.5660	2.1331	8963.7923	1972
		$F = .9840; p = $ n.s.		
Age at last offense				
Nonoffender	15.3704	1.9071	6310.1672	1736
Adult offender	15.8322	1.6579	645.9218	236
Within groups total	15.4257	1.8791	6956.0890	1972
		$F = 12.5470; p < .01$		
Juvenile career length				
Nonoffender	.7869	1.5670	4260.2083	1736
Adult offender	1.3954	1.8255	783.1482	236
Within groups total	.8597	1.6000	5043.3565	1972
		$F = 30.0571; p < .01$		

The data concerning the age and time measures for females in the 1958 cohort are reported in Tables 6.5 and 6.6. Before examining these results it is important to recall that adult criminality was extremely rare among females as only 540 women, or 3.9% of the 14,000 females in the cohort, were recorded as adult criminals. Among the 1,972 delinquent females, there were only 236 adult criminals, or a prevalence of roughly 12%. The very low prevalence of adult criminals among female delinquents will make predictions even more difficult than was the case for males.

Despite this constraint, Table 6.5 confirms that females follow the same age patterns as were observed for males. That is, female delinquents, regardless of race and socioeconomic status, who begin their delinquency careers early, and those delinquents who commit their last delinquent events at later juvenile ages, have significantly higher odds of becoming adult criminals. Likewise, a female delinquent who has a long career, or one who commits her last delinquent act closer to her 18th birthday, has significantly higher odds of becoming an adult crimi-

TABLE 6.5

Logistic Regression of Adult Offender Status on Delinquency Timing Measures, Race, and Socioeconomic Status for Females

		Coeff.	s.e.	Exp(B)
Age at				
First juvenile offense		−.1366**	.0369	.8724
Last juvenile offense		.2611**	.0498	1.2984
White	(610)	.8305	1.6902	2.2945
Black	(1296)	1.1956	1.6878	3.3054
Hispanic	(62)	.1075	1.7381	1.1134
Socioeconomic status		−.3628*	.1753	.6957
Constant		−5.0464**	1.8347	
Juvenile career length		.1366**	.0369	1.1463
Transition time		−.1246**	.0459	.8829
White	(610)	.8305	1.6902	2.2945
Black	(1296)	1.1956	1.6878	3.3054
Hispanic	(62)	.1075	1.7381	1.1134
Socioeconomic status		−.3628*	.1753	.6957
Constant		−2.8044	1.6912	

*p<.05   **p<.01

nal. Unlike males, however, it seems that low social status among females, and not race, is associated with adult criminality.

In Table 6.6 we duplicate the discrete measure analysis that we reported above for males. For most procedures, the female results mirror those for males. We found significant effects for transition time, age at onset, and career length. Concerning transition time, the less time remaining the greater the odds of adult crime. Unlike males, however, the odds do not follow a linear pattern as time remaining until age 18 decreases. Similarly, when age at onset groups from 11 and under, through age 16, are compared to late starters (17), the data indicate that all these age at onset points have a significantly greater chance of adult crime compared to the very late starters. Also like males, the career length measure was significant, and socioeconomic status had a significant effect.

TABLE 6.6

Logistic Regression of Adult Offender Status on Discrete Delinquency Timing Measures, Career Length, Race, and Socioeconomic Status for Females

Transition time (mos)		Coeff.	s.e.	Exp(B)
1	(21)	1.7052*	.7233	5.5024
2–3	(38)	1.9783**	.5967	7.2302
4–6	(96)	1.6428**	.5062	5.1695
7–12	(206)	1.5165**	.4505	4.5563
13–18	(246)	1.3193**	.3911	3.7408
19–24	(252)	1.1822**	.3778	3.2615
25–36	(470)	.4036	.3148	1.4973
Age at onset				
11	(159)	1.7404*	.7083	5.6997
12	(184)	2.1711**	.5879	8.7683
13	(314)	1.9968**	.5252	7.3653
14	(348)	1.4673**	.4976	4.3376
15	(447)	1.4617**	.4191	4.3132
16	(336)	1.0779**	.3955	2.9386
Career length		−.0493**	.0911	.9519
White	(610)	1.1013	2.7407	3.0080
Black	(1296)	1.4380	2.7391	4.2125
Hispanic	(62)	.3730	2.7708	1.4521
Socioeconomic status		−.3617*	.1774	.6965
Constant		−5.4121	2.7859	

*$p<.05$ **$p<.01$

All of these age or timing-based measures were significant for both males and females. The results suggest that starting early, continuing through the juvenile status years, and being active right up to the point of becoming an adult (age 18), are important delinquency precursors of adult criminality. Of course, one might inquire as to the reason for these effects. As we noted at the outset of the chapter, perhaps these age measures point to a sequence of beginning a career, then reinforcing said career, then becoming committed to the deviant life-style as such reinforcement takes effect over time.

Alternatively, all of these age measures, taken together, could serve merely as a proxy for the frequency of offending and it is the frequency of offending that really is associated with a delinquent going on to adult crime. The age measures may make frequent delinquency possible, and it is the frequency of delinquent acts, not age or time, that is predictive of adult crime status. We investigate these issues in the next set of analyses (Tables 6.7 to 6.12).

Frequency of Delinquency and Adult Status

Table 6.7 gives descriptive data for three delinquency frequency measures: total delinquent events, total nonstatus offenses, and total Sellin-Wolfgang index offenses (an observable degree of injury, theft, or damage). The latter two measures represent only a limited accounting for offense seriousness and are examined here only to provide a comparison to the overall, global measure of delinquency. The predictive value of offense seriousness will be examined in greater detail in the next two chapters.

Table 6.7 indicates that male delinquents who go on to commit adult crimes have significantly different frequencies of delinquency than do male delinquents who desist from crime during their juvenile years and are never arrested as adults, at least until age 26. Among males, the adult criminals committed an average of two more delinquencies of any type than did the adult nonoffenders. When status offenses are excluded from the delinquency total, the adult criminals committed on average 1.6 more offenses than did delinquents who desisted. Last, the delinquent-criminals committed about twice as many Selin-Wolfgang index crimes as did the delinquents who desisted.

In Table 6.8 we turn to the issue of predicting adult crime status by adding a frequency measure of delinquency to the age and time variables that we examined in the previous analyses. If frequency of delinquency is an intervening variable between the age and time measures and adult status, then the significance of these age and time effects

TABLE 6.7
Mean Number of Select Delinquency Totals by Adult Offender Status for Males

	Mean	Standard deviation	Sum of squares	Cases
Total delinquent events				
Nonoffender	2.7171	3.3089	27471.1633	2510
Adult offender	4.6693	5.1685	48191.5435	1805
Within groups total	3.5337	4.1884	75662.7068	4315
		$F = 228.0767; p < .01$		
Total nonstatus offenses				
Nonoffender	2.0625	2.6931	18197.1797	2510
Adult offender	3.6781	4.1882	31643.9856	1805
Within groups total	2.7384	3.3994	49841.1653	4315
		$F = 237.1434; p < .01$		
Total index offenses				
Nonoffender	1.1506	1.9523	9563.0741	2510
Adult offender	2.2000	3.1234	17598.8000	1805
Within groups total	1.5896	2.5095	27161.8741	4315
		$F = 183.6005; p < .01$		

should disappear when frequency is included in the models. If on the other hand, these age and time measures have independent effects on making a transition to adult status, then inclusion of frequency categories should not affect these other factors and could, instead, add another significant main effect to the prediction of adult crime.

In the top half of Table 6.8, we employed our standard three-level categorization of delinquency prevalence (i.e., 1, 2 to 4, 5 or more) in the logistic analysis, while in the bottom half of the table, we employed a four-level measure (1, 2 to 4, 5 to 9, and 10 or more) which was used to provide an expanded examination of chronic offending and thus differentiate between chronic delinquents and very chronic delinquents. The regression results for both of these analyses are definitive in several respects owing to the effects that are significant and the particular patterns of these effects.

First, concerning the analysis in the top half of Table 6.8, we note that the frequency of delinquency has a significant and strong effect on adult crime status. When compared to one-time offenders, the nonchronic recidivists have significantly greater odds (1.62) of becoming

TABLE 6.8

Logistic Regression of Adult Offender Status on Alternative Delinquent Event Groups, Delinquency Timing Measures, Race, and Socioeconomic Status for Males

		Coeff.	s.e.	Exp(B)
White	(1412)	.4923	.2741	1.6361
Black	(2768)	.6237**	.2720	1.8658
Hispanic	(125)	.3723	.3043	1.4510
Socioeconomic status		−.1343	.0764	.8743
Timing				
First juvenile offense		.0648**	.0298	1.0670
Career length		.0766**	.0356	1.0796
Transition time		−.1218**	.0231	.8853
2–4 offenses	(1529)	.4841**	.0886	1.6228
5+ offenses	(982)	1.0486**	.1249	2.8537
Constant		−1.7192**	.6318	
White	(1412)	.4916	.2740	1.6350
Black	(2768)	.6216**	.2719	1.8618
Hispanic	(125)	.3709	.3042	1.4490
Socioeconomic status		−.1350	.0764	.8737
Timing				
First juvenile offense		.0644**	.0298	1.0665
Career length		.0732**	.0359	1.0759
Transition time		−.1217**	.0231	.8854
2–4 offenses	(1529)	.4916**	.0893	1.6349
5–9 offenses	(654)	1.0298**	.1277	2.8005
10+ offenses	(328)	1.1313**	.1730	3.0996
Constant		−1.7120**	.6136	

**p<.01

an adult offender. When we move to the chronic delinquent category, these odds increase to 2.85. These conditional odds are important because they reflect controls for the age–time measures and the demographic factors of race and socioeconomic status. Among these control variables, all of the age–time measures were significant and the effect of being a black male delinquent was also significant.

Second, when we expand the chronic offender category to differentiate between the chronic delinquents with 5 to 9 offenses and those with 10 or more offenses, we confirm that any level of delinquency beyond a one-time status is associated with adult crime status shown in the lower half of Table 6.8). More important, the results confirm that the likelihood of adult crime increases strongly as level of prior delinquency increases.

Third, as we hypothesized above, the inclusion of delinquency involvement operates as another significant main effect on making the transition from delinquency to adult crime. Moreover, the inclusion of this factor does not generally reduce or diminish the effect of the age–time measures. That is, the effects of having a long career or having a short time remaining until the delinquent becomes eligible for adult crime do not depend on the delinquent having accumulated a large number of delinquencies. The effects of delinquency group, career length, and transition time are additive.

But, Table 6.8 shows a change in the sign of the age at first offense effect. Previously, the age at which a delinquent started was negatively associated with adult status—the earlier a delinquent started, the greater the chance of becoming an adult criminal. We now see, however, that this early onset was merely a factor that increased the likelihood of accumulating a higher number of delinquencies, and it was this greater involvement in delinquency that was responsible for going on to adult crime. The age at onset coefficient, after controlling for number of delinquencies, career length, and transition time, is now significant and positive, thus indicating that the late starters also are postured for increased odds of adult criminality because of the short time remaining in which they can abandon a deviant life-style which has only recently begun.

In the analyses reported in Table 6.9, we used two different measures of delinquency frequency. In the first, we differentiated among delinquents who had committed only status offenses, one nonstatus offense, 2 to 4 nonstatus offenses, 5 to 9 nonstatus offenses, and 10 or more nonstatus offenses. Our objective was to examine increasing levels of delinquency involvement for which the accumulation of status offenses did not pose a factor. By excluding status offenses, we can examine more directly the frequency group into which a delinquent falls when such frequency is based on more serious delinquent acts.

The results in Table 6.9 indicate that delinquents who committed only one nonstatus offense are not significantly different from status offenders in making a transition to adult crime. However, as delinquents committed more offenses of any type more serious than juvenile status events, the odds of continuing this life-style as an adult significantly increased. In addition, the delinquency timing measures are significantly associated with adult crime, as is being a black male delinquent.

In the lower half of Table 6.9, we employ a measure of the frequency of Sellin-Wolfgang index crimes to further explore the extent of delinquency, while explicitly providing for a gross measure of the seriousness

TABLE 6.9
Logistic Regression of Adult Offender Status on Alternative Delinquent Offense
Groups, Delinquency Timing Measures, Race, and Socioeconomic Status for Males

		Coeff.	s.e.	Exp(B)
White	(1412)	.4931	.2741	1.6374
Black	(2768)	.6551**	.2720	1.9254
Hispanic	(125)	.3899	.3041	1.4768
Socioeconomic status		−.1349	.0764	.8738
First juvenile offense		.0676**	.0296	1.0699
Career length		.0979**	.0346	1.1028
Transition time		−.1123**	.0232	.8938
1 Nonstatus	(1697)	−.0156	.1151	.9845
2–4 Nonstatus	(1383)	.4675**	.1265	1.5959
5–9 Nonstatus	(515)	.9803**	.1586	2.6652
10+ Nonstatus	(216)	1.0494**	.2095	2.8561
Constant		−1.7688	.6323	
White	(1412)	.4843	.2742	1.6230
Black	(2768)	.6100**	.2721	1.8404
Hispanic	(125)	.3641	.3040	1.4393
Socioeconomic status		−.1317	.0763	.8766
First juvenile offense		.0843**	.0298	1.0880
Career length		.1482**	.0335	1.1598
Transition time		−.1207**	.0231	.8863
One Index	(1329)	.1864**	.0806	1.2049
2–4 Index	(981)	.5423**	.0979	1.7200
5–9 Index	(275)	.8855**	.1599	2.4243
10+ Index	(85)	.6452**	.2581	1.9063
Constant		−1.9601**	.6379	

**$p<.01$

of the delinquency career. These results confirm the results obtained for
the two global measures of delinquency reported in Table 6.8 and the
frequency of nonstatus offenses discussed above. Thus, as involvement
in delinquency of an index character increases, there is a corresponding
increase in the conditional odds of continuing a criminal lifestyle as an
adult. Black male delinquents also reflect significantly higher odds of
adult crime, even after controlling for the effects of these other important factors.

The situation surrounding the relationship between the frequency of delinquency and adult prevalence among females is both similar and dissimilar to that for males in the cohort. Table 6.10 shows findings similar to those for males, considering that female criminals had a more extensive delinquency career than their counterparts who did not go on to adult crime. These findings emerge, and do not diminish in strength, even though female involvement in numerous delinquencies was lower than that for males. Female delinquents who continue crime as adults committed an average of one more juvenile crime than did females who desisted. When gross measures of seriousness are examined, female delinquents who continued as adults committed twice as many nonstatus offenses and twice as many index offenses as did females who stopped as juveniles.

However, while males demonstrated one of the possible hypothesized relationships among the age and delinquency timing measure, frequency of delinquency involvement, and adult crime status, the females in the cohort exhibited the other possible effect. That is, for females the

TABLE 6.10
Mean Number of Select Delinquency Totals by Adult Offender Status for Females

	Mean	Standard deviation	Sum of squares	Cases
Total delinquent events				
Nonoffender	1.8675	1.7868	5539.5276	1736
Adult offender	2.7754	2.4383	1397.0975	236
Within groups total	1.9762	1.8765	6936.6251	1972
	$F = 48.6363; p < .01$			
Total nonstatus offenses				
Nonoffender	.7460	.9942	1714.9718	1736
Adult offender	1.4449	1.7483	718.2839	236
Within groups total	.8296	1.1114	2433.2557	1972
	$F = 82.1717; p < .01$			
Total index offenses				
Nonoffender	.4303	.7696	1027.5662	1736
Adult offender	.8686	1.2865	388.9280	236
Within groups total	.4828	.8480	1416.4942	1972
	$F = 55.5185; p < .01$			

results showed that age and timing of delinquency are not independent effects, but rather, they operate as antecedent variables that drive the frequency measures which in turn affect the transition to adult crime.

Table 6.11 indicates that the higher frequency levels of overall delinquency do increase the odds of adult crime. The odds for recidivists are 1.65 times higher than that of one-time offenders, while the odds for chronic delinquents increase to 3.58 compared to one-time offenders. When the chronic category is expanded to reflect 5 to 9 offenses vs. 10 or more offenses, the odds increase as the chronic level of delinquency is expanded. Table 6.11 shows that none of the three age–timing measures

TABLE 6.11

Logistic Regression of Adult Offender Status on Alternative Delinquent Event Groups, Delinquency Timing Measures, Race, and Socioeconomic Status for Females

		Coeff.	s.e.	Exp(B)
White	(610)	.8145	1.6837	2.2580
Black	(1296)	1.1457	1.6813	3.1445
Hispanic	(62)	.1161	1.7322	1.1231
Socioeconomic status		−.3613**	.1770	.6968
Timing				
First juvenile offense		.0088	.0629	1.0089
Career length		.0007	.0826	1.0007
Transition time		−.1101	.0596	.8958
2–4 offenses	(643)	.5025**	.1853	1.6529
5+ offenses	(147)	1.2768**	.2823	3.5852
Constant		−2.7012	2.1084	
White	(610)	.8149	1.6837	2.2589
Black	(1296)	1.1458	1.6813	3.1450
Hispanic	(62)	.1151	1.7322	1.1219
Socioeconomic status		−.3623**	.1774	.6961
Timing				
First juvenile offense		.0088	.0629	1.0089
Career length		.0001	.0828	1.0001
Transition time		−.1099	.0596	.8959
2–4 offenses	(643)	.5036**	.1857	1.6547
5–9 offenses	(123)	1.2718**	.2886	3.5672
10+ offenses	(24)	1.3147**	.5254	3.7237
Constant		−2.7019	2.1083	

**p<.01

were significant, but as before, low socioeconomic status females are at higher risk of adult crime.

In Table 6.12 we again note that none of the age and time measures were significant, but the alternate measures of delinquency frequency were associated with greater odds of adult crime. Female delinquents who accumulate more delinquent events in which status offenses are not included exhibit significantly increasing odds of adult crime. These odds range from 1.49 for 1 nonstatus offense, to 2.67 for 2 to 4 nonstatus offenses, to 6.84 for 5 to 9 nonstatus offenses, to 23.16 for 10 or more status offenses.

TABLE 6.12

Logistic Regression of Adult Offender Status on Alternative Delinquent Offense Groups, Delinquency Timing Measures, Race, and Socioeconomic Status for Females

		Coeff.	s.e.	Exp(B)
White	(610)	.7764	1.6958	2.1735
Black	(1296)	1.1417	1.6935	3.1321
Hispanic	(62)	.1899	1.7441	1.2092
Socioeconomic status		−.3678**	.1788	.6923
First juvenile offense		.0339	.0656	1.0345
Career length		.0684	.0759	1.0708
Transition time		−.0696	.0615	.9327
1 Nonstatus	(794)	.4042**	.1687	1.4981
2–4 Nonstatus	(274)	.9828**	.2103	2.6720
5–9 Nonstatus	(24)	1.9239**	.4710	6.8480
10+ Nonstatus	(4)	3.1425**	1.1851	23.1606
Constant		−3.4470	2.1582	
White	(610)	.8232	1.6959	2.2777
Black	(1296)	1.1329	1.6937	3.1046
Hispanic	(62)	.1818	1.7439	1.1993
Socioeconomic status		−.3118	.1778	.7321
First juvenile offense		.0371	.0645	1.0378
Career length		.1095	.0730	1.1157
Transition time		−.0816	.0608	.9217
One Index	(557)	.2525	.1623	1.2873
2–4 Index	(133)	1.0078**	.2333	2.7395
5–9 Index	(13)	1.2617**	.6050	3.5315
Constant		−3.2780	2.1457	

**p<.01

Similarly, as female involvement in the group of serious index offenses increases, there is a corresponding increase in the odds of adult
crime. In particular, if a female had committed either two to four such
index offenses, the odds of adult crime were 2.73, and if she had committed 5 to 9 such index offenses, the odds increased to 3.53, compared to female delinquents who committed no index crimes.

Juvenile Court Dispositions and Adult Status

Thus far we have examined the age and timing measures surrounding the prior history of the delinquents and the extent to which these
measures assist in the prediction of adult crime. We introduced measures characterizing the frequency of a delinquent's involvement in juvenile crime and whether these frequency measures affect the age and
timing effects, and furthermore, whether these frequency measures have
their own independent contribution to the prediction of adult crime. For
males both sets of factors showed significant effects, while for females
only the delinquency measures had significant effects on adult crime
status.

Because the consistency with which the level of delinquency involvement, whether measured as a continuous measure or alternative
dimensions of involvement, was associated with adult crime, it is important to investigate the context in which delinquents can accumulate
delinquency after delinquency after delinquency. Clearly, a pattern of recidivism operates as a reinforcing commitment to a deviant, delinquent,
and criminal life-style, and makes a transition to adult crime a natural
extension of this life-style.

The most natural candidate for such investigation concerns the way
in which delinquents were handled—if and when their cases were heard
in juvenile court and were disposed of with the imposition of particular
interventions. We turn to this analysis below.

Table 6.13 reports logistic regression results for models in which
race and socioeconomic status controls were added to the age and timing variables to typify how a delinquent was handled by the police and
the court. These categories are (1) police remedial only; (2) court adjustment only; (3) a combination of court adjustment and probation; (4) probation only; (5) a combination of probation and juvenile residential facility; and (6) juvenile residential facility only. In effect, these categories
reflect an increasing degree of intervention on the part of the authorities.
We also added two continuous measures of disposition: frequency of
probation and frequency of juvenile facility commitments.

TABLE 6.13

Logistic Regression of Adult Offender Status on Alternative Delinquency Timing Measures, Police and Court Disposition, Race, and Socioeconomic Status for Males

		Coeff.	s.e.	Exp(B)
White	(1412)	.5044	.2742	1.6559
Black	(2768)	.6054**	.2720	1.8320
Hispanic	(125)	.3332	.3041	1.3955
Socioeconomic status		−.1202	.0762	.8868
Age at onset		−.0833**	.0165	.9201
Transition time		−.2642**	.0255	.7678
Adjusted	(1561)	.2211**	.0848	1.2474
Adjusted/probation	(946)	.7399**	.1019	2.0956
Probation only	(212)	.4660**	.1544	1.5936
Probation/prison	(156)	1.0922**	.2023	2.9808
Prison only	(70)	.9444**	.2661	2.5714
Constant		.4752	.3931	
White	(1412)	.4977	.2738	1.6450
Black	(2768)	.5935**	.2717	1.8102
Hispanic	(125)	.3300	.3037	1.3909
Socioeconomic status		−.1220	.0762	.8851
Age at onset		−.0787**	.0166	.9244
Transition time		−.2584**	.0256	.7723
Adjusted	(1561)	.2287**	.0848	1.2570
Adjusted/probation	(946)	.4953**	.1443	1.6410
Probation only	(212)	.2711	.1746	1.3113
Probation/prison	(156)	.6818**	.3288	1.9774
Prison only	(70)	.8373**	.3469	2.3101
Frequency of probation		.1701**	.0710	1.1854
Frequency of prison		.0827	.1518	1.0862
Constant		.4020	.3941	

**$p<.01$

At first impression, the results of these analyses are startling. That is, in the top half of Table 6.13, we note that each type of court disposition, compared to the most lenient disposition of all (i.e., police remedial, in which the police release the delinquent to the custody of family and no further official actions are taken), produces significantly higher odds of the delinquent going on to adult crime. These results seem to suggest that the imposition of any court disposition, especially probation, juvenile facility, or a combination of the two, are a complete failure in deterring the delinquent from future criminal conduct as an adult. When we add the frequency of probation and facility dispositions, we find in the lower half of Table 6.13, that the increasing use of the probation disposition is an especially unsuccessful intervention in averting adult crime.

Among females, the results given in Table 6.14 show the same general result. Increasingly severe court handling of a female delinquent is accompanied by significantly higher odds of the commission of adult

TABLE 6.14

Logistic Regression of Adult Offender Status on Alternative Delinquency Timing Measures, Police and Court Disposition, Race, and Socioeconomic Status for Females

		Coeff.	s.e.	Exp(B)
White	(610)	.8220	1.6931	2.2750
Black	(1296)	1.1382	1.6907	3.1211
Hispanic	(62)	.0967	1.7413	1.1016
Socioeconomic status		−.3308	.1781	.7183
Age at onset		−.0698	.0428	.9326
Transition time		−.1320**	.0562	.8763
Adjusted	(571)	.3608**	.1757	1.4345
Adjusted/probation	(168)	1.3291**	.2239	3.7775
Probation only	(63)	1.1919**	.3230	3.2933
Probation/prison	(19)	1.2919**	.5322	3.6395
Prison only	(19)	.5103	.6503	1.6659
Constant		−1.9540	1.8470	
White	(610)	.8206	1.6931	2.2718
Black	(1296)	1.1375	1.6907	3.1189
Hispanic	(62)	.0989	1.7412	1.1040
Socioeconomic status		−.3285	.1782	.7200
Age at onset		−.0714	.0431	.9311
Transition time		−.1337**	.0564	.8749
Adjusted	(571)	.3594**	.1758	1.4324
Adjusted/probation	(168)	1.3996**	.3568	4.0536
Probation only	(63)	1.2578**	.4125	3.5176
Probation/prison	(19)	1.6066	1.0093	4.9858
Prison only	(19)	.7437	1.0377	2.1038
Frequency of probation		−.0592	.2313	.9425
Frequency of prison		−.1765	.6114	.8382
Constant		−1.9252	1.8486	

**$p<.01$

crime. Even when a particular coefficient was not significant, the sign of each and every court disposition coefficient was positive thus indicating higher odds of adult crime. While the frequency of either probation or facility dispositions were negative, these effects were not significant and the odds comparatively low compared to the other measures.

Thus, contrary to expectations, the results would seem to suggest that the juvenile court is consistently and highly ineffective in handling offenders, whether male or female. Perhaps as some of the criminological literature would have us believe, severe court dispositions, when applied to juveniles, only make matters worse by "hardening" the delinquent and making him or her even more susceptible to a continuing life of crime.

We investigated the efficacy of court dispositions further to confirm the lack of success of such dispositions or discover possibly latent effects that were being masked. In particular, we determined that an overall, or offender-based measure, which merely indicated how an offender was handled by the court across his or her career, was insufficient to determine the actual relationship between court dispositions as the career progresses offense by offense, juvenile career recidivism, and later adult crime. Court dispositions, such as probation and commitment to a residential facility, and the number of such dispositions, may be confounded with the frequency and/or the severity of delinquency. Naturally, courts may hold probation and facility commitment dispositions in abeyance until the delinquent reaches a certain point of recidivism or offense severity.

We believed that the timing of court dispositions in the delinquency career must be controlled to gage the efficacy of the dispositions. If particular court dispositions are to have any value in providing a rehabilitating experience through probation supervision or even deterring a delinquent from subsequent delinquency and/or later criminal adult conduct, then court-ordered supervision or residential commitment must occur at a propitious point in the juvenile's career. Obviously, such dispositions should occur early enough in the career to have the desired effect. If court dispositions are imposed too late in a delinquent's career—a point that is too late to influence and reorient the juvenile's commitment to illegal activities, then results such as were reported above for Tables 6.13 and 6.14 are understandable and should be expected.

In order to investigate the timing of the court dispositions, we examined a delinquent's offense career, offense by offense, and determined the point at which probation or a treatment facility disposition was imposed. Using these rank offense data, we developed a discrete measure of probation and facility commitment dispositions which reflect the specific timing of these dispositions. We used four such categories for the probation and commitment measures (1) no probation (court adjustment, a form of diversion for less serious offenders); (2) early probation; (3) midcareer probation; and (4) late career probation. With respect to rank number of offense, early, medium, and late probation were measured as follows:

1. Early: Probation 1: first, second, or third offense
               Probation 2: second, third, or fourth offense
               Probation 3: third or fourth offense
2. Medium: Probation 1: fourth, fifth, or sixth offense
               Probation 2: fifth, sixth, or seventh offense
               Probation 3: fifth, sixth, or seventh offense
3. Late: Probation 1: at or beyond the seventh offense
               Probation 2: at or beyond the eighth offense
               Probation 3: at or beyond the ninth offense

We used a parallel measurement for the timing of commitment to a residential juvenile facility.

Table 6.15 reports logistic regression results for males, using a model which includes race and socioeconomic status as control factors, a probation timing measure, the total number of delinquent events in the offender's career, and an interaction term between probation timing and the total number of events.

These results are in sharp contrast to those reported above (Table 6.13) concerning the overall court disposition measure that ignored the timing parameter. When we include timing, we now see that probation not only makes a difference, it makes a very significant difference. Thus, compared to male delinquents who were classified as "late" recipients of a probation disposition, delinquents who were adjusted (a form of court diversion) or who received an "early" or "medium" probation sentence had significantly lower odds of becoming adult offenders.

As we noted, this model includes an interaction term which we used to determine whether the imposition of probation had a significant effect across the total delinquent events continuum. The signs and significance of the interaction term signify that as the frequency of delinquency increases and as the imposition of probation occurs later and later in the career, the delinquent is likely to become an adult criminal as compared to the delinquent who, in light of early probation intervention, is a less frequent delinquent and less likely to go on to adult crime.

The results for females shown in Table 6.16 are different from the results for males. For cohort females, the timing of probation dispositions

TABLE 6.15
Logistic Regression of Adult Offender Status On Timing of Probation, Frequency of Delinquency, Race, and Socioeconomic Status for Males

		Coeff.	s.e.	Exp(B)
White	(1412)	.4530	.2730	1.5731
Black	(2768)	.5487**	.2710	1.7311
Hispanic	(125)	.2498	.3024	1.2837
Socioeconomic status		−.1096	.0753	.8962
No probation	(3002)	−2.0319**	.4665	.1311
Early probation	(895)	−1.4415**	.4772	.2366
Medium probation	(298)	−1.2074**	.5408	.2990
Total delinquent events		−.0230	.0277	.9773
Events by probation				
No probation		.1436**	.0313	1.1544
Early probation		.1384**	.0377	1.1484
Medium probation		.1043**	.0423	1.1100
Constant		.6557	.5353	

**$p<.01$

appears to make no difference in predicting adult crime status. The coefficients for the various probation timing categories are high in magnitude and are in the expected direction (negative), but the standard errors are high and none of these effects produce conditional odds ratios that reach statistical significance.

This absence of significant probation effects among females must be placed within a context of the overall distribution of court dispositions for females. That is, 1,722 of the 1,972 female delinquents, or 87.3%, had never received a probation disposition. They had been remedialled by the police or adjusted at the juvenile court stage. Among the 250 female delinquents (12.7%) who had received probation, 195 (9.9%) received early probation, 40 (2.0%) received medium probation, and just 15 (0.8%) received late probation. Thus, prevalence of probation for females, and especially of midcareer or late career probation, is too low to form a meaningful basis for comparison.

In Table 6.17 we address the issue of the effectiveness of court dispositions committing male delinquents to the custody of a treatment facility. We again used a timing measure that consisted of the same four categories as for probation (i.e., none, early, medium, and late). Only one

TABLE 6.16

Logistic Regression of Adult Offender Status on Timing of Probation, Frequency of Delinquency, Race, and Socioeconomic Status for Females

		Coeff.	s.e.	Exp(B)
White	(610)	.7636	1.6895	2.1459
Black	(1296)	1.0890	1.6871	2.9712
Hispanic	(62)	.0262	1.7379	1.0265
Socioeconomic status		−.3064	.1777	.7361
No probation	(1722)	−3.3585	1.9010	.0348
Early probation	(195)	−2.0297	1.9165	.1314
Medium probation	(40)	−2.6332	2.0676	.0718
Total delinquent events		−.1411	.1837	.8684
Events by probation				
No probation		.3161	.1895	1.3717
Early probation		.2427	.1994	1.2747
Medium probation		.2591	.2094	1.2958
Constant		−.0929	2.5359	

main effect coefficient for commitment timing is significant—the effect of no facility commitment vs. the late imposition of commitment. This parameter indicates that juveniles who were never sentenced to a treatment facility have significantly lower odds of adult crime compared to delinquents who were sent to a juvenile facility late in their delinquency careers. Neither the early nor medium imposition of a commitment disposition is significantly more effective in reducing adult crime compared to late commitment.

These main effects ignore possible interactions between timing of facility commitment and either the frequency or severity of the offenses in the delinquent's career. A model containing a facility commitment by frequency interaction term did not produce any significant effects. However, a severity by commitment interaction term did indicate a significant effect. That is, among less serious offenders, imposition of commitment at midcareer compared to late in the career reduces the odds of adult crime.

On the whole, however, investigating the timing of commitment to a facility among male delinquents does not appear to reveal any appreciable and consistent value to this disposition in reducing the propensity for adult crime. As with probation for females reported above, however,

TABLE 6.17
Logistic Regression of Adult Offender Status on Timing of Prison, Frequency and Severity of Delinquency, Race, and Socioeconomic Status for Males

		Coeff.	s.e.	Exp(B)
White	(1412)	.4366	.2722	1.5475
Black	(2768)	.5245	.2702	1.6896
Hispanic	(125)	.2318	.3014	1.2608
Socioeconomic status		−.1231	.0748	.8842
No prison	(4089)	−1.9244**	.7598	.1460
Early prison	(54)	−.9034	1.1195	.4052
Medium prison	(57)	−2.4890	1.3778	.0830
Total delinquent events		.0217	.0256	1.0219
Events by prison				
No prison		.1193**	.0282	1.1268
Early prison		.0168	.0698	1.0169
Medium prison		.0963	.1052	1.1011
Average severity		−.1044	.0935	.9009
Severity by prison				
No prison		.1308	.0937	1.1398
Early prison		.1561	.1102	1.1689
Medium prison		.3349**	.1685	1.3977
Constant		.5449	.8030	

**$p<.01$

the distribution of commitments among males shows very little dispersion. That is, the overall distribution is highly skewed; 4,089 of the 4,315 male delinquents, or 94.8%, had never been committed to a treatment facility. Further, the distribution is particularly skewed toward the later imposition of the commitment to a facility; 54 males were sentenced to a facility early and at midcareer, while over twice as many, 115, were sentenced to a facility late in the career,

Thus, commitments to juvenile facilities for males might have been effective under the following two scenarios: First, if more delinquents had received such a disposition; or second, if commitments to a residential facility were imposed much earlier in the delinquency career (even among the small number of males (236) who did receive such a sentence). Regardless, all we can say here is that committing a male delinquent to a juvenile facility did not appear to be an effective disposition in reducing the likelihood of adult crime in the 1958 cohort.

In fact, given the lateness, as measured by rank number of offense, with which such commitments were imposed, one could infer a particular motivation for commitment to a juvenile facility. The late imposition of facility commitment is more akin to a "just deserts" philosophy of finally punishing the offender for his transgressions, rather than a deterrence or rehabilitation ideal, which would have been pursued much earlier in the delinquent's career.

In Table 6.18 we report the facility commitment timing data for females. Not surprisingly, in light of the female probation data and male prison data given previously, we do not find any significant prison timing effects for females. Further, only 38 of the 1,972 female delinquents received a prison sentence, with 17 each in the early and midcareer periods and only four late recipients. Clearly, this skewed distribution of prison timing categories is insufficient to form a meaningful basis for comparison.

TABLE 6.18

Logistic Regression of Adult Offender Status on Timing of Prison, Frequency and Severity of Delinquency, Race, and Socioeconomic Status for Females

		Coeff.	s.e.	Exp(B)
White	(610)	1.0729	2.7776	2.9238
Black	(1296)	1.3868	2.7761	4.0018
Hispanic	(62)	.2863	2.8072	1.3315
Socioeconomic status		−.3527**	.1789	.7028
No prison	(1934)	4.0834	63.2196	59.3496
Early prison	(17)	.2852	63.3942	1.3300
Medium prison	(17)	4.7224	63.2594	112.4373
Total delinquent events		.0244	4.8065	1.0247
Events by prison				
No prison		.1697	4.8066	1.1850
Early prison		.3210	4.8146	1.3785
Medium prison		−.4609	4.8176	.6307
Average severity		.0465	16.5822	1.0476
Severity by prison				
No prison		.0063	16.5822	1.0063
Early prison		.2078	16.6017	1.2309
Medium prison		2.1587	16.6242	8.6595
Constant		−7.8347	63.2804	

**p<.01

The final analysis in this chapter is to investigate the comparative effects when both probation timing and facility commitment timing are included in the same model. Our purpose here is to confirm the results obtained in the separate models when probation and prison commitments are considered simultaneously in the same model, and thus the effects of each are controlled. This will ensure that the significant probation effects (for males) are not an artifact of the prison timing measure, or that the absence of significant prison effects is due to a suppression effect of probation.

Table 6.19 indicates that controlling for the main effect of facility timing, and an interaction effect between facility timing and offense severity, does not affect the statistical significance of probation timing for males. Thus, there are significant main effects for no probation vs.

TABLE 6.19
Logistic Regression of Adult Offender Status on Timing of Probation and Prison, Frequency and Severity of Delinquency, Race, and Socioeconomic Status for Males

		Coeff.	s.e.	Exp(B)
White	(1410)	.4547	.2730	1.5757
Black	(2768)	.5397*	.2710	1.7155
Hispanic	(125)	.2500	.3024	1.2840
Socioeconomic status		−.1132	.0755	.8930
No probation	(3002)	−1.6656**	.5707	.1891
Early probation	(895)	−1.0743**	.5791	.3415
Medium probation	(298)	−.9780	.5974	.3761
Total delinquent events		−.0190	.0309	.9811
Events by probation No probation		.1064**	.0413	1.1122
Early probation		.0997*	.0466	1.1049
Medium probation		.0874*	.0458	1.0914
No prison	(4089)	−.1070	.5836	.8985
Early prison	(54)	1.3371	.7857	3.8080
Medium prison	(57)	.3599	.9894	1.4332
Severity by prison No prison		.0340	.0397	1.0346
Early prison		−.0671	.0706	.9351
Medium prison		.0357	.1007	1.0364
Constant		.3903	.6371	.5401

*p <.05   **p <.01

late probation, and for early probation vs. late probation. Further, when the frequency of the delinquency and probation timing interaction term is examined, we find that all categories have significant effects. These effects indicate that as frequency of delinquency declines, any type of disposition, compared to late probation, produces significantly lower odds of adult crime. Our confidence in this result is bolstered by the fact that these results were obtained while controlling for the effects of race, socioeconomic status, total delinquent events, facility timing, and an offense severity by facility timing interaction. Clearly, as the probation disposition is applied later and later, especially for frequent delinquents, the probability of adult crime status increases.

The complete court disposition model for females is shown in Table 6.20. These results indicate, as before, that there are no significant effects

TABLE 6.20

Logistic Regression of Adult Offender Status on Timing of Probation and Prison, Frequency and Severity of Delinquency, Race, and Socioeconomic Status for Females

		Coeff.	s.e.	Exp(B)
White	(610)	1.0124	2.7724	2.7521
Black	(1296)	1.3466	2.7709	3.8445
Hispanic	(62)	.2736	2.8023	1.3147
Socioeconomic status		−.2825	.1791	.7539
No probation	(1722)	−2.7975	1.5892	.0610
Early probation	(195)	−1.4287	1.6099	.2396
Medium probation	(40)	−2.2530	1.8124	.1051
Total delinquent events		−.0529	4.9077	.9485
Events by probation				
No probation		.2473	.1560	1.2805
Early probation		.1601	.1682	1.1737
Medium probation		.2169	.1867	1.2423
No prison	(1934)	5.7475	55.1258	313.4131
Early prison	(17)	2.5972	55.2045	13.4260
Medium prison	(17)	8.2819	55.1429	3951.5060
Severity by prison				
No prison		−.0102	4.9089	.9899
Early prison		.1361	4.9159	1.1458
Medium prison		−.2424	4.9115	.7847
Constant		−6.6789	55.2030	

for female delinquents concerning the timing of either probation or facility commitment, or for the possible interaction between probation and the frequency of delinquency, or between facility commitment and the severity of delinquency.

Summary

In this chapter we restricted our analyses to the delinquent subset of the 1958 cohort, 4,315 males and 1,972 females, in order to investigate three distinct aspects of the delinquency career that were hypothesized to be related to the likelihood that a delinquent would continue his or her career into of adult criminality. The three dimensions of the delinquency career we investigated were (1) the age and timing factors of the delinquency career; (2) the frequency of delinquent acts; and (3) the various juvenile court dispositions (and their timing) that were applied to the delinquents as their careers progressed.

Age and Timing of Delinquency

In the first set of analyses in this chapter we investigated several dimensions of age and delinquency. We analyze the relationship between adult criminality and the age at onset and age at last offense for the delinquency career. However, because beginning a delinquency career at an early age does not guarantee that the delinquent will have a lengthy juvenile career, we used the two age measures to calculate a third age measure—actual juvenile career length. Lastly, we reconceptualized age at last offense and expressed it as the difference between the age at last offense and the delinquent's 18th birthday, thus indicating the length of time that the delinquent had available before he or she made the transition to adult status.

Our results concerning the relationship between the age and timing measures of delinquency and the odds of the delinquent going on to adult crime were definitive for males in the cohort. When various transition time categories were compared to the longest category (three or more years between last offense and age 18), all such categories were significantly more likely to make a transition to adult crime except the category closest to the comparison group (i.e., the 2- to 3-year category). These results thus indicated that when a delinquent commits his last offense anywhere from one month before his 18th birthday to his 15th birthday, he is significantly more likely than delinquents who did not have any official acts of delinquency recorded between ages 15 and 17, to commit an adult crime.

In order to ensure that the results surrounding "time remaining" were genuine, we also included age-at-onset categories to confirm that analysis was not picking up a "late starters effect." That is, late starters—by virtue of beginning late—must have a comparatively short time period remaining, and this short time remaining would influence the "time remaining" results artificially. These data show that only males who began their careers comparatively late, in the last 2 years of their period at risk (i.e., ages 15 and 16), were not significantly more likely to become adult criminals compared to those very late starters, who began at age 17. The results also indicated that two particular ages, 13 and 14, had the strongest conditional odds of becoming adult criminals.

In addition to including age at onset, we also included the career length measure, race, and socioeconomic status as control variables. The results indicate that career length was significant and show that the longer the career the greater likelihood of adult crime. The results for socioeconomic status were not significant, but the effect of being a black male in the cohort was significant.

The age and timing results indicated that females followed the same pattern as was observed for males. That is, female delinquents, regardless of race and socioeconomic status, who began their delinquency careers early and who committed their last delinquent events later, had significantly higher odds of becoming adult criminals. Similarly, female delinquents with long careers, or who commit their last delinquent acts closer to their 18th birthday, have significantly higher odds of becoming adult criminals. Among females, unlike males, it seems that low social status, and not race, is consistently associated with adult criminality.

When we considered the "time remaining data" for females, the results mirrored those for males. We found significant effects for transition time, age-at-onset, and career length. Concerning transition time, the less time remaining the greater the odds of adult crime. Unlike males, however, the odds did not follow a linear pattern as time remaining decreases. Similarly, when age-at-onset groups from 11 and under through age 16 were compared to late starters (at age 17), the data indicate that all the age-at-onset ages had a significantly greater chance of adult crime compared to the very late starters. Also as with males, the career length measure was significant and showed that a longer delinquency career is associated with the likelihood of adult status, even after controlling for the period of time remaining.

Frequency of Delinquency

Because all of the age or career timing measures were significant for both males and females, the most basic explanation is that starting early, continuing through the delinquency years, and then being active right up to the point of becoming an adult (at age 18) are important delinquency career related precursors of adult criminality. We considered an alternative explanation that all of these age measures taken together could merely function as a proxy for the frequency of offending, and it is this frequency that really is associated with a delinquent proceeding to adult crime. The age measures may merely make frequent delinquency possible and it is frequency, not age or time, that is predictive of adult crime status.

Thus we examined two possible outcomes when the frequency of delinquency is considered in the same prediction models as the age and timing measures. First, if frequency of delinquency is an intervening variable between the age and time measures and increased odds of adult crime status, then the significance of these age and time effects should disappear when frequency is included in the models. Second, if on the other hand, these age and time measures have independent effects on making a transition to adult status, then inclusion of frequency categories should not affect these other factors, and could instead, add another significant main effect to the prediction of adult crime.

Consistent with the second hypothesis, the inclusion of delinquency involvement operated as another significant main effect on making the transition from delinquency to adult crime for males. Further, the inclusion of this factor did not generally reduce the effect of the age and time measures. That is, the effects of having a long career or having a short time remaining until the delinquent becomes eligible for adult crime, did not depend on the delinquent having accumulated a large number of delinquencies. The effects of delinquency group, career length, and transition time were significant additive effects.

We also employed discrete measures of two alternate groupings of delinquency frequency. In one analysis we differentiated among delinquents who had: just status offenses, one nonstatus offense, 2 to 4 nonstatus offenses, 5 to 9 nonstatus offenses, and 10 or more nonstatus offenses. Our intent here was to examine increasing levels of delinquency involvement which did not include the accumulation of status offenses. The results indicated that delinquents who committed only one nonstatus offense were not significantly different from status offenders in making a transition to adult crime. However, as delinquents committed more offenses of any type more serious than juvenile status events, there were significantly increasing odds of continuing this life-style as an adult. In addition, the delinquency timing measures continued to be significant and so was the effect of being a black male delinquent.

Our second alternate measure was the frequency of index crimes which provided for a gross measure of the seriousness of the delinquency career. These results confirmed the results obtained for the two other measures of delinquency. Thus, as involvement in delinquency of an index character increased, there was a corresponding increase in the conditional odds of continuing a criminal lifestyle as an adult. As usual, black male delinquents also reflected significantly higher odds of adult crime even after controlling for the effects of these other important factors.

For females we found support for the other hypothesized relationships among the age and delinquency timing measures, frequency of delinquency involvement, and adult crime status. That is, for females the results showed that age and timing of delinquency were not independent effects, but rather, they operated as antecedent variables that increased the frequency measures which in turn affected the transition to adult crime.

For females, the higher frequency levels of overall delinquency substantially and significantly increased the odds of adult crime. Female delinquents who accumulated more delinquent events in which status offenses are not included exhibited significantly increased odds of adult crime. Likewise, when we examined female involvement in the group of serious index offenses, we found that as involvement increased, there was a corresponding increase in the odds of adult crime. In particular, if a female had committed either 2 to 4 such index offenses, the odds were 2.7, while if she had committed 5 to 9 such index offenses, the odds increased to 3.5, compared to female delinquents who committed no such index crimes.

Juvenile Court Dispositions

We examined the juvenile court dispositions the delinquents had received to investigate the context in which delinquents could accumulate many delinquent offenses and thereby establish such a strong pattern of recidivism that making a transition to adult crime was merely a natural extension of their previous delinquent life-style. We first examined an overall measure of court dispositions which typified how a delinquent was handled by the police and the court throughout his or her career.

These aggregate results suggested that the juvenile court was consistently and highly ineffective in handling offenders, whether male or female.

We investigated the efficacy of court dispositions further, and we determined that an overall, or offender-based, measure that merely indicated how an offender was handled by the court across his or her career, was insufficient to determine the actual relationship between court dispositions, offense by offense, and juvenile recidivism and later adult crime.

Therefore, we tested the timing of both probation and juvenile facility dispositions to show whether the disposition was imposed early in the delinquency career, during a point in midcareer, or later in the career. For males we found that the early imposition of probation was associated with significantly lower chances of the delinquent going on to commit adult crime. This "early" probation effect remained strong despite controls for other factors.

We did not find any consistent value for the use of commitment to a juvenile facility for males. We also did not find any significant effects for either probation or juvenile facility for females.

The absence of any effects for the facility commitment disposition for males compared to the effectiveness of early probation dispositions may be because residential commitment was used sparingly and was most often much too late in the delinquency career to determine its possible value. Similarly, both type of dispositions were imposed too infrequently among females for analyses of their value in preventing adult crime. Thus, it remains to be seen whether the increased use of facility commitments, and an accompanying change in the timing of such dispositions, may have a beneficial effect in diverting delinquents away from further delinquent conduct and ultimately prevent the transition to adult crime. The results presented here do indicate, however, that a delayed imposition of facility commitments is an ineffective means of controlling habitual juvenile offenders and does not deter them from adult criminality.

Predicting Adult Crime Status from Type of Delinquency

In this chapter we begin to examine the relationship between adult criminality in the 1958 birth cohort and the nature or seriousness of prior juvenile offending. We know from our findings in the two previous chapters the importance of the frequency and timing of offending, but now our concern is to determine whether the commission of some forms of delinquency are more likely to lead to offending later in life after the delinquent becomes an adult. We will then extend this focus to include an analysis of the juvenile careers of delinquents who may engage in specialized delinquency or concentrate in certain offenses.

Of course, Healy and Bronner reported in 1926 that continued offending or desisting from crime rarely had any relation to the type of offense previously committed (1926: 177). Even so, it is important for us to examine this question because at least two generations have progressed through their crime-prone years since the time of the Healy and Bronner research, statutes have identified new offenses, justice systems have expanded, and technological advances have provided new methods of analysis. As we improve our efforts to predict criminality, we must understand more about the substantive forms of delinquency, as well as the sheer volume of delinquent conduct, especially as they relate to adult offending.

Consideration of delinquency types is important because the delinquency phenomenon has a myriad of features, any of which might affect the transition to adult crime. Some forms of delinquency may have personal and lasting effects that extend well beyond the delinquency years into adulthood. For example, a solitary offense in which serious injury was inflicted, particularly in an unplanned, spontaneous, or impulsive manner, might be more likely to alter the life course than a single incident of a less serious nature. Other forms may exist merely as the "nonutilitarian, malicious, and negativistic" youthful expressions noted by Albert Cohen (1955). Peer influence may serve as the initial catalyst to career offending, whether through gentle encouragement, instruction, or pressure from the group. Alternately, peers may be cast aside and adult offending may be more likely to emerge among delinquents whose juvenile offenses were committed on the delinquent's own initiative.

The police and juvenile court officials might be more likely to intervene in the life of a juvenile if certain types of offenses are committed. Society at large surely tends to view property crimes with greater ambivalence and much less concern than personal injury and violent offenses. Whether this lack of clarity exists because of the greater value implicitly placed on most human life or because of the vast prevalence of property violations, the perceived result is greater tolerance and more lenient punishment of property offenders. The reciprocity argued by symbolic interactionists between official intervention and subsequent offending suggests that adult offender status may vary by type of delinquency for this reason.

There are quite clearly a number of ways in which offense types may be viewed and several considerations can affect the development of various classifications. In all crime typologies, however, it is important to separate violations involving property from those which involve personal injury. It is also imperative that consideration of type of offending include attention to the seriousness of the loss or harm. It is not our intent to develop a mutually exclusive and comprehensive scheme of offending classes, but rather to isolate specific features associated with offending that have theoretical and policy relevance for understanding the transition to adult offender status.

Throughout this chapter we will discuss the following nine independent measures of type of offending by which the critical elements of delinquency may be distinguished.

- *Major violence* includes the offenses of homicide, rape, robbery, aggravated assault, and aggravated sexual intercourse.
- *Robbery* is treated as an independent offending class because of its unique combination of property and personal crime elements and because it alone is primarily a street crime.
- *Injury* denotes any statute violation in which there was actual physical harm to a person regardless of the degree of injury which may have ranged from minor harm to death.
- *Major property* crimes are burglary, theft, automobile theft, arson, and vandalism in excess of $500.
- *Theft* is a property-related variable in which the victim suffered some loss of money or property.

- *Weapon* offenses merit separate consideration because a youth in possession of a weapon, regardless of whether the weapon is used, is considered a potentially serious situation.
- *Drug* offenses are recognized both for their offensiveness and because of public perceptions that drug offenders are unstable and potentially at-risk for other types of violations.
- *Status* offenses include runaway, truancy, and curfew violations.
- Offenses committed with one or more *co-offenders* are examined individually because of the theoretical acclaim granted to the influence of peers on offending and the serious policy interventions aimed at youth gangs.

Type of Delinquency and Adult Status

Each of the nine indicators of type are first treated as dichotomous measures to distinguish between juvenile delinquents with any involvement of the specified type and delinquents who committed no offense of that kind. We examine offending type separately for males and females in an effort to avoid confounding effects due to variation in offending by gender. Finally, as was true of the preceding chapter, the analyses in the first half of this chapter by necessity are restricted to the subset (n = 6,287; 4,315 males; 1972 females) of the 1958 cohort with officially recorded delinquency.

Offense Types for Males

Table 7.1 reports the number and percentage of adult offenders across the nine measures of delinquency type for males. For each and every type of delinquency, the prevalence of adult offending is higher among delinquents with any involvement of the form specified compared to delinquents who never engaged in the particular form of delinquency. Among the male delinquents with an official record of any form of major violence, 56.2% were also arrested as adults compared to only 36.7% of the nonviolent delinquents. Similar relationships were shown for other forms of violence.

Among delinquents with any record of robbery, 58.8% continued offending as adults compared to only 38% of the delinquents with no robbery experience. Over half (55.5%) of the delinquents who committed an injurious offense became adult offenders in comparison to 36.9% of other male delinquents. This pattern also was shown among youths who had at some point in their delinquency careers possessed or used a weapon; 56% of whom were arrested as adults. For each of these measures of violence or potential personal injury, the prevalence ratios indicate that for male delinquents continuing a criminal career is 1.5 times more likely when one or more police contacts were the result of activities within these categories than among delinquents with no recorded violence.

Among the male delinquents with one or more serious property offenses, 51.4% later offended as adults compared to only 36% of the other delinquents. A similar relationship also appeared when only theft was examined. Over half (56%) of the male delinquents with any drug offenses had an adult arrest in comparison to 40% of the males without a drug offense. Prevalence of adult crime was higher among males with a recorded status offense (47.5%) than other forms of delinquency (37.9%), but the majority in each category did not offend as adults. Similarly,

TABLE 7.1

Number and Percentage of Adult Offender Status by Select Delinquency Type Measures for Males

	Nonoffender		Offender	
	N	%	N	%
Major violence offenses	494	43.8	634	56.2
No major violence	2,016	63.3	1,171	36.7
Robbery offenses	326	41.2	465	58.8
No robbery	2,184	62.0	1,340	38.0
Injury offenses	509	44.5	636	55.5
No injury	2,001	63.1	1,169	36.9
Major property offenses	793	48.6	840	51.4
No major property	1,717	64.0	965	36.0
Theft offenses	929	48.5	987	51.5
No theft	1,581	63.9	818	34.1
Weapon offenses	479	44.0	609	56.0
No weapon	2,031	62.9	1,196	37.1
Drug offenses	274	46.4	317	53.6
No drugs	2,236	60.0	1,488	40.0
Status offenses	931	52.5	843	47.5
No status	1,579	62.1	962	37.9
Co-offender offenses	1,658	54.2	1,403	45.8
No co-offender	852	67.9	402	32.1

when any delinquency with a co-offender was reported, 45.8% of the males also offended as adults compared to 32.1% of the delinquents who always acted alone.

In the next set of tables we report the results of logistic regression analyses in which adult crime status is predicted from the type of delinquency experience. As with the previous analyses in this volume, we controlled for race and socioeconomic status and we examined males and females separately. Further, for all analyses we included the extent of career delinquency as a main effect to ensure that any main effects due to a particular offense type measure were not spurious. That is, when we examine a particular offense type, a significant main effect could be observed that was not genuine, but rather, was spurious to the effect of being a chronic delinquent. However, by including the discrete measure pertaining to the frequency of delinquency (i.e., one-time, recidivist, and chronic recidivist) we ensure that any offense type that is found to be significant is a genuine relationship.

Moreover, we also included interaction effects between the discrete frequency measure and the various offense type dichotomies to determine if any specification effects could be uncovered. That is, by using the one-time offender as the omitted category, we can investigate whether being a recidivist and having committed a particular offense type versus being a chronic recidivist and having committed a particular offense type is differentially predictive of adult crime status compared to the one-time delinquent.

Table 7.2 displays a model which focuses on whether the delinquent had ever committed a major violence offense. The results indicate that there is a significant coefficient for black males (.5478) and for each of the two discrete frequency of delinquency measures (recidivist, .6779; chronic, 1.4105). There is also a significant effect for whether the delinquent had been a violent delinquent (.4520) indicating that such delinquents have about 1.5 times the odds of becoming an adult offender compared to delinquents without any violent offenses in their delinquency career. The interaction effect was not significant. Thus, after controlling for the considerable influence on adult crime of the extent of the delinquency career, there is significant discriminating power to the status of being a violent delinquent.

Table 7.3 presents a model which focuses on the important offense type of robbery, an offense type that can involve violence, theft, intimidation, and weapon use. As above, there are significant effects for black delinquents (.5421) and for recidivists (.6936) and chronic recidivists (1.3659). Also as above, there is a significant effect for the specific offense type. Delinquents who had committed at least one robbery have condi-

TABLE 7.2

Logistic Regression of Adult Offender Status on Race, Socioeconomic Status, Delinquency Status, and any Major Violence Offenses for Males

		Coeff.	s.e.	Exp(B)
White	(1412)	.4990	.2739	1.6471
Black	(2768)	.5478*	.2720	1.7295
Hispanic	(125)	.2787	.3035	1.3214
Socioeconomic status	(1612)	−.0990	.0753	.9057
Recidivist	(1529)	.6779**	.0814	1.9698
Chronic	(982)	1.4105**	.1202	4.0980
Major violence	(1128)	.4520**	.1839	1.5714
Delinquent group by major violence				
Recidivist by major violence		−.1911	.2183	.8261
Chronic by major violence		−.3328	.2279	.7169
Constant		−1.4523**	.2761	

*p<.05   **p<.01

tional odds of adult crime that are approximately 1.75 times higher than delinquents who never engaged in a robbery event. There is no significant interaction effect.

In Table 7.4 we consider delinquent events which involved actual injury to a victim, regardless of the level of harm inflicted or the particular legal label attached to the offense by the police. The results show that injury offense conduct does not have a significant effect on the likelihood of adult crime. Among the race categories, the results indicate that when compared to the overall race effect on the likelihood of an adult arrest, only blacks have a significantly higher odds of adult crime. The two levels of delinquency frequency are significant and have substantial odds of adult crime status.

In Tables 7.5 and 7.6 we move away from violence-related offenses to two alternate property offense types. Table 7.5 concerns the effect of the delinquent having been charged at least once with a major property offense (burglary, larceny, vehicle theft, arson, vandalism). Table 7.6 concerns an offense in which actual theft occurred regardless of the circumstances.

Tables 7.5 and 7.6 display significant coefficients for black delinquents, recidivists, and chronic recidivists, all of which indicate that the odds of adult crime are much greater for these delinquents than their counterparts. The results also indicate that neither of the property of-

TABLE 7.3

*Logistic Regression of Adult Offender Status on Race, Socioeconomic Status,
Delinquency Status, and any Robbery Offenses for Males*

		Coeff.	s.e.	Exp(B)
White	(1412)	.4974	.2737	1.6445
Black	(2768)	.5421*	.2719	1.7197
Hispanic	(125)	.2754	.3032	1.3171
Socioeconomic status	(1612)	−.0978	.0753	.9068
Recidivist	(1529)	.6936**	.0782	2.0009
Chronic	(982)	1.3659**	.1057	3.9194
Robbery	(791)	.5577*	.2411	1.7466
Delinquent group by robbery				
Recidivist by robbery		−.3241	.2779	.7232
Chronic by robbery		−.3314	.2743	.7179
Constant		−1.4367**	.2757	

*p<.05   **p<.01

TABLE 7.4

*Logistic Regression of Adult Offender Status on Race, Socioeconomic Status,
Delinquency Status, and any Injury Offenses for Males*

		Coeff.	s.e.	Exp(B)
White	(1412)	.4989	.2740	1.6469
Black	(2768)	.5682*	.2719	1.7651
Hispanic	(125)	.2803	.3035	1.3236
Socioeconomic status	(1612)	−.0995	.0753	.9053
Recidivist	(1529)	.6259**	.0820	1.8699
Chronic	(982)	1.3615**	.1172	3.9021
Any injury	(1145)	.2002	.1793	1.2217
Delinquency group by injury				
Recidivist by injury		.1579	.2138	1.1710
Chronic by injury		−.0331	.2239	.9675
Constant		−1.4437**	.2762	

*p<.05   **p<.01

TABLE 7.5

Logistic Regression of Adult Offender Status on Race, Socioeconomic Status, Delinquency Status, and any Major Property Offenses for Males

		Coeff.	s.e.	Exp(B)
White	(1412)	.4778	.2734	1.6126
Black	(2768)	.5660*	.2713	1.7612
Hispanic	(125)	.2735	.3030	1.3145
Socioeconomic status	(1612)	−.1042	.0753	.9010
Recidivist	(1529)	.6848**	.0875	1.9834
Chronic	(982)	1.2449**	.1469	3.4726
Major property	(1633)	.0749	.1402	1.0778
Delinquency group by major property				
Recidivist by major property		−.0019	.1758	.9981
Chronic by major property		.1947	.2086	1.2150
Constant		−1.4260**	.2761	

*p<.05 **p<.01

TABLE 7.6

Logistic Regression of Adult Offender Status on Race, Socioeconomic Status, Delinquency Status, and any Theft Offenses for Males

		Coeff.	s.e.	Exp(B)
White	(1412)	.4925	.2741	1.6364
Black	(2768)	.5591*	.2721	1.7491
Hispanic	(125)	.2769	.3037	1.3190
Socioeconomic status	(1612)	−.1019	.0753	.9032
Recidivist	(1529)	.6688**	.0924	1.9519
Chronic	(982)	1.3735**	.1844	3.9491
Theft	(1916)	.2333	.1270	1.2628
Delinquent group by theft				
Recidivist by theft		−.0541	.1637	.9474
Chronic by theft		−.0958	.2272	.9087
Constant		−1.4660**	.2773	

*p<.05 **p<.01

fense types is associated with significantly higher chances of becoming an adult offender. Thus, regardless of whether the male delinquent was charged with a serious property offense or actually committed an offense that involved property theft, the chances of making a transition to adult crime are not significantly different from other delinquents.

Table 7.7 indicates that if a delinquent was ever charged with any possession or use of a weapon as a juvenile, such conduct significantly heightened the odds of adult crime. This result is observed even though Table 7.7 also shows that there are the usual significant effects for black delinquents and the two levels of delinquency frequency.

Table 7.8 examines the effect on adult crime status of whether the delinquency career included a drug offense. We find that there is no significant effect associated with drugs. Similarly, Table 7.9 indicates that whether the delinquent had ever been charged with a status offense does not increase the odds of adult crime. However, for each of these models there are significant effects associated with being a black delinquent, a recidivist, or a chronic recidivist.

Table 7.10 displays the last of the nine offense types. The particular measure that we are using concerns whether the delinquent's delinquency history includes his having been arrested for a delinquent act that he committed with at least one co-offender. These results display two important findings. First, there are the usual significant main effects for black delinquents and recidivists but the main effect for chronics is

TABLE 7.7

Logistic Regression of Adult Offender Status on Race, Socioeconomic Status, Delinquency Status, and any Weapon Offenses for Males

		Coeff.	s.e.	Exp(B)
White	(1412)	.5036	.2738	1.6546
Black	(2768)	.5581*	.2718	1.7474
Hispanic	(125)	.2779	.3034	1.3204
Socioeconomic status		−.1009	.0753	.9040
Recidivist	(1529)	.6991**	.0812	2.0119
Chronic	(892)	1.3914**	.1165	4.0203
Weapon	(1088)	.5003*	.1733	1.6493
Delinquent group by weapon				
Recidivist by weapon		−.2719	.2116	.7619
Chronic by weapon		−.3269	.2187	.7212
Constant		−1.4690**	.2762	

*$p<.05$ **$p<.01$

TABLE 7.8

Logistic Regression of Adult Offender Status on Race, Socioeconomic Status,
Delinquency Status, and any Drug Offenses for Males

		Coeff.	s.e.	Exp(B)
White	(1412)	.4662	.2738	1.5940
Black	(2768)	.5578*	.2717	1.7468
Hispanic	(125)	.2784	.3033	1.3210
Socioeconomic status	(1612)	−.1139	.0754	.8923
Recidivist	(1589)	.6348**	.0786	1.8867
Chronic	(982)	1.3448**	.0936	3.8375
Drugs	(591)	−.0293	.2032	.9711
Delinquent group by drugs				
Recidivist by drugs		.4309	.2482	1.5387
Chronic by drugs		.4327	.2606	1.5415
Constant		−1.3981**	.2757	

*$p<.05$ **$p<.01$

TABLE 7.9

Logistic Regression of Adult Offender Status on Race, Socioeconomic Status,
Delinquency Status, and any Status Offenses for Males

		Coeff.	s.e.	Exp(B)
White	(1412)	.4855	.2738	1.6250
Black	(2768)	.5782*	.2718	1.7828
Hispanic	(125)	.2793	.3034	1.3222
Socioeconomic status	(1612)	−.1089	.0752	.8968
Recidivist	(1589)	.7520**	.0906	2.1211
Chronic	(982)	1.4949**	.1428	4.4590
Status	(1774)	−.0249	.1276	.9754
Delinquency group by status				
Recidivist by status		−.1086	.1647	.8971
Chronic by status		−.0623	.1973	.9396
Constant		−1.4164**	.2770	

*$p<.05$ **$p<.01$

TABLE 7.10
Logistic Regression of Adult Offender Status on Race, Socioeconomic Status, Delinquency Status, and any Co-Offending Offenses for Males

		Coeff.	s.e.	Exp(B)
White	(1412)	.4861	.2742	1.6259
Black	(2768)	.5860*	.2721	1.7969
Hispanic	(125)	.2816	.3037	1.3252
Socioeconomic status	(1612)	−.1046	.0753	.9007
Recidivist	(1589)	.5099**	.1319	1.6651
Chronic	(982)	.6373	.3543	1.8914
Co-offenders	(3061)	.0023	.1055	1.0023
Delinquency group by co-offenders				
Recidivist by co-offenders		.2463	.1616	1.2793
Chronic by co-offenders		.8275**	.3675	2.2877
Constant		−1.4296**	.2808	

*$p<.05$ **$p<.01$

not significant. Second, however, we note that there is a significant inter-action effect between chronic delinquency status and co-offender status. These results suggest that when the delinquent is a chronic offender and he commits at least one of his offenses with a co-offender, the odds of adult crime status are significantly increased.

Thus far, we have examined nine separate logistic regression models which were used to estimate the effects of certain types of delinquency, race, socioeconomic status, and recidivism status on the likelihood that the delinquent would move on to adult offender status among male delinquents. In every model, whether the offender was black was a significant factor and any level of delinquency beyond a status of one-time offender was also significant. More important, we found significant effects associated with four of the offense type measures. Three of these measures, major violence, robbery, and weapon possession suggest that when the delinquency career involves any aspect of violence or the potential for violence, there are significantly increased odds of later adult crime. For the fourth offense type, we found a specification effect for which being a co-offender was significant for chronic delinquents and increased their odds of adult crime.

Offense Types for Females

Before examining the offense type results for females, it is important to note that the results in the previous two chapters showed that females are less likely than males to offend as adults; indeed, only 12% of the female delinquents were arrested as adults compared to 42% of the male delinquents. Given the lower overall prevalence of adult crime among females, we might also expect lower rates of adult offending among females regardless of the particular form of delinquent conduct they may have committed compared to the situation for males in which recidivism and the correlates of it were consistently associated with adult crime status.

Table 7.11 indicates that with the exceptions of status offenses (n = 979) and co-offending (n = 722), there is a very low prevalence of the various offense types among females compared to males. However, despite this low prevalence, the chances of adult offending is higher among female delinquents with any law violations of all the types specified. Over one-fourth of the females with any major violence, property, or robbery experience as youths also were arrested as adults compared to approximately 10% of other delinquents. For these three types of delinquency, the prevalence ratios indicate that female delinquents continuing their criminal careers is about 2.5 times more likely than delinquents without such an experience. Nearly one-fifth of females with any police contact related to drug offenses, weapons, theft, or injury violations also proceed to adult crime compared to 10% of other female delinquents. The prevalence of adult crime is higher, but not appreciably, between those with a status offense and those who committed only non-status delinquency. Similarly, the prevalence of adult offending is slightly higher among females who had at least one co-offender.

The next nine tables show the logistic regression models of adult offending based on delinquency type among female delinquents. Generally, the results for female delinquents reveal few specific offense types that have a significant association with adult crime status. However, the specific offense types that are significant suggest that there are offense pathways from delinquency to crime that females follow and these pathways are almost always different from those observed for males.

Table 7.12 indicates, like the case for males, that a female delinquent who ever engaged in a major violence offense (n = 140) has significantly higher odds (2.28:1) of becoming an adult criminal than her nonviolent counterpart. The main effect of any major violence (.8253) is significant despite controlling for the effects of recidivism and chronic recidivism which were also significant and showed increasing odds of adult crime.

TABLE 7.11

Number and Percentage of Adult Offender Status by Select Delinquency Type
Measures for Females

	Nonoffender		Offender	
	N	%	N	%
Major violence offenses	104	74.3	36	25.7
No major violence	1,632	89.1	200	10.9
Robbery offenses	29	70.7	12	29.3
No robbery	1,707	88.4	224	11.6
Injury offenses	231	82.2	50	17.8
No injury	1,505	89.0	186	11.0
Major property offenses	159	73.3	58	26.7
No major property	1,577	89.9	178	10.1
Theft offenses	385	82.1	84	17.9
No theft	1,351	89.9	152	10.1
Weapon offenses	104	79.4	27	20.6
No weapon	1,632	88.6	209	11.4
Drug offenses	75	78.9	20	21.1
No drugs	1,661	88.5	216	11.5
Status offenses	979	87.8	136	12.2
No status	757	88.3	100	11.7
Co-offender offenses	722	84.7	130	13.3
No co-offenders	1,014	90.5	106	9.5

Tables 7.13 and 7.14 indicate that the other two forms of violence, robbery (n = 41) and injury (n = 281) respectively, are not significant predictors of adult crime status.

Tables 7.15 and 7.16 concern the two serious property offenses. Table 7.15 indicates that being charged with a serious property offense ranging from burglary to vandalism involves only 217 of the 1972 female delinquents and such involvement is not associated with adult crime status. Table 7.16, however, indicates the presence of an interaction effect. That is, chronic female delinquents are likely to continue on to adult crime regardless of other factors including whether they ever committed theft, but there is no main effect for the recidivists. Among recidivist females, if they also committed offenses which actually involved theft, then the chances of adult crime are significantly enhanced.

The relationship between possession of a weapon by female delinquents and adult crime is shown in Table 7.17. Here we observe that few

TABLE 7.12
Logistic Regression of Adult Offender Status on Race, Socioeconomic Status, Delinquency Status, and any Major Violence Offenses for Females

		Coeff.	s.e.	Exp(B)
White	(610)	.7866	1.6809	2.1959
Black	(1296)	1.0794	1.6785	2.9429
Hispanic	(62)	.0856	1.7291	1.0894
Socioeconomic status	(667)	−.3313	.1764	.7180
Recidivist	(643)	.5885**	.1617	1.8013
Chronic	(147)	1.1773**	.2540	3.2456
Major violence	(140)	.8253*	.4031	2.2826
Delinquent group by major violence				
Recidivist by major violence		−.5602	.5525	.5711
Chronic by major violence		.0643	.5873	1.0664
Constant		−3.2773*	1.6798	

*p<.05   **p<.01

TABLE 7.13
Logistic Regression of Adult Offender Status on Race, Socioeconomic Status, Delinquency Status, and any Robbery Offenses for Females

		Coeff.	s.e.	Exp(B)
White	(610)	1.0417	2.7568	2.8340
Black	(1296)	1.3673	2.7553	3.9246
Hispanic	(62)	.3130	2.7865	1.3675
Socioeconomic status	(667)	−.3415	.1766	.7107
Recidivist	(643)	.5912**	.1547	1.8062
Chronic	(147)	1.2225**	.2309	3.3958
Robbery	(41)	−4.0563	15.7262	.0173
Delinquent group by robbery				
Recidivist by robbery		3.4680	15.7442	32.0715
Chronic by robbery		5.2421	15.7343	189.0587
Constant		−3.5107*	2.7560	

*p<.05   **p<.01

TABLE 7.14

Logistic Regression of Adult Offender Status on Race, Socioeconomic Status, Delinquency Status, and any Injury Offenses for Females

		Coeff.	s.e.	Exp(B)
White	(610)	.7822	1.6787	2.1862
Black	(1296)	1.1043	1.6762	3.0170
Hispanic	(62)	.0674	1.7269	1.0697
Socioeconomic status	(667)	−.3189	.1761	.7269
Recidivist	(643)	.6552**	.1674	1.9256
Chronic	(147)	1.2578**	.2709	3.5176
Injury	(281)	.4440	.3185	1.5589
Delinquent group by injury				
Recidivist by injury		−.5978	.4304	.5500
Chronic by injury		.0304	.4904	1.0308
Constant		−3.3051*	1.6777	

*p<.05   **p<.01

TABLE 7.15

Logistic Regression of Adult Offender Status on Race, Socioeconomic Status, Delinquency Status, and any Major Property Offenses for Females

		Coeff.	s.e.	Exp(B)
White	(610)	.7806	1.6864	2.1828
Black	(1296)	1.1031	1.6839	3.0135
Hispanic	(62)	−.0043	1.7352	.9957
Socioeconomic status	(667)	−.3262	.1779	.7217
Recidivist	(643)	.4452**	.1698	1.5608
Chronic	(147)	.9769**	.2810	2.6563
Major property	(217)	.5439	.3448	1.7227
Delinquent group by major property				
Recidivist by major property		.4876	.4412	1.6284
Chronic by major property		.6280	.5147	1.8738
Constant		−3.3001*	1.6854	

*p<.05   **p<.01

TABLE 7.16
*Logistic Regression of Adult Offender Status on Race, Socioeconomic Status,
Delinquency Status, and any Theft Offenses for Females*

		Coeff.	s.e.	Exp(B)
White	(610)	.7673	1.6872	2.1539
Black	(1296)	1.0724	1.6846	2.9224
Hispanic	(62)	.0307	1.7354	1.0312
Socioeconomic status	(667)	−.3084	.1768	.7346
Recidivist	(643)	.2961	.1890	1.3445
Chronic	(147)	1.0783**	.3000	2.9396
Theft	(469)	−.1342	.2932	.8744
Delinquent group by theft				
Recidivist by theft		.8164*	.3710	2.2624
Chronic by theft		.7253	.4743	2.0653
Constant		−3.2118*	1.6868	

*p<.05   **p<.01

(n = 131) females engage in delinquent conduct with a weapon and such use is not significantly associated with adult crime.

The model reported in Table 7.18 contains the drug offense measure and the results for this model are highly interesting. First, uncovering drug use among females leads to the emergence of a significant socioeconomic status effect that as socioeconomic status decreases, the chances of adult crime increase significantly. Second, each of the recidivism levels is also significant and carries with it increased odds of adult crime. Third, the main effect of drugs is significant and has associated odds of adult crime (3.68:1) that are second only to chronic recidivism (3.94:1) in magnitude. Fourth, there is also, however, a significant interaction effect between drug use and recidivism.

The last two tables concerning offense types involve analysis of status offenses and co-offending. Table 7.19 shows that the presence versus absence of status offenses in the delinquency career is not significantly related to adult crime status. The final table for female delinquents, Table 7.20, shows that the odds of an adult arrest do not significantly increase whether or not the delinquent engaged in delinquent conduct with any co-offenders.

The nine models testing the effects of various forms of delinquency, socioeconomic status, race, and frequency of delinquency on adult of-

TABLE 7.17
Logistic Regression of Adult Offender Status on Race, Socioeconomic Status,
Delinquency Status, and any Weapon Offenses for Females

		Coeff.	s.e.	Exp(B)
White	(610)	.7833	1.6813	2.1886
Black	(1296)	1.1009	1.6789	3.0068
Hispanic	(62)	.0582	1.7296	1.0599
Socioeconomic status	(667)	−.3176	.1761	.7279
Recidivist	(643)	.5908**	.1612	1.8055
Chronic	(147)	1.4642**	.2344	4.3242
Weapon	(131)	.7443	.4306	2.1049
Delinquent group by weapon				
Recidivist by weapon		−.5065	.5588	.6026
Chronic by weapon		−.8356	.6197	.4336
Constant		−3.2928*	1.6802	

*p<.05   **p<.01

TABLE 7.18
Logistic Regression of Adult Offender Status on Race, Socioeconomic Status,
Delinquency Status, and any Drug Offenses for Females

		Coeff.	s.e.	Exp(B)
White	(610)	.7582	1.6785	2.1345
Black	(1296)	1.1161	1.6758	3.0528
Hispanic	(62)	.0556	1.7268	1.0572
Socioeconomic status	(667)	−.3469*	.1781	.7069
Recidivist	(643)	.6392**	.1595	1.8949
Chronic	(147)	1.3722**	.2252	3.9440
Drugs	(95)	1.3041**	.4220	3.6844
Delinquent group by drugs				
Recidivist by drugs		1.3511**	.6201	.2589
Chronic by drugs		−.4220	.7191	.6557
Constant		−3.3123*	1.6773	

*p<.05   **p<.01

TABLE 7.19

Logistic Regression of Adult Offender Status on Race, Socioeconomic Status,
Delinquency Status, and any Status Offenses for Females

		Coeff.	s.e.	Exp(B)
White	(610)	.7910	1.6896	2.2055
Black	(1296)	1.1172	1.6872	3.0562
Hispanic	(62)	.0986	1.7378	1.1036
Socioeconomic status	(667)	−.3217	.1766	.7249
Recidivist	(643)	.7172**	.2365	2.0486
Chronic	(147)	1.7754**	.7775	5.9025
Status	(1115)	−.3433	.2191	.7095
Delinquent group by status				
Recidivist by status		−.0462	.3247	.9548
Chronic by status		−.1890	.8190	.8278
Constant		−3.1348	1.6898	

*p<.05   **p<.01

TABLE 7.20

Logistic Regression of Adult Offender Status on Race, Socioeconomic Status,
Delinquency Status, and any Co-offending Offenses for Males

		Coeff.	s.e.	Exp(B)
White	(610)	.7353	1.6929	2.0861
Black	(1296)	1.0900	1.6905	2.9742
Hispanic	(62)	.1445	1.7408	1.1555
Socioeconomic status	(667)	−.3539	.1777	.7019
Recidivist	(643)	.3560	.2183	1.4276
Chronic	(147)	.7631*	.3912	2.1448
Co-offenders	(852)	.2127	.2128	1.2370
Delinquent group by co-offenders				
Recidivist by co-offenders		.3997	.3105	1.4914
Chronic by co-offenders		.8593	.4768	2.3616
Constant		−3.3128*	1.6948	

*p<.05

fender status for females show only one offense type, major violence, that carried the same results as those found for males. As a juvenile, police contact for any major violence offense increases the risk of becoming an adult offender for female and male delinquents.

Whether the female delinquent engaged in any robbery, injury, major property, weapon, status, or co-offending did not significantly affect her chances of committing a crime as an adult. However, unlike males, female delinquents who engaged in theft offenses or drug offenses did exhibit significantly enhanced odds of becoming an adult criminal.

In looking at the nature of delinquency and how it relates to adult offending, we have determined that the commission of particular offense types does increase the likelihood of continuity between the delinquency and adult criminal careers for both males and females. The relevant offenses for males include the specific delinquent acts of major violence, robbery, weapon use, and being a co-offender, while the offenses for females include major violence, theft, and drugs. These results are based on the entire pool of delinquents in the cohort, without regard for the frequency of their contacts with police. In addition, offense type was defined broadly as any involvement. This means that a one-time delinquent, a chronic delinquent with one experience of the type noted, and a chronic delinquent whose entire offenses are of that particular type, are grouped together and treated alike.

To help distinguish among these delinquents and the varying degrees by which offenses of particular types might be committed, the next set of analyses will focus on delinquents with varying experience in the nine different types of delinquency, from those with little or no such experience to considerable experience (i.e., more than 50% of the career).

Delinquency Concentration and Adult Status

In this section we attempt a natural extension of our analyses on the topic of specific offense types by examining the association between adult crime status and delinquency careers that have a particular concentration within one specific offense type. The assumption underlying this line of inquiry is that juveniles who primarily engage in one form of offending or at least commit the majority of their delinquencies within a particular type, might be more apt to develop expertise, and thus, such expertise reinforces the repeat commission of the offense and specialization develops. A possible consequence of this reinforced specialization is that the delinquent's career is more likely to continue into adulthood.

Clearly, the topic of offense specialization, or "versatility in offending," as it has often been called, occupies a central place in criminological research. As Bursik (1980) has noted, concern over specialization dates back to the pioneering work of Clifford Shaw in the 1930s, which was concerned with the dynamic social processes surrounding delinquency. Farrington, Snyder, and Finnegan (1988) have also noted that, from a theoretical standpoint, research on offense specialization or versatility is an important way of shedding light on the number of dimensions underlying delinquency. From the standpoint of policy, J. Cohen (1986) has observed that, because crime control policies focus on particular categories of offenders, knowledge of offense specialization may be useful in focusing crime control efforts on offenders who are most likely to continue to exhibit particular offense types that are of policy concern, for example, predatory offenders.

Despite the importance of the topic of delinquency specialization, there is considerable variation in what research has told us about the phenomenon. Indeed, the literature is replete with conclusions that specialization is far less common than a general delinquency career that involves varieties of conduct (Farrington, 1986; Klein, 1984; Wolfgang, Figlio, and Sellin, 1972). Some studies have found evidence of some specialization, however, in the form of repeated involvement in property crime (Bursik, 1980; Petersilia, 1980; Peterson, Pitman, and O'Neal, 1962; Peterson et al., 1981; Rojeck and Erickson, 1982; and Wallerstedt, 1984), personal crime (Farrington, 1978; Peterson et al., 1962; Peterson et al., 1981; and Petersilia, 1980) and status offenses (S.H. Clarke, 1975; Rojeck and Erickson, 1982; Kobrin et al., 1980; Tielman and Peterson, 1981). Prior research has also suggested that specialization might become more evident as careers become more established (Bursik, 1980; Farrington, 1986; Quay and Blumen, 1968).

The preceding notwithstanding, there are comparatively few studies that report specialization results for substantively meaningful samples of juvenile offenders. There are several possible reasons for the comparative lack of offense specialization studies and the accumulation of a consistent body of results.

First, a very substantial share of contemporary research with juvenile subjects utilizes self-report data on offending. Although the self-report technique is generally believed to provide more complete data on an offender's delinquency career owing to the absence of the possible selection effects and potential biases present in official criminal history data, it is quite clear that retrospective self-reports from respondents do not permit the precise sequencing of the illegal acts reported, especially when the subject reports many offenses per year per offense type.

Second, even when official data are employed, and even when these data represent the complete delinquency history of the subjects, problems still remain. If the criminal history data include only rap sheets and do not include offense descriptions or investigation reports in which the details of the delinquent events are detailed, the possibility of classification errors in typifying offenses as one type versus another are very likely. Further, the usually small sample sizes and the absence of sufficient numbers of high-rate offenders preclude the generalization of results to offender groups for whom specialization is more likely to be a meaningful construct.

Our effort here concerning delinquency specialization or versatility is different from prior research in several major respects. First, we are treating delinquency specialization as an independent variable rather than a dependent measure. Our interest is to investigate its explanatory power as a delinquency precursor of adult crime status. Second, because the juvenile career of the 1958 cohort delinquents is fully completed, our characterization of specialization is neither interim nor tentative. Third, because we have the entire pool of a delinquent's offenses as well as the police investigation report narratives, we can measure offense specialization on the basis of much more extensive information than was possible in other studies. Last, we have conceptualized specialization as a career concept rather than an offense by offense analysis that focuses on transitions between particular offense pairs.

In order to measure specialization, the proportion of the delinquency career involving particular offense types was calculated for each of the nine types of delinquency. Each proportion was then recoded as a three-level discrete measure depicting no involvement in the given offense type, 1% through 49% of the career within the offense type, and 50% or more of all offenses concentrated within the particular offense type. This procedure is less restrictive than the usual markov models or stochastic models of specialization which analyze immediately adjacent events as the basis of specialization.

In our view, it seems entirely valid to consider as specialists those delinquents who concentrate in a primary offense type by committing 50% or more of their acts within the category, yet may vacillate among a range of offense types between any given transition number. Moreover, we are hypothesizing that these "concentrators" may be the delinquents who are more likely to become adult offenders because of this concentration and the reinforcement of the delinquent role associated with such concentration.

There is one remaining explanatory note that must precede the presentation of the results pertaining to offense concentration. That is, in this stage of the analyses surrounding offense type concentration, we will no longer use the entire pool of delinquents, but rather, we will employ a select subsample of the delinquents. The subsample consists of those delinquents who committed at least three delinquent events as juveniles. We are making this selection of recidivists with at least three offenses because from a conceptual standpoint, it is necessary for a delinquent to have a minimum number of offenses before specialization, or concentration as we have chosen to call the phenomenon, can legitimately occur. Clearly, a juvenile with only one delinquent act cannot be considered a specialist. Even among the pool of two-time offenders, who have merely one opportunity to change offense type or repeat the previous offense, it would be difficult to draw valid conclusions about whether offense concentration occurred.

We suggest, therefore, that restricting the cases for analysis to the subsample who have at least three offenses, represents the barest minimum number of offenses necessary to analyze validly specialization or concentration. Among the 4,315 male delinquents, 1,806, or 41.9%, could be classified in the select subset. For females, the number of recidivists with at least three offenses was much lower, 411 of the 1,972 delinquents, or 20.8%.

Offense Concentration among Males

The next nine tables report logistic regression results concerning the likelihood of adult crime status based on delinquency concentration within a single offense type, total number of delinquent events, race, and socioeconomic status. Table 7.21 begins the series of findings for males and concerns concentration in major violence offenses. We note first of all, that only 112, or 6%, of the select delinquents had a 50% or greater concentrated in such delinquencies, 752, or 41.6%, showed a violence concentration of from one to 49%, and the remaining 942 offenders, or 52.2% committed no violent offenses as juveniles. The logistic regression results indicate that neither of the violence concentrations had significantly higher odds of adult crime status than did the delinquents with no violence in their juvenile careers. The only factor that had a significant effect on adult crime status was frequency of delinquency.

Table 7.22 presents the data pertaining to robbery offenses. The distribution of robbery events is highly skewed and reflects only a very small prevalence of robbery among the select recidivists. There were only 44 delinquents, or 2.4%, who had a high concentration and 590 offenders, or 32.7%, who committed the lower concentration level of from one to 49%. The regression results indicated that, compared to delin-

TABLE 7.21
Logistic Regression of Adult Offender Status on Race, Socioeconomic Status,
Delinquency Status, and Major Violence Concentration for Males

		Coeff.	s.e.	Exp(B)
White	(436)	1.1883	1.0309	3.2815
Black	(1320)	1.0613	1.0292	2.8903
Hispanic	(46)	.9394	1.0498	2.5586
Socioeconomic status	(523)	−.0900	.1136	.9140
Delinquency frequency		.0478**	.0112	1.0490
Major violence				
LE 49%	(752)	.1564	.1087	1.1692
GE 50%	(112)	.2526	.2101	1.2874
Constant		−1.1883	1.0309	

**$p<.01$

quents who never committed robbery events, the odds of adult crime status increase for delinquents with some robbery experience, but not among those delinquents for whom robbery constitutes the majority of their delinquencies. The probability of adult offending again increased as the frequency of delinquency increased.

Similarly, Table 7.23 shows that delinquent careers with some involvement in injurious offenses, but not those careers that had a high concentration of injury offenses, are more apt than delinquents without injury offenses to continue their careers as adults. Like the case of major violence and robbery, neither socioeconomic status nor race achieved significance in the models but frequency of recidivism was significant.

The major property offenses were comparatively more extensive in the delinquency careers of the select male recidivists. There were 204, or about 11%, who committed the majority of their delinquent acts in this category, while 938 delinquents, or about 52% who had lesser involvement in these serious property offenses. When compared to the three-time offenders who never committed any major property crimes, neither concentration level had significantly higher odds of making the transition to adult crime.

Table 7.25 presents the data pertaining to offenses that actually involved a theft component regardless of the legal category of the offense. We note that such theft offenses were very prevalent in the careers of the male recidivists with 322, or 18%, reflecting high concentration, and 992, or 55%, of lesser concentration. The regression results indicate that, in

TABLE 7.22

Logistic Regression of Adult Offender Status on Race, Socioeconomic Status, Delinquency Frequency, and Robbery Concentration for Males

		Coeff.	s.e.	Exp(B)
White	(436)	1.1861	1.0310	3.2742
Black	(1320)	1.0216	1.0295	2.7776
Hispanic	(46)	.9370	1.0499	2.5523
Socioeconomic status	(523)	−.0863	.1137	.9174
Delinquency frequency		.0445**	.0111	1.0455
Robbery				
LT 49%	(590)	.2819*	.1139	1.3256
GE 50%	(44)	.4059	.3252	1.5007
Constant		−1.1586	1.0308	

*p<.05 **p<.01

addition to the frequency of delinquency measures, some theft experience has a significant main effect on the likelihood of adult offender status. The negative sign associated with the coefficient (-.1662) for less than 50% of the delinquency career devoted to theft indicates, interestingly, that the chances of adult arrests are greater among the omitted category of delinquents with no thefts.

TABLE 7.23

Logistic Regression of Adult Offender Status on Race, Socioeconomic status, Delinquency Frequency, and Injury Concentration for Males

		Coeff.	s.e.	Exp(B)
White	(436)	1.1858	1.0297	3.2734
Black	(1320)	1.0708	1.0279	2.9176
Hispanic	(46)	.9460	1.0487	2.5753
Socioeconomic status	(523)	−.0921	.1138	.9121
Delinquency frequency		.0434**	.0110	1.0444
Injury				
LT 49%	(760)	.2997*	.1053	1.3495
GE 50%	(91)	.1946	.2248	1.2149
Constant		−1.2198	1.0299	

*p<.05 **p<.01

TABLE 7.24

Logistic Regression of Adult Offender Status on Race, Socioeconomic Status,
Delinquency Frequency, and Major Property Concentration for Males

		Coeff.	s.e.	Exp(B)
White	(436)	1.1547	1.0310	3.1732
Black	(1320)	1.0738	1.0293	2.9264
Hispanic	(46)	.9176	1.0500	2.5033
Socioeconomic status	(523)	−.0915	.1136	.9125
Delinquency frequency		.0494**	.0112	1.0507
Major property				
LT 49%	(938)	.1036	.1090	1.1091
GE 50%	(204)	.0057	.1628	1.0058
Constant		−1.1731	1.0313	

**p<.01

In Table 7.26 we turn to the issue of whether the concentration of
weapon offenses in the delinquency career is predictive of adult crime
status. Only a small proportion of the select delinquents, about 4%, or 69
delinquents, were classified at the high concentration level of 50% or
greater indicating that the majority of their delinquent acts involved
weapon possession. However, the logistic regression results indicate
that having such a high concentration of weapon offenses is significantly

TABLE 7.25

Logistic Regression of Adult Offender Status on Race, Socioeconomic Status,
Delinquency Frequency, and Theft Concentration for Males

		Coeff.	s.e.	Exp(B)
White	(436)	1.1614	1.0286	3.1945
Black	(1320)	1.0476	1.0271	2.8508
Hispanic	(46)	.9051	1.0477	2.4721
Socioeconomic status	(523)	−.0849	.1138	.9186
Delinquency frequency		.0463**	.0110	1.0474
Theft				
LT 49%	(992)	−.1662*	.0778	.8468
GE 50%	(322)	.0889	.0669	1.0929
Constant		−1.0991	1.0290	

*p<.05   **p<.01

TABLE 7.26

Logistic Regression of Adult Offender Status on Race, Socioeconomic Status, Delinquency Frequency, and Weapon Concentration for Males

		Coeff.	s.e.	Exp(B)
White	(436)	1.2061	1.0284	3.3403
Black	(1320)	1.0879	1.0266	2.9680
Hispanic	(46)	.9342	1.0472	2.5452
Socioeconomic status	(523)	−.0946	.1135	.9097
Delinquency frequency		.0489**	.0111	1.0502
Weapon				
LT 49%	(743)	.1515	.1057	1.1635
GE 50%	(69)	.4948*	.2631	1.6401
Constant		−1.2180	1.0286	

$*p<.05$ $**p<.01$

associated with adult crime compared to delinquents who never committed any offenses with weapons. Further, being charged with the carrying of a weapon in less than 50% of a delinquent's offenses did not have a significant effect on adult status.

Table 7.27 indicates the results concerning the relationship among drug offenses and making the transition to adult crime among the three time or greater recidivists. These results indicate both concentrations of drug offenses were comparatively rare among the recidivists as only 20.8% of the recidivists had any drug offenses in their delinquency careers. Despite this low prevalence, the logistic regression results indicate that both levels of drug concentration carry significant effects on adult crime status. If the recidivist had some drug offenses in his career, the odds are 1.4 times greater that he will move on to adult crime. If the majority of the recidivist's delinquencies involve drugs, then the chances of adult crime are nearly 2 times greater in comparison to recidivists with no drug offenses.

The data in Table 7.28 concerning status offenses present results from a very different prevalence basis compared to drug offenses. That is, unlike drug offenses which involves a small minority of recidivists, status offenses involved a majority of the recidivists as 62% of these select delinquents had some involvement in status offending. Surprisingly, in comparison to delinquents who never committed a status offense, delinquents with some status offending and those for whom it is a focus of their juvenile careers have significantly greater odds of an adult arrest.

TABLE 7.27

Logistic Regression of Adult Offender Status on Race, Socioeconomic Status,
Delinquency Frequency, and Drug Offense Concentration for Males

		Coeff.	s.e.	Exp(B)
White	(436)	1.1339	1.0310	3.1076
Black	(1320)	1.0734	1.0292	2.9253
Hispanic	(46)	.9132	1.0499	2.4923
Socioeconomic status	(523)	−.1057	.1138	.8997
Delinquency frequency		.0522**	.0107	1.0536
Drugs				
LT 49%	(336)	.3311**	.1268	1.3925
GE 50%	(40)	.6746*	.3436	1.9633
Constant		−1.2020	1.0308	

*p<.05 **p<.01

These status offense results are interesting in terms of their association with the accumulation of more and more delinquencies. That is, from the point of view of cumulative recidivism and the consistently significant effect that we have seen for the frequency of delinquency measure, it may have been expected that recidivists who committed other offense types as well as a few status offenses may have greater odds of adult crime simply because of the cumulative total of their delinquent acts. However, it is entirely unexpected that when the greatest contribu-

TABLE 7.28

Logistic Regression of Adult Offender Status on Race, Socioeconomic Status,
Delinquency Frequency, and Status Offense Concentration for Males

		Coeff.	s.e.	Exp(B)
White	(436)	1.1785	1.0311	3.2496
Black	(1320)	1.1117	1.0293	3.0394
Hispanic	(46)	.9241	1.0499	2.5197
Socioeconomic status	(523)	−.0918	.1138	.9122
Delinquency frequency		.0498**	.0112	1.0510
Status				
LT 49%	(909)	.1605*	.0737	1.1741
GE 50%	(214)	.1359*	.0731	1.1456
Constant		−1.2477	1.0314	

*p<.05 **p<.01

tor to a recidivist's career delinquency total comes from the status offense dimension, that such trivial delinquency would carry significantly higher odds of adult crime later in life.

The last analysis for the male recidivists concerns the relationship between being a co-offender type delinquent and the likelihood of adult crime. Here we are trying to distinguish between delinquents who commit their offenses in concert with other offenders and those delinquents who engage in solitary acts of delinquency. The marginal frequencies indicate that few delinquents can be classified as solitary offenders as only 170, or 9.5% of the recidivists, committed their delinquent acts alone. Compared to these solitary offenders, the chances of adult offending increase to 1.57:1 among recidivists with less than 50% co-offenders and increase to 1.63:1 among recidivists with a high concentration of co-offenders.

The analysis of offense concentration for the select male recidivists produced two consistent findings. First, the frequency of delinquency measure was consistently significant in predicting adult crime status. The more offenses a delinquent accumulated the higher the likelihood of adult crime. Second, adult offending status was not significantly affected by race or by the socioeconomic status of the male recidivist.

In addition to these findings, the offense concentration analyses revealed that adult crime status was more likely among those delinquents who concentrated their juvenile offending within particular offense types. However, these effects did not consistently indicate that the re-

TABLE 7.29
Logistic Regression of Adult Offender Status on Race, Socioeconomic Status,
Delinquency Frequency, and Co-offending Concentration for Males

		Coeff.	s.e.	Exp(B)
White	(436)	1.1783	1.0314	3.2487
Black	(1320)	1.1173	1.0295	3.0566
Hispanic	(46)	.9022	1.0502	2.4651
Socioeconomic status		−.0511	.0598	.9502
Delinquency frequency		.0478**	.0109	1.0489
Co-offenders				
LE 49%	(809)	.4558**	.1758	1.5774
GE 50%	(827)	.4907**	.1727	1.6335
Constant		−1.6244	1.0409	

*p<.05   **p<.01

cidivists who were classified at the higher as opposed to the lower concentration level had the higher odds of adult crime status. Overall,
among the nine offense concentration analyses, the results were significant for seven offense types.

For three offense types (robbery, injury, and theft), adult crime was
significantly related to the commission of offenses at the lower concentration level (from 1 to 49%). In one measure, the possession of a
weapon, the higher concentration level was significantly related to adult
crime. For the remaining three offense types (drugs, status, and co-offending), the particular concentration level did not discriminate very
well as both concentration levels, when compared to delinquents who
had never committed these three offense types, were significantly associated with adult crime status.

Offense Concentration among Females

The analyses just discussed for male delinquents who had committed at least three juvenile offenses was repeated for the pool of 411 female recidivists with at least three delinquent acts. The findings show
fewer significant factors for females, as four of the offense types were related to adult crime. Before discussing these findings, however, it is important to underscore not only that the prevalence of adult crime status
is much lower among females, but also, that the nature of juvenile offending differs substantially by gender.

First, females outnumber males in the total 1958 Philadelphia birth
cohort (14,000 versus 13,160); however, only 14.6% of the females became delinquents in comparison to 42.8% of the males. When we consider recidivism as we have in the analyses above, we note that there
were 1,806 male delinquents, or 41.9% of all male delinquents, included
within the subsample of recidivists with at least three juvenile offenses.
By comparison, only 411 females, or 20.8% of all female delinquents,
meet this criterion. Within the subsample, females had committed an average of 4.66 juvenile offenses compared to 6.66 offenses on average for
the select male recidivists. As such, male delinquents were twice as
likely as female delinquents—who were already less common—to be included within the analyses of offense concentration as well as more
likely to have accumulated more offenses.

Meaningful differences also exist between females and males when
the concentration of juvenile offending by offense type is compared. For
example, 57.4% of the females in the subsample compared to only 11.8%
of the males, committed over half of their juvenile career in status offenses. Only 14.6% of the females had no status offenses, compared to

38.1% of the males. Females also more often offended alone; 42.8% had no co-offenders compared to 9.5% of the males. Nearly half of the males (45.2%) committed the majority of their delinquency with someone, but the same was true of only 23.4% of the females. Aside from status offenses and the 30 females with considerable theft experience, almost no females concentrated their offending in any single crime category. Moreover, the majority of female recidivists also had not committed any major violence (82.7%), robbery (92.5%), injury (73.2%), drug offenses (91.7%), weapon offenses (83.2%), or serious property crime (74.9%). The male recidivists were more likely to have any experience in each of the crime categories.

Finally, when our concern turns to adult offending status among this subsample of recidivists, the gender gap is very evident. Among this group of three-or-more-time delinquents, only 93 females, or 22.6%, continued their criminal careers as adults compared to 1,020 males, or 56.5%, who were arrested as adults. These statistics serve to forewarn us that logistic regression models used to estimate the effects of delinquency concentration, number of offenses, socioeconomic status, and race are constrained by the small number of subjects and the low levels of offending. In fact, aside from status offending, co-offending and theft, the very few females who specialize in one type of delinquency virtually preclude analyses of specialization effects in those types and allow comparisons based only on the category of some involvement.

TABLE 7.30
*Logistic Regression of Adult Offender Status on Race, Socioeconomic Status,
Delinquency Frequency, and Major Violence Concentration for Females*

		Coeff.	s.e.	Exp(B)
White	(109)	.7325	3.3880	2.0802
Black	(289)	1.1919	3.3830	3.2934
Hispanic	(12)	.8529	3.4254	2.3463
Socioeconomic status	(112)	−.3811	.3200	.6831
Delinquency frequency		.0314	.0446	1.0319
Major violence				
LE 49%	(68)	.7230**	.2986	2.0606
GE 50%	(3)	.5004	1.2355	1.6494
Constant		−2.5112	3.3865	.4584

**p<.01

TABLE 7.31

Logistic Regression of Adult Offender Status on Race, Socioeconomic Status, Delinquency Frequency, and Robbery Concentration for Females

		Coeff.	s.e.	Exp(B)
White	(109)	.7396	3.3880	2.0951
Black	(289)	1.2542	3.3828	3.5051
Hispanic	(12)	.8164	3.4253	2.2622
Socioeconomic status	(112)	−.3861	.3202	.6797
Delinquency frequency		.0348	.0448	1.0355
Robbery				
LT 49%	(30)	.7337	.4111	2.0827
GE 50%	(1)	−4.0992	13.4997	.0166
Constant		−2.4885	3.3866	

Table 7.30 concerns the effect of major violence offenses on adult crime status for females. The concentration data indicate that females have a minimal involvement in violent acts of delinquency as only 17.3% of the female recidivists committed any level of this crime type. However, the female recidivists (68, 16.5%) who committed some serious violent crime as juveniles were significantly more likely to be arrested as adults. There was no significant effect for the three (0.72%) females recidivists who had a high concentration of major violence.

Tables 7.31 and 7.32 show no significant findings for the relationship between adult crime status and the other two measures of violence-type offenses, robbery and injury. These tables also demonstrate the comparatively low prevalence of violence-related delinquency in female careers.

Table 7.33 shows with respect to major property offenses, that like the situation for major violence discussed above, such offenses are rare among females. However, also like the major violence data, we see that the odds of adult offending increase among females with some serious property delinquency in comparison to delinquents with no such offenses.

Interestingly, Table 7.34 shows that female delinquents who commit some theft offenses are less likely to continue on to adult crime than delinquents with no theft component in their delinquency career. Apparently, female involvement in acts of theft in their youth is a particular aspect of delinquency that a woman can leave behind her when she becomes an adult.

TABLE 7.32

Logistic Regression of Adult Offender Status on Race, Socioeconomic Status, Delinquency Frequency, and Injury Concentration for Females

		Coeff.	s.e.	Exp(B)
White	(109)	.7132	3.3881	2.0406
Black	(289)	1.2494	3.3829	3.4883
Hispanic	(12)	.8085	3.4254	2.2446
Socioeconomic status	(112)	−.3533	.3191	.7024
Delinquency frequency		.0460	.0442	1.0471
Injury				
LT 49%	(105)	.2564	.2710	1.2923
GE 50%	(5)	.7312	.9284	2.0777
Constant		−2.5610	3.3865	

Tables 7.35, 7.36, and 7.37 show that neither weapon use, drug offenses, nor juvenile status offenses have a significant effect on adult crime. It is entirely expected that neither weapon use nor drugs would be likely to have an effect on adult crime. Each of these offenses shows only minimal involvement among female recidivists—16.7% for weapons and 8.3% for drugs. However, a priori, one might expect a different result for status offenses. That is, it would be expected that many females would engage in some status offending but fewer would specialize in this dimension and this high concentration might be related to adult

TABLE 7.33

Logistic Regression of Adult Offender Status on Race, Socioeconomic Status, Delinquency Frequency, and Major Property Concentration for Females

		Coeff.	s.e.	Exp(B)
White	(109)	.7317	3.3887	2.0786
Black	(289)	1.2460	3.3831	3.4764
Hispanic	(12)	.6118	3.4281	1.8437
Socioeconomic status	(112)	−.4274	.3274	.6522
Delinquency frequency		.0160	.0455	1.0161
Major property				
LT 49%	(94)	1.1061**	.2728	3.0226
GE 50%	(9)	1.1742	.6928	3.2356
Constant		−2.6527	3.3873	

**$p<.01$

TABLE 7.34

Logistic Regression of Adult Offender Status on Race, Socioeconomic Status,
Delinquency Frequency, and Theft Concentration for Females

		Coeff.	s.e.	Exp(B)
White	(109)	.7212	3.3882	2.0568
Black	(289)	1.2042	3.3830	3.3343
Hispanic	(12)	.7543	3.4257	2.1260
Socioeconomic status	(112)	−.3587	.3214	.6986
Delinquency frequency		.0407	.0442	1.0416
Theft				
LT 49%	(140)	−.3647*	.1854	.6944
GE 50%	(30)	.0745	.1948	1.0774
Constant		−2.2719	3.3891	.5026

*p<.05

crime. What we find instead is that the vast majority of females, 85%, had involvement in status offending and 57% specialized in this offense type.

In Table 7.38, the final model shows that the majority (235, 57.1%) of female recidivists act with someone else when they commit their delinquencies. Regardless of the particular level with which they engage in this co-offending, there is a significant association between co-offending and the probability of adult crime. Females who commit their offenses

TABLE 7.35

Logistic Regression of Adult Offender Status on Race, Socioeconomic Status,
Delinquency Frequency, and Weapon Concentration for Females

		Coeff.	s.e.	Exp(B)
White	(109)	.9901	5.5679	2.6916
Black	(289)	1.5504	5.5648	4.7134
Hispanic	(12)	1.0324	5.5907	2.8077
Socioeconomic status	(112)	−.3954	.3173	.6734
Delinquency frequency		.0501	.0433	1.0514
Weapon				
LT 49%	(65)	.0498	.3188	1.0511
GE 50%	(4)	−5.1360	11.1206	.0059
Constant		−2.7771	5.5670	.6179

TABLE 7.36
*Logistic Regression of Adult Offender Status on Race, Socioeconomic Status,
Delinquency Frequency, and Drug Offense Concentration for Females*

		Coeff.	s.e.	Exp(B)
White	(109)	.7795	3.3891	2.1804
Black	(289)	1.3333	3.3834	3.7936
Hispanic	(12)	.6365	3.4326	1.8898
Socioeconomic status	(112)	−.4232	.3212	.6550
Delinquency frequency		.0528	.0430	1.0542
Drugs				
LT 49%	(32)	.2989	.4380	1.3484
GE 50%	(2)	1.5660	1.4871	4.7875
Constant		−2.6032	3.3873	

alone are much less likely to make the transitions to adult crime when
their delinquency career is over.

Summary

This chapter has examined the relationships between adult offending status and various measures concerning the types of delinquent acts
committed during the delinquency career. We provided two related but

TABLE 7.37
*Logistic Regression of Adult Offender Status on Race, Socioeconomic Status,
Delinquency Frequency, and Status Offense Concentration for Females*

		Coeff.	s.e.	Exp(B)
White	(109)	.6356	3.3885	1.8882
Black	(289)	1.1765	3.3831	3.2430
Hispanic	(12)	.7434	3.4263	2.1031
Socioeconomic status	(112)	−.4063	.3229	.6661
Delinquency frequency		.0680	.0437	1.0703
Status				
LT 49%	(115)	.3179	.2149	1.3743
GE 50%	(236)	.1804	.1786	1.1977
Constant		−2.3441	3.3871	.4889

TABLE 7.38
Logistic Regression of Adult Offender Status on Race, Socioeconomic Status,
Delinquency Frequency, and Co-Offending Concentration for Females

		Coeff.	s.e.	Exp(B)
White	(109)	.6433	3.3895	1.9028
Black	(289)	1.1323	3.3834	3.1027
Hispanic	(12)	.7188	3.4279	2.0519
Socioeconomic status	(112)	−.3361	.1626	.7145
Delinquency frequency		.0437	.0443	1.0446
Co-offenders				
LE 49%	(146)	.7117*	.2889	2.0375
GE 50%	(89)	.9234**	.3253	2.5179
Constant		−3.1332	3.3910	

*p<.05   **p<.01

distinct types of analyses. In the first set of analyses we examined a series of dichotomous measures reflecting whether the delinquent had ever committed one of the nine specific offense types. We looked separately at serious violence and property crimes, robbery, drug offenses, possession or use of weapons, theft and injury offenses regardless of their severity level, status offenses, and the presence of co-offenders. Although not exhaustive of all possibilities, these offense types capture a very wide variety of the possible forms of delinquency and cover the full spectrum of severity.

In looking at the nature of delinquency and how it was related to adult offending status, we found that the commission of particular offense types did increase the likelihood of continuity between the delinquency career and the subsequent adult criminal careers for both males and females.

There were particular offenses that were relevant for males. These included the delinquent acts associated with major violence, robbery, weapon use, and being a co-offender. For females, the significant offense types included major violence, theft, and drugs. These results were based on the entire pool of delinquents in the cohort, without regard for the career frequency of their contacts with police. In addition, offense type was defined broadly to include any level of involvement. This means that a one-time delinquent, a chronic delinquent with one experience of the type noted, and a chronic delinquent whose entire offense career was of that particular type, were grouped together and treated alike.

In the second set of analyses, we selected the pool of delinquents who had accumulated at least three offenses in their delinquency career. We selected these recidivists in order to examine another aspect of delinquency offense types, the concept of offense specialization. We decided that an alternative way to investigate the concept of offense specialization was to ignore the issue of offense sequencing offense by offense across the usual transition matrices and focus instead on the extent to which a delinquency career could be classified and studied in terms of the particular concentration with which a delinquent committed the select offense types that we designated for analysis.

We differentiated between two levels of concentration. The first category, low concentration, comprised those select delinquents whose delinquency career showed from 1% to 49% commission of a particular offense. The other category, high concentration or specialists, committed at least 50% of their career offenses in a particular offense type.

The analysis of offense concentration for the select male recidivists produced a range of findings. Adult crime status was more likely among those delinquents who concentrated their juvenile offending within particular offense types. Among the nine offense concentration analyses, the results were significant for seven offense types. For three offense types (robbery, injury, and theft), adult crime was significantly related to the commission of offenses at the lower concentration level (from 1% to 49%). In one measure, the possession of a weapon, the higher concentration level was significantly related to adult crime. For the remaining three offense types (drugs, status, and co-offending), the particular concentration level did not discriminate very well as both concentration levels, when compared to delinquents who had never committed these three offense types, were significantly associated with adult crime status.

In addition to these concentration findings, we found that the frequency of delinquency measure was consistently significant in predicting adult crime status. As with all of the analyses reported in this volume thus far, the more offenses a male delinquent accumulated the higher the likelihood of adult crime. Also, adult offending status was not significantly affected by the race or by the socioeconomic status of the male recidivist.

In addition to the marked gender differences that were reported for the dichotomous offense types, there were gender differences concerning offense concentration. The findings indicated that in only four of nine measures was offense concentration significantly related to adult crime status. Female recidivists with some involvement in three offenses, major violence, major property, and theft, had significantly higher odds of adult crime than females with no involvement. However, high concentration, or specialization in our terms, was not related to adult crime. For one offense type, co-offending, was related to adult crime status for both concentration levels.

Predicting Adult Crime Status from the Severity of the Delinquency Career

In the previous chapter we explored the relationships between the type of offenses that had been committed by the offenders in the 1958 cohort and their influence on the probability of adult crime. We first examined the type of offenses (using dichotomous offense measures) committed by the entire pool of delinquents to determine whether the commission of particular offense types was associated with the likelihood that the delinquent would continue into adult crime. Then in an effort to examine the association between delinquency and the familiar concept of specialization, offense switching, or "versatility in offending"—as it is often labeled, or "offense concentration," as we have chosen to refer to the phenomenon—we restricted our analyses to the subsample who had committed at least three offenses as juveniles.

As we explained, it is necessary for a delinquent to have a minimum number of offenses before the issue of delinquency specialization is relevant and can be properly investigated. That is, a one-time offender, by definition, cannot exhibit specialization. Likewise, a two-time offender has had but one opportunity to either repeat the prior offense type or to switch to another. In the absence of another offense rank or transition number, it is premature to identify a "pattern" on the basis of only two observations. Thus, it seemed to us that three offenses are the minimum number necessary to permit analyses of offense specialization. Under the same assumption, we will continue to use the group of delinquents with at least three offenses here as we investigate the topic of offense severity and offense escalation in particular.

This chapter will address the issue of whether delinquency careers that exhibit evidence of what may be termed *offense severity escalation*, demonstrate a higher probability of adult crime. The question of offense escalation parallels that of offense specialization, but concerns not whether offense type repeats have a higher chance of occurrence, but rather, whether delinquent offenses show a pattern of increased severity as the juvenile career progresses. This progression in severity may differentially posture the delinquent for a more likely transition to adult crime as compared with those delinquents who exhibit no such progression, and thus, no change in severity as they accumulate offenses.

That is, as the delinquency career progresses it is plausible to envision several seriousness patterns. First, delinquents commit the same type of offenses and inflict the same amount of harm on the community or a victim and, therefore, exhibit little if any severity escalation. Second, offenders might switch to more serious offense types which involve greater degrees of harm with a consequent increase in the severity of harm. Third, offenders may commit the same offense type again but the repeat offense may be less serious than the previous (e.g., a lesser degree of physical harm to the victim in an assault or lesser property loss in a robbery). Last, offenders may exhibit neither a constant severity nor a continually increasing or decreasing pattern, but rather, show a fluctuating pattern of severity with upward and downward swings in the severity of their delinquent acts.

The seriousness of juvenile offenses concerns our investigation of subsequent criminal career development because individuals who engage in serious crime at an early age may be more likely to continue their offensivity, and the gravity of their ensuing behavior may even escalate. Support for the hypothesis that criminality continues as the result of serious initial offending was found in three prior studies.

First, in the St. Louis Follow-Up Study of psychiatric patients and matched controls, Robins (1966) found that her dichotomous measure of crime severity was a strong predictor of subsequent behavior—no child without frequent or serious antisocial behavior became a sociopathic adult. Second, Wolfgang, Figlio, and Sellin (1972) reported support for a relationship between seriousness and crime continuation in the 1945 Philadelphia Birth Cohort Study—boys who committed nonindex first offenses were somewhat more likely to stop after the first offense than were boys who inflicted some bodily or property harm. Third, the Rand Corporation survey of 624 California inmates found that, "Respondents who committed a serious crime before age 16 tended to report more adult crime, commit more types of crime, commit violent crimes at a higher rate, and hold professional criminal attitudes" (Petersilia, 1980: 347).

Neither the 1945 Philadelphia Birth Cohort Study (Wolfgang et al., 1972: 282), nor the Racine, Wisconsin, birth cohorts (Shannon, 1978: 135; 1980) found evidence of a systematic progression in severity among offenders. After testing the notion of career escalation and achieving non-significant results, studies by Bursik (1980), Hamparian et al. (1978: 129–130), Klein (1979), and Rojek and Erickson (1982) arrived at essentially the same conclusion found in the Philadelphia and Racine cohort investigations.

Alternatively, the topic of escalation has been operationalized in terms of whether offenders move to more serious offense types as they accumulate additional crimes rather than in terms of the comparative severity of offenses, especially repeat-offense sequences. The offense switching approach was used by Rojek and Erickson, and they reported "there is no evidence that the probability distributions of the five types of offenses shift in any way toward more serious offenses" (1982: 17). Farrington, Snyder, and Finnegan (1988), using a similar operationalization, examined whether the frequency of serious offenses was correlated with offense transition number and found some evidence of specialization.

The results of previous research concerning the effect of crime severity on subsequent delinquent or criminal behavior, attests to the need for further research to determine whether youths who commit offenses of a serious nature are more likely than others to commit crimes upon reaching adulthood. Many investigations, including several longitudinal studies, employing various research designs and with data drawn from numerous sources, have been attempted. As our review of this literature in Chapter 3 revealed, some of the issues have received considerable attention by researchers while others were given only casual mention in a few studies. The review has shown that none of these important research issues have been rigorously examined to the degree sufficient to achieve resolution.

Cohen (1986) has thoroughly reviewed the approaches to escalation and has noted that offense switches to more serious varieties of offenses as the offending career advances is not the only way to analyze offense severity changes. She has endorsed the approach of measuring escalation in terms of an examination of the average severity of successive offenses. We have adopted this approach in this study.

Juvenile Severity and Adult Status for Males

Basic Measures of Offense Severity

Table 8.1 reports logistic regression results concerning the probability of adult crime by race, socioeconomic status, and the frequency and average severity of delinquent acts. We have seen from prior results that

TABLE 8.1

Logistic Regression of Adult Offender Status on Race, Socioeconomic Status, Delinquency Frequency, and Average Juvenile Severity for Males

	Coeff.	s.e.	Exp(B)
White	1.1713	1.0297	3.2262
Black	1.0640	1.0280	2.8979
Hispanic	.8924	1.0487	2.4411
Socioeconomic status	−.0855	.1138	.9181
Delinquency frequency	.0692**	.0283	1.0717
Average juvenile severity	.0639**	.0262	1.0660
Frequency by severity	−.0033	.0042	.9967
Constant	−1.4705	1.0402	

**$p<.01$

an especially strong predictor of adult crime was the extent of the delinquency career, whether this extent was measured as a continuous frequency variable, or as a discrete variable using delinquency categories (i.e., one-time, recidivist, and chronic recidivist). We report the results in Table 8.1 to establish the basic finding that both frequency and average severity have strong, significant, and independent effects on adult crime status. It is noteworthy that the absence of a significant interaction effect attests to the fact that average severity effect does not depend upon the underlying frequency of delinquency—as the delinquent's average severity increases, the probability of adult crime similarly increases, regardless of the frequency of the delinquent acts.

Table 8.1 establishes that delinquents with a higher average severity across their delinquency career have a significantly higher likelihood of continuing their illegal conduct as adults. These results do not indicate the mechanisms or the context in which offense severity produces higher odds of adult crime, however; they only establish that offense severity, and possibly escalation in severity, are worthy of further analyses.

In the next three tables, we investigate preliminary measures of escalation in an effort to specify the severity effect. We have constructed three basic measures of the changes in offense severity across the delinquency career in an attempt to delineate evidence of escalation and its possible association with adult crime status.

Table 8.2 reports on the first alternative severity measure, which calculates the difference between the delinquent's maximum or peak offense severity and his average severity across all his delinquent acts. We were concerned here with the relative differences in the departure of the severity peak from the offender's own baseline, and whether the probability of adult crime status increases as the maximum versus average difference increases. The logistic analysis includes race and socioeconomic status as basic control variables, and also includes a control for the frequency of delinquent acts to ensure that the severity effects are genuine and important, "net of the effect" of this other very strong predictor. Table 8.2 includes coefficients for four dummy effects (each category is a range of 4.9 severity points) compared to the omitted category of "less than a 4.9 point difference" between the maximum offense severity and the average offense severity.

The results in Table 8.2 show two basic findings. First, each of the four categories of "maximum versus average offense severity," compared to the omitted category representing "little or no difference between the maximum and the average," has a significant effect on the probability of adult crime independent of the effect of delinquency frequency, race, and socioeconomic status. Simply, compared to a delinquent who commits all his offenses within a narrow range of severity, a delinquent who has a difference of as little as 5 severity points between

TABLE 8.2

Logistic Regression of Adult Offender Status on Race, Socioeconomic Status, Delinquency Frequency, and Maximum Juvenile Severity vs. Average Severity for Males

	Coeff.	s.e.	Exp(B)
White	1.1647	1.0308	3.2050
Black	1.0477	1.0291	2.8512
Hispanic	.8769	1.0500	2.4033
Socioeconomic status	−.0919	.1143	.9122
Delinquency frequency	.0608**	.0179	1.0626
Maximum juvenile severity vs. average juvenile severity			
5–9.9 pt. diff.	.2554*	.1132	1.2910
10–14.9 pt. diff.	.5840**	.1724	1.7933
15–19.9 pt. diff.	.9873**	.3439	2.6841
GE 20 pt. diff.	.9663**	.3358	2.6282
Frequency by maximum vs. average juvenile severity	−.0020	.0011	.9980
Constant	−1.3156	1.0324	

*$p<.05$ **$p<.01$

his maximum and his average has significantly greater odds of becoming an adult criminal.

The second basic finding concerns the fact that as the difference increases, there is a consequent increase in the odds of adult crime. Thus, compared to delinquents in the omitted group, the delinquents in the first category (5–9.9 points) have a coefficient of .2554, which was significant at the .05 level, and produce adult crime odds 1.29 times higher. The coefficients for the second (10–14.9 points), the third category (15–19.9 points), and the fourth category (20 or more pts.) are all significant at the .01 level and generally produce increasing odds of adult crime. Thus, Table 8.2 generally suggests that a delinquency career with variation in the severity of delinquent acts is associated with adult crime status.

In Table 8.3 we present a second alternative severity measure, a familiar variance type measure—the range between the lowest and highest offense severity scores. We are treating this "spread" in the offense severity across a delinquency career as a possible indicator of severity escalation. A narrow spread indicates that a delinquent committed offenses with similar severity scores and did not, therefore, exhibit an escalation-type pattern. On the other hand, a spread in offense severity indicates that the delinquent either committed a mix of offenses of varying seriousness or committed the same type of offense with varying degrees of harm.

As with the previous analysis reported in Table 8.2, we used a 5-level measure with the lowest category omitted and derived coefficients for the other four categories. We also used the same class limits (i.e., 4.9 severity points) as the maximum versus average variable. The results for the second escalation measure confirm what we learned in Table 8.2. That is, as the range between a delinquent's lowest and highest offense severity scores gets larger, there is a significant increase in the likelihood that the delinquent will make the transition to adult crime. Compared to delinquents who had a severity score range of less than 5 points, delinquents with a wider range in severity generally exhibit a greater likelihood of becoming an adult criminal. In particular, delinquents with a range of 15 to 20 seriousness points are about twice as likely, and delinquents with a 20-point or wider range are about three times more likely, to become adult criminals compared to the omitted category (i.e., less than 5 points).

Table 8.3 also indicates a significant interaction effect between the frequency of delinquency and the severity score range. The coefficient is significant, but more important, it has a negative sign. The negative sign indicates that delinquents with a high frequency have a higher chance of

TABLE 8.3
Logistic Regression of Adult Offender Status on Race, Socioeconomic Status,
Delinquency Frequency, and Juvenile Severity Range for Males

	Coeff.	s.e.	Exp(B)
White	1.1640	1.0278	3.2026
Black	1.0396	1.0261	2.8282
Hispanic	.8568	1.0471	2.3555
Socioeconomic status	−.0808	.1146	.9224
Delinquency frequency	.0665**	.0191	1.0688
Juvenile severity range			
5–9.9 pt. diff.	.4678**	.1501	1.5964
10–14.9 pt. diff.	.4458**	.1467	1.5617
15–19.9 pt. diff.	.6793**	.1879	1.9725
GE 20 pt. diff.	1.1778**	.2739	3.2471
Frequency by juvenile severity range	−.0017*	.0008	.9983
Constant	−1.5300	1.0326	

$*p<.05$ $**p<.01$

adult crime regardless of their range in severity scores. This is expected as a chronic delinquent may continually repeat the same type of serious offense and thus not produce any appreciable range in severity scores. But, the negative sign also indicates that even at the lower end of the frequency distribution, delinquents who exhibit changes in seriousness (and as such changes produce an increasing difference between their least and most serious offenses) are more likely to go on to adult crime than would be normally expected of low frequency delinquents.

We have thus far established that when a delinquent's maximum offense severity increasingly departs from either the severity score for his least serious offense or from the average severity across all his offenses, his probability of adult crime increases significantly. In the next table we take up a related issue of the percentage increases in offense severity.

Table 8.4 examines the third and last alternative escalation measure. This measure represents the cumulative percentage difference in an offender's delinquent acts across his career. That is, the percentage difference between the first and the second offense, the second and the third offense, and so on, were calculated and then these percentage differences were summed to reflect the "net difference" in offense severity changes. This measure is used to show whether the severity increase findings observed above come from a single dissimilar offense that rep-

TABLE 8.4
Logistic Regression of Adult Offender Status on Race, Socioeconomic Status, Delinquency Frequency, and Juvenile Severity Cumulative Percentage Increases for Males

	Coeff.	s.e.	Exp(B)
White	1.1632	1.0301	3.2003
Black	1.0898	1.0282	2.9738
Hispanic	.8931	1.0493	2.4426
Socioeconomic status	−.0957	.1142	.9087
Delinquency frequency	.4036**	.1546	1.4972
Juvenile severity cumulative percentage increases			
LT 100%	1.1838*	.5951	3.2669
100%	1.6549**	.6000	5.2328
200%	1.4171*	.6093	4.1250
300–500%	1.5465**	.6090	4.6952
GE 600%	1.8152**	.7293	6.1424
Frequency by juvenile severity cumulative % increases			
LT 100%	−.3448*	.1563	.7084
100%	−.3585*	.1558	.6987
200%	−.3631*	.1562	.6955
300–500%	−.3665*	.1578	.6932
600%	−.4235**	.1796	.6548
Constant	−2.5356	1.1763	

*p<.05 **p<.01

resents a substantial departure from an otherwise stable pattern of low severity scores, or whether the increases in offense seriousness represent a substantial change in the offender's severity scores.

We have isolated five groups of cumulative percentage changes: (1) less than 100%; (2) exactly 100%; (3) exactly 200%; (4) 300 to 500%; and (5) 600% or higher; in comparison to the omitted category of "no appreciable changes" or a percentage decrease. The findings given in Table 8.4 show that any extent of cumulative percentage increases in offense severity produces a significant likelihood that the delinquent will continue the delinquency career into adulthood. Generally, the higher the percentage increase, the greater the odds of adult crime. The significance pattern for the coefficients indicates that only for the 200% increase category do the odds of adult crime *not* increase linearly as the percentage increases.

The significant interaction effect observed between the frequency of delinquent acts and the cumulative percentage increase categories indicates, as before, that the effect of the severity score increase works especially well at the lower level of delinquency frequency. Thus, offenders who committed the lower range of offenses exhibit substantial odds of adult crime if they also accumulated an increasing degree of offense severity increases.

In these preliminary analyses of offense seriousness we have established the need to investigate the dynamics of offense seriousness further. First, we have seen that the average offense severity of a male's delinquent acts is associated with adult crime. Second, we have also seen that delinquents who exhibit variation in seriousness scores (whether such variation is measured by [1] the difference between his peak score and his average score; [2] the difference between his peak score and his lowest score; or [3] the net percentage change across the increases and decreases across his entire career) have significantly higher odds of making a transition to adult crime status.

The Timing of Changes in Offense Severity

The first few analyses reported above did confirm that the seriousness of delinquent conduct is an important consideration in examining a delinquent's propensity for adult crime. While important, however, these preliminary analyses do not address the possible relevance that the timing of severity changes may have on the delinquent's increasing probability of adult crime. There are very different policy implications for juvenile justice if it is established that offense severity differences predictive of adult crime occur at different stages of the delinquency career. Severity differences early in a career, for example, may be much more susceptible to judicious and strategic intervention than is the case late in a delinquency career.

In order to examine this timing issue, we calculated additional variables. First, because each of the delinquents in the restricted pool of offenders that we are using here had at least three delinquent offenses, we calculated the average severity of this set of offenses that was common to all delinquents in the subset. Second, we then calculated the average severity of several groups of subsequent offenses: (1) the fourth through seventh; (2) the eighth through fourteenth; and (3) the fifteenth through last. Third, we calculated the difference between the average severity of the set of early offenses (first, second, third) and these three other sets of offenses (and the differences among the three continuation sets as well).

With these average offense severity variables and the differences between the means of subsequent offense sets, we can examine the timing of offense severity changes and its effects on the likelihood of adult crime.

Table 8.5 reports the logistic regression results for the usual control variables (race, socioeconomic status, and frequency of delinquency) and three new severity variables—average severity for first three offenses, a discrete variable expressing the difference between the average severity of the first three offenses and the fourth through seventh offenses, and the interaction effect. The five categories for the severity difference variable—much lower, lower, same, higher, and much higher—produce dummy effects in comparison to the omitted category (desisted at third offense). Thus, we are contrasting the severity difference possibilities between the average severity of the first three offenses and the

TABLE 8.5

Logistic Regression of Adult Offender Status on Race, Socioeconomic Status, Delinquency Frequency, Severity of Offenses 1–3, and Severity 4–7 vs. 1–3 for Males

	Coeff.	s.e.	Exp(B)
White	1.1466	1.0256	3.1476
Black	1.0550	1.0240	2.8721
Hispanic	.8749	1.0451	2.3987
Socioeconomic status	−.0721	.1147	.9304
Delinquency frequency	.0393**	.0118	1.0401
Average juvenile severity offenses 1–3	.0876**	.0261	1.0915
Severity 4–7 vs. 1–3			
Much lower	.3685	.3397	1.4455
Lower	.3255	.3832	1.3848
Same	.5361*	.2708	1.7093
Higher	.6645*	.2947	1.9436
Much higher	.7877**	.2254	2.1983
Severity 1–3 by severity 4–7 vs. 1–3			
Much lower	−.0392	.0406	.9616
Lower	−.0220	.0671	.9783
Same	−.0614	.0537	.9405
Higher	−.0945	.0602	.9098
Much higher	−.0994	.0450	.9054
Constant	−1.6674	1.0342	

*$p<.05$ **$p<.01$

fourth through seventh offense compared to delinquents who stop at three delinquencies.

The results given in Table 8.5 report the familiar result that there are no significant race or socioeconomic status effects in the probability of adult crime. These findings also show the usual result that the extent of delinquency is a significant predictor of adult crime status. The new findings, however, bear directly on the relationship between the seriousness of delinquency, the timing of such serious delinquency, and the propensity for adult crime. These important results warrant a detailed discussion.

First, Table 8.5 shows that the severity of a delinquent's first three offenses has a significant coefficient (.0876, p <.01) that is higher than that of delinquency frequency (.0393, p <.01). This is the first time that we have seen a variable displace delinquency frequency as the strongest predictor of adult crime.

Second, the results also indicate that delinquents who continue as recidivists to at least a fourth offense, but who show either a substantial decrease or a slight decrease in the severity of their fourth through seventh offenses, are no more likely to become adult criminals than delinquents who desisted at the third offense. Simply, additional recidivism beyond the third offense is not a sufficient condition for significantly increasing the odds of adult crime.

Third, when an offender does goes on to a fourth, fifth, sixth, or seventh offense, and the average severity of such additional offenses is either the same, higher, or much higher than the average for the first set, then such delinquents have significantly increasing odds of making a transition to adult crime. These results indicate that the additional recidivism must carry with it a severity level the same as a prior high level for offenses one through three, or an increasing severity score for offenses four through seven, before such recidivism increases the odds of adult crime.

Last, one of the interaction effects was significant–the coefficient for severity 1 to 3 with the "much higher" level for severity 4–7. The negative sign of this coefficient indicates that when the prior offense severity for the initial set of offenses moves toward the lower end of the distribution and the severity score of the first set of additional recidivism—offenses 4 through 7—is at the highest level, then the delinquent has significantly greater odds of becoming an adult offender.

These results taken together would suggest the following. As the average severity of a delinquent's first three offenses increases, there also is a significant increase in the probability of adult crime. Accumulating additional offenses does not significantly increase such odds unless one of two conditions exists. First, if the delinquent continues, or surpasses, his prior high level of seriousness during his next set of offenses (4–7), then recidivism increases the risk of adult crime. Second, however, even an offender with a lower seriousness for his starting offenses can increase his chances for adult crime if he escalates his severity level during his additional recidivism.

Given the importance of the results shown in Table 8.5, we decided to continue to investigate the timing of severity changes throughout the career to find other timing points that might influence adult crime status. We added two additional sets of severity score differences—the 8th through the 14th offense and the 15th offense and beyond—and calculated the difference between the average score for these sets and the av-

TABLE 8.6

Logistic Regression of Adult Offender Status on Race, Socioeconomic Status, Delinquency Frequency, Severity of Offenses 1–3, Severity 4–7 vs. 1–3, Severity 8–14 vs. 1–3, Severity 15–53 vs. 1–3 for Males

	Coeff.	s.e.	Exp(B)
White	1.1534	1.0261	3.1690
Black	1.0529	1.0244	2.8660
Hispanic	.8605	1.0457	2.3643
Socioeconomic status	−.0703	.1150	.9321
Delinquency frequency	.0369	.0262	1.0376
Average juvenile severity offenses 1–3	.0877**	.0261	1.0916
Severity 4–7 vs. 1–3			
Much lower	.3513	.3402	1.4209
Lower	.3312	.3865	1.3926
Same	.5047	.2743	1.6565
Higher	.5765*	.3011	1.7798
Much higher	.7094**	.2324	2.0327
Severity 8–14 vs. 1–3			
Lower	.3672	.2911	1.4437
Same	−.0961	.2896	.9084
Higher	.2860	.2085	1.3311
Severity 15–53 vs. 1–3			
Lower	−.6149	.5264	.5407
Higher	−.2447	.3692	.7829
Constant	−1.6614	1.0373	

*p<.05 **p<.01

erage score for the first three offenses. The results are reported in Table 8.6.

The findings concerning the impact of the severity of additional recidivism stages make an important contribution to our analysis of the probability of adult crime. First, the significant coefficient for the frequency of delinquency disappears. Second, the average severity of the first three offenses remains significant. Third, the difference between average score of the fourth through fifth offenses and the first three offenses has significant effects for recidivists who have higher or much higher severity scores for the fourth through fifth offenses. Last, there are no significant effects at any difference levels for subsequent recidivism (i.e., 8–14 or 15+) in predicting adult crime.

The Severity of Early Delinquency

The results in Table 8.6 indicate that it is the severity of a delinquent's first few offenses, rather than the extent of his recidivism or the average severity of his recidivism that is predictive of adult crime status. As the last step in our investigation of severity scores we turn to an analysis of the first three offenses.

Table 8.7 displays the logistic regression results for a model in which the average severity of the first three offenses has been replaced by the individual severity scores of the first three offenses. There is a significant effect of delinquency frequency, as was true in the model reported in Table 8.5. In addition, we see that there are significant positive effects for the severity of the first and the second offenses; as the severity of these offenses increases, the probability of adult crime similarly rises. There also is a significant interaction between the two. This interaction shows that even when the severity scores of these offenses move to opposite ends of the continuum, a high severity score for one of the offenses is significantly associated with adult crime status.

When we consider the severity of the third offense, the results show that the third offense alone is not associated with adult crime. Similarly, the relationship between the first and third offenses does not add any explanatory value to the model. However, there is a significant interaction effect between the second and third offense. This means that the chances of adult crime increase if the third offense severity is high and the second offense severity is low.

The results in Table 8.7, based on the individual severity scores of the first three offenses, suggest that delinquents who begin their careers with serious offenses, or who escalate between their first and second offenses, or between their second and third offenses, have significantly

TABLE 8.7

Logistic Regression of Adult Offender Status on Race, Socioeconomic Status, Delinquency Frequency, Severity of First, Second, and Third Offenses for Males

	Coeff.	s.e.	Exp(B)
White	1.1484	1.0310	3.1532
Black	1.0504	1.0293	2.8588
Hispanic	.8878	1.0500	2.4297
Socioeconomic status	−.0883	.1140	.9154
Delinquency frequency	.0561**	.0108	1.0577
First offense severity	.0275*	.0139	1.0279
Second offense severity	.0309**	.0117	1.0313
First offense severity by second offense severity	−.0317*	.0110	.9983
Third offense severity	.0158	.0113	1.0159
First offense severity by third offense severity	.0016	.0015	1.0016
Second offense severity by third offense severity	−.0020*	.0010	.9980
Constant	−1.4263	1.0342	

*$p<.05$ **$p<.01$

greater odds of becoming an adult criminal. Further, adding measures that capture either the extent of subsequent recidivism or the severity of such recidivism does not contribute any additional explanatory value to that gleaned from the first three offenses.

Juvenile Severity and Adult Status for Females

The parallel analyses that we conducted on the set of female recidivists who had committed at least three offenses did not parallel the findings that we have reported above for males. In fact, there was an almost total absence of significant results. Before we present a brief exposition of these findings for females, it is important to highlight the vastly different career and seriousness parameters which operate for the males and females in the 1958 cohort.

First, among the 1,972 female delinquents in the 1958 cohort, there were only 411, or 20.8%, who qualified as three-time or more recidivists. By comparison, of the 4,315 male delinquents, 1,806, or 41.9%, could be classified as three-time or greater recidivists. Thus, males were twice as likely as females to be included in the select set of recidivists that we are using in the present analyses and in the later part of Chapter 7.

Second, the gender difference gets even wider in the prevalence of adult crime. That is, only 93 of the 411 female recidivists, or 22.6%, made a transition to adult crime, while 1,020 of the 1,806 male recidivists, or 56.5%, made such a transition to criminal status. Thus, the gender effect for the dependent variable in this study (adult crime status) shows that over 2 1/2 times as many male recidivists become adult criminals as their female counterparts.

Last, the various predictor variables that we have been including in our models are characterized by substantial gender differences, even though the pool requires that a delinquent have at least three offenses for inclusion in our analyses. While females had committed 4.66 juvenile offenses, males had accumulated 6.66 delinquent acts. The average severity of female offenses (2.77) was about one-half of that achieved by males (5.51). Similarly, the average maximum severity of any female act was less than half that achieved by males (6.73 vs. 13.85).

These few statistics are sufficient to indicate the constraints under which our prediction models for females must operate. First, female recidivism was less prevalent in the cohort than was the case for males. Second, the male recidivists in the select pool accumulated many more offenses and committed a much greater range of severity for their offenses than did females. Last, very few females in the select pool of recidivists made a transition to adult crime compared to their male counterparts. Thus, there are fewer females who exhibit the criterion measure and their predictor variables exhibit much less variation in seriousness with which to make the predictions.

Basic Measures of Offense Severity

Table 8.8 presents an analysis of the overall frequency and severity measures and their relationship to adult crime status for females. The results indicate that these two aspects of the delinquency career for females, unlike the case for males, are not significantly related to adult crime status. That is, neither the number of delinquents acts in the delinquency career nor the average severity of these acts, helps predict whether the female delinquent will make a transition to adult crime status.

Tables 8.9, 8.10, and 8.11 display the results for the three alternative severity measures that were developed to capture the peaks, the range, and the cumulative changes in offense severity throughout the juvenile career. We note first in Table 8.9 that when we compare the various cate-

.

TABLE 8.8

Logistic Regression of Adult Offender Status on Race, Socioeconomic Status,
Delinquency Frequency, and Average Juvenile Severity for Females

	Coeff.	s.e.	Exp(B)
White	.7266	3.3885	2.0681
Black	1.2647	3.3831	3.5421
Hispanic	.6623	3.4303	1.9392
Socioeconomic status	−.3328	.3217	.7169
Delinquency frequency	−.0352	.0848	.9654
Average juvenile severity	−.0302	.1204	.9703
Frequency by severity	.0304	.0245	1.0308
Constant	−2.4471	3.4037	

gories of peak severity (the highest severity score for any delinquent offense) there are no significant differences in adult crime status. Second,
we observe in Table 8.10 that the particular range of offense severity
scores for female delinquencies does not facilitate the prediction of
whether the female delinquent will make a transition to adult crime.
Third, with respect to Table 8.11, we further see that, even when we compute the cumulative net increase in offense severity across a female's
delinquency career, the various categories are not significantly different
in distinguishing whether the delinquent will continue her career as an
adult.

These basic severity results indicate that alternate measures of the
severity of delinquency across a female's delinquency career are, unlike
the case for males, entirely unsuccessful in differentiating which delinquents will continue to commit illegal acts as adults.

The Timing of Changes in Offense Severity

In Tables 8.12 and 8.13 we turn to the issue of whether the delinquency career may be characterized as having stages (i.e., early,
medium, late) in which severity score changes may influence the delinquent's propensity for adult crime. Table 8.12 presents results that are
both similar and dissimilar to those obtained for males. The results are
similar in that the average severity of a female offender's early delinquency career—the first three offenses—is significantly associated with
the likelihood that she will continue as an adult. As the severity of this

TABLE 8.9

Logistic Regression of Adult Offender Status on Race, Socioeconomic Status,
Delinquency Frequency, and Maximum Juvenile Severity vs.
Average Severity for Females

	Coeff.	s.e.	Exp(B)
White	.7328	3.3881	2.0808
Black	1.2970	3.3829	3.6582
Hispanic	.7787	3.4265	2.1787
Socioeconomic status	.3373	.3208	.7137
Delinquency frequency	.0479	.0647	1.0490
Maximum juvenile severity vs. average juvenile severity			
5–9.9 pt. diff.	−.3042	.3624	.7377
10–14.9 pt. diff.	.0312	.6204	1.0317
15–19.9 pt. diff.	.1281	1.2893	1.1366
GE 20 pt. diff.	1.1321	1.4235	3.1022
Frequency by maximum vs. average juvenile severity	.0014	.0072	1.0014
Constant	−2.5297	3.3904	

TABLE 8.10

Logistic Regression of Adult Offender Status on Race, Socioeconomic Status,
Delinquency Frequency, and Juvenile Severity Range for Females

	Coeff.	s.e.	Exp(B)
White	.7361	3.3886	2.0877
Black	1.2478	3.3833	3.4827
Hispanic	.6752	3.4295	1.9644
Socioeconomic status	−.4056	.3225	.6666
Delinquency frequency	.0208	.0665	1.0210
Juvenile severity range			
5–9.9 pt. diff.	.3616	.3124	1.4356
10–14.9 pt. diff.	.2785	.4760	1.3211
15–19.9 pt. diff.	−.0246	.7395	.9757
GE 20 pt. diff.	.7849	1.0912	2.1922
Frequency by juvenile severity range	.0020	.0055	1.0020
Constant	−2.5993	3.3931	

TABLE 8.11

Logistic Regression of Adult Offender Status on Race, Socioeconomic Status, Delinquency Frequency, and Juvenile Severity Cumulative Percentage Increases for Females

	Coeff.	s.e.	Exp(B)
White	.6020	3.3895	1.8258
Black	1.3094	3.3835	3.7038
Hispanic	.7735	3.4277	2.1674
Socioeconomic status	−.4234	.3336	.6548
Delinquency frequency	−.0364	.3138	.9643
Juvenile severity cumulative percentage increases			
LT 100%	−.6416	1.2780	.5264
100%	−.2486	1.3272	.7799
200%	−.2028	1.4298	.8164
300–500%	−1.2817	1.6592	.2776
GE 600%	1.3850	2.8036	3.9950
Frequency by juvenile severity cumulative % increases			
LT 100%	.0458	.3262	1.0469
100%	.0450	.3224	1.0461
200%	.2080	.3365	1.2312
300–500%	.0759	.3988	1.0788
600%	−.5079	.7863	.6018
Constant	−1.8960	3.5883	

set of early offenses increases, the chances of adult crime status also increase.

The results are dissimilar from those obtained for males in terms of the fact that, for females, examining the severity changes that occur between the first three offenses and the second set, offenses 4 through 7, does not reveal any additional significant effects in predicting adult crime.

Similarly, when we expand the delinquency career in Table 8.13 to include four sets of offense stages (i.e., offenses 1 to 3, 4 through 7, 8 through 14, and 15 and above), the results are identical to those just obtained in Table 8.12. There are no significant severity effects beyond the first three offenses. That is, the early delinquency career, and only the early career of females, is statistically useful in making predictions about the likelihood of adult crime.

TABLE 8.12

Logistic Regression of Adult Offender Status on Race, Socioeconomic Status, Delinquency Frequency, Severity of Offenses 1–3, and Severity 4–7 vs. 1–3 for Females

	Coeff.	s.e.	Exp(B)
White	.5894	3.3896	1.8029
Black	1.1369	3.3839	3.1172
Hispanic	.7086	3.4309	2.0312
Socioeconomic status	−.2849	.3279	.7521
Delinquency frequency	.0359	.0535	1.0366
Average juvenile severity offenses 1–3	.1654*	.0757	1.1798
Severity 4–7 vs. 1–3			
Much lower	1.2160	.9394	3.3736
Lower	1.5992	1.2117	4.9491
Same	.2829	.5146	1.3269
Higher	1.0898	.6280	2.9736
Much higher	−.0735	.7452	.9291
Severity 1–3 by severity 4–7 vs. 1–3			
Much lower	−.1324	.1288	.8760
Lower	−.4498	.3240	.6378
Same	−.2242	.2525	.7991
Higher	−.2513	.1791	.7778
Much higher	.1363	.2902	1.1461
Constant	−2.9000	3.3934	

*$p < .05$

The Severity of Early Delinquency

In Table 8.14 we present the results of our analysis in which we attempted to uncover the pattern of severity scores across the first three offenses that is responsible for the "early severity" effect that we have observed above. For males, we found a particular pattern suggesting that if either the first or second offense were very serious or if the third offense represented an escalation over the second offense, the chances of adult crime increased significantly. For females, we were not able to uncover any such patterns. Thus, taken together, the average severity of a female's delinquency career is predictive of adult crime, but, this effect does not apply to the individual scores of the first three offenses.

TABLE 8.13
*Logistic Regression of Adult Offender Status on Race, Socioeconomic Status,
Delinquency Frequency, Severity of Offenses 1–3, Severity 4–7 vs. 1–3, Severity 8–14
vs. 1–3, Severity 15–53 vs. 1–3 for Females*

	Coeff.	s.e.	Exp(B)
White	.8609	5.5691	2.3652
Black	1.3624	5.5655	3.9056
Hispanic	.9824	5.5943	2.6709
Socioeconomic status	−.2900	.3347	.7482
Delinquency frequency	.0404	.1242	1.0412
Average juvenile severity offenses 1–3	.1653*	.0757	1.1798
Severity 4–7 vs. 1–3			
Much lower	1.2161	.9490	3.3740
Lower	1.5278	1.2661	4.6078
Same	.3235	.5631	1.3819
Higher	.9818	.6742	2.6692
Much higher	−.0626	.7634	.9393
Severity 8–14 vs. 1–3			
Lower	.8090	1.0371	2.2456
Same	−.1616	.9178	.8508
Higher	.3639	.7979	1.4390
Severity 15–53 vs. 1–3			
Lower	−6.2834	14.8360	.0019
Higher	−.2333	1.7688	.7919
Constant	−3.1483	5.5807	

*$p<.05$

Severity Summary

This chapter has attempted to address the issue of whether the offense seriousness exhibited across delinquency careers affects the probability of adult crime. We investigated whether particular patterns of offense severity, and in particular, changes in such offense severity, are associated with significantly greater odds of continuing a delinquency career into adulthood. We analyzed three principal aspects of offense severity: overall measures of seriousness across the whole career; the severity of offenses at particular stages in the delinquency career; and finally the decomposition of early seriousness.

TABLE 8.14

*Logistic Regression of Adult Offender Status on Race, Socioeconomic Status,
Delinquency Frequency, Severity of First, Second, and Third Offenses for Females*

	Coeff.	s.e.	Exp(B)
White	.6861	3.3888	1.9860
Black	1.2217	3.3835	3.3931
Hispanic	.6590	3.4306	1.9329
Socioeconomic status	−.3117	.3268	.7322
Delinquency frequency	.0581	.0432	1.0598
First offense severity	.0480	.0424	1.0491
Second offense severity	.0429	.0420	1.0438
First offense severity by second offense severity	.0015	.0076	1.0015
Third offense severity	.0622	.0361	1.0642
First offense severity by third offense severity	−.0008	.0085	.9992
Second offense severity by third offense severity	−.0036	.0039	.9964
Constant	−2.9147	3.3903	

Our findings show distinct gender differences in the relationship between delinquency severity and adult crime status. First, all the alternative measures of the overall severity scores in the delinquency careers of males produced significant factors in differentiating the transition to adult crime status. For females, however, there were no such effects.

Second, for males, we found particular career points in which offense severity patterns were significantly associated with adult crime. These patterns indicated that offense severity early in the career, specifically the first three offenses, and offense severity escalation in the next stage, offenses 4 through 7, were significantly related to adult crime. There were no significant severity patterns beyond these two stages. For females, significant results were obtained only for the early stage.

Third, for males we found that the individual severity scores of the first and second offense in the career and escalation by the third offense were predictive of adult crime status. For females, there were again no such effects.

The results concerning the severity score effects for males, especially the results surrounding the first three offenses, represent an important aspect of the delinquency career in which propitious intervention might have the greatest yield. That is, these "early" career effects dovetail with the findings presented in previous chapters and pose important implications for juvenile justice policy. Thus, we have found strong evidence that how a delinquent begins his delinquency career, and the severity pattern of the next few offenses, have definitive effects which significantly increase the likelihood of this type of delinquent exhibiting substantially higher odds of going on to adult crime.

9

Summary of Results

Our objective in this study has been to follow the entire population of the 1958 Philadelphia birth cohort as it moved from the legal status of juvenile to that of adult. We have been able to observe the transition from the acts that comprised the delinquency career to those that comprised the adult criminal careers through the age of 26. The principal focus of this investigation has centered on the issue of the continuity versus discontinuity between the delinquent career and the adult criminal career. Our investigation revealed that continuity was by far the most likely transition. Cohort members were most likely to continue as adults as they had behaved as juveniles. Because we found that delinquents showed the greatest likelihood of committing adult crime, we subsequently tried to uncover what it is about juvenile delinquency that might make delinquents more likely to continue their illegal conduct as adults and why other delinquents desisted from such conduct.

This predominant focus on delinquency and its connection to adult criminality necessarily calls for a research design and an associated data collection process that allows an investigation such as this to make valid inferences about career continuity. More important, it must be able to uncover the specific aspects of delinquency that are associated with higher risks of adult crime. Although cross-sectional research is not incapable of examining these important dynamics surrounding criminal careers, the longitudinal approach, especially the birth cohort method, is the most viable and productive way to study the multitude of issues that surround delinquent and adult careers in crime and the transition between the two. With cross-sectional research, even multiwave panel designs, there are internal and external validity problems that hinder the investigation of criminal careers.

When research uses samples drawn from disparate locales or across time periods representing vastly different social milieus, there is a danger that what is being uncovered about delinquency may be an artifact of the underlying contexts (either social or legal) and may not represent a meaningful basis for studying the continuity between delinquency and crime. Comparatively, the present research has used a birth cohort design, which holds constant many of the potential sources of error and misclassification.

First, the 1958 cohort consists of all those persons born in the target year who had demonstrated continuous residence in the city of Philadelphia at least from age 10 through age 17. The residence restriction, by eliminating migratory cases, not only ensures that each cohort member was exposed to the environment at the same time, but also guarantees that all cohort members will face the same period at risk of delinquency, a span of 8 years. This ensures that any prevalence or incidence differences across cohort members are not an artifact of a differential period of residence and a consequently shorter period within which to engage in delinquent conduct.

Second, although the social environments of cohort members may differ across the various areas of the city, the criminal justice environment was the same for all cohort members. The policies and procedures for law enforcement, especially in the handling of juvenile offenders, were the same for all 1958 cohort subjects. Likewise, official juvenile court policy followed the same statutory provisions for the disposition of all delinquents in the 1958 cohort. Naturally, this consistency in official policy does not preclude the possibility of differences in the informal handling of delinquents in the cohort, either by the police or by juvenile court authorities. However, the uniformity of the criminal justice process applied to the 1958 cohort at least ensures that differences in either the extent or character of delinquency are not an artifact of the system and, more probably, differences across cohort members are reflective of real differences in behavior.

Third, the criminal history data were comprehensive and represent the complete record of a cohort member's delinquency or adult criminality through the age of 26. These data were uncensored and represent the most complete accounting possible of a cohort member's involvement in illegal behavior.

From the records of the Juvenile Aid Division of the Philadelphia Police Department we obtained the delinquency data for the cohort. These data consisted of *all* the police contacts recorded for a juvenile, whether or not the offense resulted in official arrest processing. Thus, delinquency was measured in terms of police contacts for offenses, not just those offenses that resulted in arrests. From the records of the Philadelphia District Attorney, the Court of Common Pleas, and the Philadelphia Police Department, we compiled the records of adult arrests.

We supplemented these juvenile and adult rap sheets with the police investigation reports, which contain the essential details concerning the offense, and with the arrest reports. These details include information about physical injury, property theft or damage, use of weapons, and any other relevant information about the event, victim, or offender that we deemed important. From the records of the Juvenile Court Division of the Court of Common Pleas for Philadelphia we collected data pertaining to how the case was handled by the juvenile court system. This handling ranges from possible diversion by an intake worker to adjustment or adjudication (i.e., probation or commitment to a juvenile treatment facility) by a juvenile court judge.

The 1958 birth cohort has the following particulars. The cohort is composed of 13,160 male subjects, of which 6,216 (47.2%) are white, 6,561 (49.9%) are black, 355 (2.7%) are Hispanic, and 28 (.2%) are Asian or American Indian. Of these male cohort subjects, 6,414 (48.7%) are low socioeconomic status, while 6,746 (51.3%) are high socioeconomic status. The 1958 cohort also contains 14,000 females, of which 6,636 (47.4%) are white, 6,968 (49.8%) are black, 370 (2.6%) are Hispanic, and 25 (.2%) are Asian or American Indian. Among females, the socioeconomic status distribution shows that 6,948 (49.6%) are low socioeconomic status, and 7,052 (50.4%) are high socioeconomic status. These data indicate very even distributions by gender, race, and socioeconomic status overall, and by race and socioeconomic status within gender categories. This absence of skewness precludes the possibility that any of the results are reflective of deficiencies in the relative sizes of the demographic subsets across the 1958 cohort.

The 1958 cohort thus contains a large number of subjects for which juvenile and criminal history data have been available longitudinally from the onset of the delinquency career through the age of 26. This number of subjects and the completeness of the criminality measures are unparalleled and have enabled us to examine career contingencies that were unavailable to previous researchers.

This study was based upon the complete delinquency careers and the adult arrest records of crime through age 26 of a large birth cohort consisting of 27,160 persons. Because of the size of the population, the length and completeness of the criminal history data collected and analyzed, and the number of offenders and volume of behaviors uncovered, the findings achieve a degree of significance that cannot be overemphasized.

We have described our results and have included only the most necessary supporting tables which highlight the findings of this research. They concern a number of criminological topics that are of contemporary concern to the discipline and to the public policy sector that labors to design and implement measures to respond to crime and criminals. The most significant of our results, because of the regularity and consistency with which they were reported, should be viewed with close attention.

Basic Measures of Continuity and Discontinuity

The initial stage of our investigation was to obtain general descriptive information about the prevalence of adult criminality in the 1958 birth cohort and across the various demographic subgroups. Fortunately for public safety concerns and for policy-making issues, adult offending, at least as we observed it through the age of 26, was a rare occurrence. Most nondelinquents (over 90%) and about two-thirds of the delinquents had no adult arrest record. However, there was some variation by sex, race, and socioeconomic status. As fully expected, males were considerably more likely than females to commit both delinquency and adult crime. Socioeconomic status was inversely related to offending, as is usually the case. And, as is so often the case, the prevalence of adult crime was somewhat higher among black members of the cohort.

Because the prevalence of adult crime status differed most dramatically by gender, separate analyses of the transition from juvenile status to that of the adult stage of life were used to identify gender-specific effects in the likelihood of adult offending. The first notable pattern discovered was that career continuity was more common than discontinuity. That is, adult crime was considerably more likely among former delinquents, while law-abiding juveniles more often remained noncriminal as adults. This finding appeared regardless of race or socioeconomic status for the 1958 cohort overall, as well as separately among males and females.

Moreover, we found that, not only was the simple dichotomous attribute of delinquency predictive of adult criminality, but we observed that the number of juvenile offenses a delinquent accumulated during the delinquency career was even more predictive of juvenile-to-adult continuity, for both males and females. We also found that the higher the socioeconomic status, the lower the odds of adult criminality. For both males and females, the data indicated no race effect on adult offender status, thereby suggesting that the number of juvenile offenses and socioeconomic status effects were independent of the oft-noted race differences.

Although we looked in only a limited fashion at recidivism during the adult period of ages 18 through 26, the results clearly indicated that as the number of delinquencies increased, there was an attendant increase in repeat adult criminality. Once again, this relationship existed for males and females, regardless of race or socioeconomic status.

We also examined one important component of discontinuity, the offender who began his or her career only during the adult time frame. The delinquents who continued their criminality as adults were a much different group of offenders than those 1,526 members of the cohort who began criminal careers as adults only. The juveniles who continued offending as adults were less likely to commit only one adult offense and were more likely to be adult recidivists, particularly frequent adult recidivists, compared to those offenders who began illegal behavior only after the age of 17. Among males, this relationship remained regardless of either socioeconomic status or race. Among females, the results were in the same direction as for males, but achieved statistical significance only for black females and low socioeconomic status females.

These comparisons between delinquents who continued offending as adults and offenders who began as adults led us to conclude that the "virgin" adult offenders were not a disproportionately frequent or serious group of criminals. The results surrounding the virgin adult offenders bolstered our subsequent analyses, which were directed at understanding how adult offending might be linked with particular aspects of delinquency careers. Further, we were interested in how such careers might be differently handled to realize more effective crime control policies in the juvenile system. Of course, the virgin adult offenders were beyond the scope of this volume from the beginning. But, it was important to discover that such adult-only offenders were a qualitatively and quantitatively different phenomenon, which should be pursued elsewhere.

Our research, therefore, subsequently progressed with an exclusive focus on the delinquents in the 1958 cohort. This group represents a large group of young persons with varying kinds of delinquent conduct and with extensive differences in the frequency and severity of such conduct. Because these delinquents were known to the police and to juvenile court officials, and because these persons showed the highest propensity for adult crime, and frequent adult crime especially, it is their adult criminality that might have been prevented with the right juvenile justice interventions. It is these 1958 cohort delinquents that comprise the policy focus of this volume.

In order to discern continuity versus discontinuity between the delinquent career and the adult career, we examined a series of factors associated with delinquency that may increase the chances for some delinquents to continue offending as adults. The delinquency careers in the cohort were thus characterized according to age, timing of offenses, and the frequency of the juvenile offenses. The delinquency careers were also differentiated in terms of the ways in which police and juvenile court officials handled each delinquent offense, particularly the type and timing of court dispositions. Attention also was given to delinquents with experience in certain types of juvenile offenses, those whose offending was concentrated within one of nine crime types, and those whose delinquency escalated in seriousness. Gender-specific analyses and controls for race and socioeconomic status were included with each of these specific dimensions of the delinquency career to determine the unique contribution to prediction accuracy concerning adult offending.

Age, Timing, and Frequency of Juvenile Offenses

Our results with respect to these basic aspects of delinquency careers revealed some notable differences across delinquents. The findings indicated that starting a delinquency career early, continuing this career throughout adolescence, and being active just as the juvenile period ends (age 17) are important predictors of adult criminality. In addition, we found that being a so-called "late starter" did not necessarily insulate one against adult crime. Thus, those delinquents whose delinquency began late also were at high risk of adult criminality if there was a very short time remaining in which they could discontinue their delinquency career.

We also found that as delinquents committed more misdemeanors and felonies of any type, their chances of continuing these careers as adults also increased substantially. For males, both the age and timing of delinquency and the total number of offenses assisted in predicting adult crime. For females, however, only the frequency measures had significant effects on adult crime status.

Juvenile Justice Intervention

We next were interested in the context in which delinquents can continue with recidivism and somehow be allowed to accumulate more and more delinquent offenses. They thereby demonstrated a commitment to illegal conduct that was substantially more likely to continue into adulthood. Our focus then shifted to an analysis of the ways in which delinquents were handled, if and when their cases were brought to juvenile court, were adjudicated, and received official intervention. We examined first the range of interventions that each delinquent received and the number of such interventions across the delinquency career. Next, we investigated the timing of probation and out-of-home placement, in comparison to informal remedial police handling and unofficial adjustment by juvenile court officials to determine whether the imposition of select dispositions was differentially successful, depending on the stage of the delinquency career in which such dispositions were imposed.

We initially found for both males and females that, compared to the most lenient disposition, in which the police release the youth to the custody of his or her family without further action, every form of court intervention was associated with an *increased risk* of adult criminality. These overall delinquency career results suggested that the juvenile court was consistently and highly ineffective in handling offenders, whether male or female. However, we considered that the overall ineffectiveness of juvenile court sanctions might be inconclusive, owing to the fact that a mere accounting of the type and frequency of sanctions makes it nearly impossible to disentangle the effects of frequent juvenile offending from the type and frequency of sanctions applied. Simply, we hypothesized that high-frequency offenders can accumulate the more severe dispositions and can accumulate more of them, and regardless of these dispositions, high frequency delinquents have by far the greatest likelihood of adult crime.

To overcome this dilemma, we extended the analysis of sanctions to include the timing of court dispositions, or more specifically, the specific stage of the delinquency career during which probation or institutionalization was imposed. The results focusing on the timing of interventions showed a dramatic difference from the overall court disposition analyses. When the timing, by rank number of offense was considered, the probation disposition was not only shown to have a negative effect on adult crime status, but the imposition of probation very early in the male offender's delinquency career made a considerable difference for male delinquents. Among the lower-frequency delinquents, any type of disposition compared to late probation produced significantly less risk of adult crime. When probation was administered later and later, especially for high-rate delinquents, the probability of adult criminality escalated dramatically.

We did not find any consistent value in reducing the odds of adult crime concerning the use of out-of-home commitments to a juvenile treatment facility for males. The absence of any effects for the facility commitment disposition for males, compared to the situation of the demonstrated effectiveness of early probation dispositions, may have been because facility commitments were dispositions which were used very sparingly. Perhaps they were applied to the wrong delinquents. Regardless, these commitments generally were imposed much too late in the delinquency career among males to produce a measurable effect in reducing adult crime. Perhaps the imposition of these commitments late in the career indicates that such dispositions were imposed for punitive rather than rehabilitative purposes.

We did not find any significant effects for either probation or juvenile facility for females. Both types of dispositions were used sparingly among females, thus constraining analyses of their value in preventing adult crime. Further, the timing of official dispositions appears to have no significant effect on adult criminality. There are no significant effects for female delinquents concerning the timing of either probation or out-of-home placement, nor for the possible interaction between probation and the frequency of delinquency, nor between commitment and the severity of delinquency. Most females were handled informally by the police or adjusted at the initial court stage and never received any probation disposition.

It remains to be seen, of course, whether the increased use of facility commitments and an accompanying change in the timing of such dispositions may have a beneficial effect in diverting delinquents away from further delinquent conduct and ultimately preventing the transition to adult crime. The results presented here for an entire cohort do indicate, however, that a delayed imposition of facility commitments is ineffective for controlling habitual juvenile offenders. It does not deter them from adult criminality in any meaningful way. Most important, the results indicate that the infrequent use or the delayed use of probation vitiates what appears to have been a highly effective yet relatively benign sanction.

Type of Delinquency and Adult Status

We investigated the nature of the delinquent conduct that comprised the delinquency career by selecting nine offense types, which cover a representative range of illegal behavior: major violence, robbery, injury, major property, theft, weapon use, drugs, status offenses, and co-offending crimes. It was not our intent to develop a mutually exclusive and comprehensive scheme of offending classes, but rather to isolate specific features of delinquency which may be associated with offending and which have theoretical and policy relevance for understanding the transition to adult offender status.

We tested nine models, which were used to estimate the effects of the specific types of delinquency, race, socioeconomic status, and recidivism status on the likelihood that the delinquent would move on to adult offender status. For the male delinquents in the cohort, we found in every model, that for blacks, any level of delinquency beyond the status of one-time offender was also significant. More important, we found significant effects associated with four of the offense type measures. Three of these delinquency measures, major violence, robbery, and weapon possession, suggested that when the delinquency career involves any aspect of violence or the potential for violence, there were significantly increased odds of later adult crime. For the co-offender offense type, we found a specification effect. Being a co-offender was significant for chronic delinquents and increased their odds of adult crime.

The nine models testing the effects of various forms of delinquency, socioeconomic status, and race on adult offender status for females confirmed that females follow particular delinquency pathways as they move to adult crime status. This is important, owing to the lower overall prevalence of adult crime among females. Only 12% of the female delinquents were arrested as adults compared to 42% of the male delinquents. In light of this, we might also have expected lower rates of adult offending among females, regardless of the particular form of delinquent conduct they may have committed compared to the situation for males.

However, despite the very low prevalence of adult criminals among females, we have discovered delinquency correlates for females that are predictive of adult crime status. Among the nine models we used, only one offense type, major violence, carried the same results as those found for males. As a juvenile, police contact for any major violence offense increased the risk of becoming an adult offender for both female and male delinquents. Whether the female delinquent engaged in any robbery, injury, major property, weapon, status, or co-offending did not significantly affect her chances of committing a crime as an adult. However, unlike males, female delinquents who engaged in theft or drug offenses exhibited significantly enhanced odds of becoming an adult criminal.

Delinquency Concentration and Adult Status

In looking at the nature of delinquency and how it might differentially posture some delinquents for adult offending, we were able to determine that the commission of particular offense types did increase the likelihood of continuity between delinquency and crime for both males and females. These results were based on all delinquents in the cohort, without regard to the frequency of their contacts with police. In addition, offense type was measured as a dichotomous attribute, reflecting *any* involvement in a particular type offense. The offense-type analyses thus ignored the distinction among one-time delinquents, recidivists, and chronic delinquents, and grouped together all delinquents and treated them alike, regardless of possible differing involvement across offense types.

As a natural extension of the analyses on the topic of specific offense types, we examined the association between adult crime status and delinquency careers that had a particular concentration within one specific offense type. Our assumption underlying this line of inquiry was that juveniles who primarily engage in one form of offending, or at least commit the majority of their delinquencies within a particular type, might be more apt to develop expertise in, and thus commitment to, particular crime contexts. In turn, this expertise and commitment reinforces the repeat commission of the offense and, in effect, the offender specializes. A possible consequence of this specialization is that the delinquent's career is more likely to continue into adulthood.

In the offense concentration analyses we no longer used the entire pool of delinquents and we used instead a select subsample of the delinquents. The subsample consisted of those delinquents who had accumulated at least three delinquent events as juveniles. We made the selection of recidivists with at least three offenses from the conceptual standpoint that it is necessary for a delinquent to have a minimum number of offenses before specialization, or concentration, can legitimately occur. Clearly, a juvenile with only one delinquent act or even two delinquent acts cannot really be considered a specialist. Therefore, we restricted the cases for analysis to a subsample of the delinquent group in the cohort who had at least three offenses. This, we maintain, represents the minimum number of offenses necessary to analyze the phenomenon of specialization or concentration.

The findings concerning offense concentration and adult crime among males were mixed. Adult crime status was more likely among delinquents who seemingly concentrated their juvenile offending in offenses involving the possession or use of weapons. Elsewhere, adult crime was significantly distinguished by any drug offenses, status offenses, or co-offenders—whether concentrated or minimal involvement. The odds of adult offending also increased among delinquents with some, but not primarily, robbery and injury offenses. Rather than any theft, no recorded theft enhanced the likelihood of adult crime. Offense type was not a factor at all in only two models attempting to predict adult crime. Those models, however, are perhaps the most interesting because only they designate serious offending in the forms of violence and property offenses equivalent to index level felonies.

There were very few significant factors concerning offense concentration for females. We found for only four of the nine measures that offense concentration was significantly related to adult crime status. Female recidivists with some involvement in three offenses, major violence, major property, and theft, had significantly higher odds of adult crime than females with no involvement. However, high concentration, or specialization in our terms, was not related to adult crime. One offense type, the co-offending measure, was related to adult crime status for both levels.

The absence of significant findings concerning specialization for females was not entirely unexpected, especially considering the marked gender differences that have been observed throughout this study. It is worth noting these gender differences here as they frame the context of the significant results for females that we have observed. These results are important to anyone interested in studying the differing involvement of males and females in delinquency and crime.

First, it must be noted that the prevalence of delinquency was much lower among females. Only 14.6% of the females became delinquent, in comparison to 42.8% of the males. While 1,806 of the 4,315 male delinquents, or 41.9%, could be included within the subsample with at least three juvenile offenses, only 411 females, or 20.8% of the 1,972 female delinquents, could meet this criterion. Further, within the recidivist subsample, females had committed an average of 4.66 juvenile offenses compared to an average of 6.66 offenses for males. Thus, male delinquents were twice as likely as female delinquents—who were already less common—to be included within the analyses of offense concentration as well as more likely to have accumulated more offenses.

Important differences also exist between females and males when concentration of juvenile offending by type is compared. For example, 57.4% of the females in the subsample compared to only 11.8% of the males committed over half of their juvenile career in status offenses. Only 14.6% of the females had no status offense, compared to 38.1 of the males. Females also more often offended alone; 42.8% had no co-offenders compared to 9.5% of the males. Nearly half of the males (45.2%) committed the majority of their delinquency with someone, but the same was true of only 23.4% of the females. Aside from status offenses (and 30 females with considerable theft experience), almost no females concentrated their offending in any single crime category. Moreover, the majority of female recidivists also had not committed any major violence (82.7%), robbery (92.5%), injury (73.2%), drug offenses (91.7%), weapon offenses (83.2%), or serious property crime (74.9%). The male recidivists were more likely to have experience in each of the crime categories.

Finally, when our concern turns to adult offending status among this subsample of recidivists, the gender gap is very evident. Among this group of three-or-more-time delinquents, only 93 females, or 22.6%, continued their criminal careers as adults compared to 1,020 males, or 56.5%. These statistics serve to caution us that models used to estimate the effects of concentrated delinquency, number of offenses, socioeconomic status, and race are necessarily constrained by the small number of females available for analysis and the low levels of offending they exhibit. In fact, aside from status offending, co-offending and theft, the very few females who specialize in one type of delinquency virtually preclude analyses of specialization effects in those types, and allow comparisons based only on the category of some involvement.

Within this overall context, we note the following. The analyses of offense type and adult offender status involved all delinquents in the 1958 Philadelphia birth cohort. The results showed that, regardless of sex, adult crime occurred more often among delinquents with any involvement in a major violent or property crime, robbery, theft, injury, weapon, drug offense or when co-offenders were sometimes present. This also was true for status offending among male delinquents, but not for females. Moreover, the chances of adult offending escalated among delinquents who were lower socioeconomic status socioeconomic status in every model. Race never affected adult offending among females. However, black minority status increased the odds of adult crime, except in those models including serious violent and robbery offending.

When we focused on how delinquency specialization affected adult crime status, we viewed specialization as a concentration of offending within one type. Concentration was measured as 50% or more of all delinquencies within the specific offense type. The analyses were restricted to a subsample of delinquents with three or more juvenile offenses to permit their development of a concentration. Total number of juvenile offenses were controlled in each model to avoid results confounded by different levels of delinquency. These efforts helped enhance the construct validity of our tests, but even among the large cohort population we were unable to avoid some constraints due to low levels of female offending.

In addition to marked gender differences in the relationship between offense concentration and adult offending, the findings also varied from the analyses of any involvement based on type. Socioeconomic status, for example, was not a significant factor in any model of adult crime with specialization but was almost universally important with type. Race also made no difference in any models including concentration. Among male recidivists but not females, the odds of adult crime increased with higher numbers of juvenile offenses. Adult offending also was more often associated with male delinquents who concentrated their offending within categories of weapons, committed some robbery or injury offenses, any record of drug or status offenses, and among those who had acted in conjunction with co-offenders. Delinquency concentration was not an issue among females. For them, the chances of adult offending increased when their juvenile offenses sometimes involved major violence or property and any co-offenders. Among both males and females, recidivists with no theft or larceny, were more likely than those with such offenses to have an adult arrest.

Seriousness of Delinquency

The last stage in our analyses concerned whether delinquency careers that exhibit what may be termed offense severity escalation demonstrate a higher probability of adult crime. A progression in offense severity may posture the delinquent for a more likely transition to adult crime, compared with those delinquents who exhibit no such progression. The seriousness of juvenile offenses is a matter of concern in the investigation of subsequent criminal career development. The reasonable hypothesis is that individuals who engage in serious crime at an early age are more likely to continue offending, and the gravity of their ensuing behavior may escalate.

We investigated whether changes in severity were associated with the chances of adult crime. We concentrated on three aspects of severity: (1) overall career measures; (2) severity at particular stages in the delinquency career; and (3) the decomposition of early seriousness. As with the concentration analyses, in order to examine the escalation question, we again used the select subsample of delinquents who had accumulated at least three delinquent acts in their career.

Basic Measures of Offense Severity

In the preliminary analyses, using basic measures of offenses seriousness, we discovered significant effects for males. First, we observed that increasing average offense severity of a male's delinquent acts is associated with adult crime. Second, we also showed that delinquents who exhibited variation in the offense seriousness scores throughout their delinquency careers (whether such variation is measured by: [1] the difference between his peak score and his average score; [2] the difference between his peak score and his lowest score; or [3] the net percentage change across the increases and decreases across his entire career) had higher chances of committing adult crime. These findings established a need to investigate further the dynamics of offense seriousness in male delinquency careers.

The basic severity results indicated that alternate measures of the severity of delinquency across females' delinquency careers were, unlike the case for males, entirely unsuccessful in differentiating which delinquents will continue to commit illegal acts as adults.

The Timing of Changes in Offense Severity

These analyses concerning the timing of changes in offense severity indicated several important results about the dynamics of such changes and their connection to adult crime status. As the average severity of a delinquent's first three offenses increased, there was a significant increase in the probability of adult crime. Interestingly, the accumulation of additional offenses did not significantly increase the odds of adult crime, unless one of two conditions occurred. First, if the delinquent continued or surpassed his prior (offenses 1–3) high level of seriousness during his next set of offenses (4–7), then further recidivism increased the risk of adult crime. Second, however, even an offender with a lower seriousness for his starting offenses could increase his chances for adult crime if he escalated his severity level during his additional recidivism.

We decided to continue the investigation of the timing of severity changes throughout the career to find other timing points that might influence adult crime status. We added two additional sets of severity score differences, the 8th through the 14th offense, and the 15th offense and beyond, and calculated the difference between the average score for these sets and the average score for the first three offenses. The results concerning the impact of the severity of additional recidivism stages made an important contribution to our analysis of the probability of adult crime.

First, the significant coefficient for the frequency of delinquency, which had continually emerged as the strongest predictor of adult crime status, disappeared. Second, the average severity of the first three offenses remained significant. Third, however, the difference between the average score of the fourth through seventh offenses and the first three offenses had significant effects for those recidivists who escalated their severity during the fourth through seventh offenses. Last, there were no significant effects at any difference levels for subsequent recidivism (i.e., 8–14 or 15+) in predicting adult crime.

The analyses concerning the timing of severity score changes for females produced results that were both similar and dissimilar to those obtained for males. The results were similar in that the average severity of a female offender's early delinquency career (i.e., the first three offenses) was significantly associated with the likelihood that she will continue as an adult. As the severity of this set of early offenses increased, the chances of adult crime status also increased.

However, the results were dissimilar from those obtained for males. For females, examining the severity changes that occur between the first three offenses and the second set, offenses 4 through 7, did not reveal any additional significant effects in predicting adult crime. Furthermore, expanding the delinquency career to include four sets of offense stages (i.e., offenses 1 to 3, 4 through 7, 8 through 14, and 15 and above) did not produce any significant severity effects beyond the first three offenses. That is, the early delinquency career for females, and *only* the early career, was statistically useful in making predictions about the likelihood of her committing adult crime.

The Severity of Early Delinquency

The timing results, for both males and females, thus indicated that it was the severity of a delinquent's first few offenses, rather than the extent of his recidivism or the average severity of his recidivism, that was predictive of adult crime status. We then turned to an analysis of the severity across the first three offenses, to determine if discernible patterns could be uncovered.

Among males, we found that using the individual severity scores of the first three offenses indicated that offenders who begin their delinquency careers with serious offenses, or who escalate in severity between their first and second offenses, or between their second and third offenses, have significantly greater odds of becoming an adult criminal. Further, adding measures that capture either the extent of subsequent recidivism or the severity of such recidivism did not contribute any additional explanatory value to that gleaned from the first three offenses.

These early career results indicate the extremely important fact for males that the delinquent's first few offenses and their relative severity indicated significantly increased odds of adult criminality, regardless of what else occurred in the remainder of the delinquency career.

For females in the 1958 cohort, our analysis failed to indicate any "early severity" patterns. Thus, taken together, the average severity of a female's delinquency career is predictive of adult crime, but this effect does not apply to the individual scores of the first three offenses.

All the alternative measures of overall severity in the delinquency careers of males produced significant factors in differentiating the transition to adult crime status. For females, however, there were no such effects. For males, we found particular career points in which offense severity patterns were significantly associated with adult crime. These patterns indicated that the offense severity early in the career, specifically the first three offenses, and offense severity escalation in the next stage, offenses 4 through 7, were significantly related to adult crime. There were no significant severity patterns beyond these two stages. For females, significant results were obtained only for the early stage. For males we also found that the individual severity scores of the first and second offense in the career and escalation by the third offense were predictive of adult crime status. For females, there were again no such effects.

The results concerning the severity score effects for males, especially the results surrounding the first three offenses, represent an important aspect of the delinquency career in which propitious intervention might have the greatest yield. That is, these "early" career effects dovetail with the findings presented in previous chapters and pose important implications for juvenile justice policy. Thus, we have found strong evidence that how delinquents begin their delinquency careers and the severity pattern of the next few offenses have definitive effects that significantly increase the likelihood of some delinquents going on to adult crime.

In the final chapter we will discuss the implications of our principal findings. We will discuss how these results might be used to alter existing juvenile justice policies and practices in ways that should improve their effectiveness. By dealing with juvenile offenders more productively, officials may be able to prevent many delinquency careers from progressing into the realm of adult crime.

10

Implications for Theory and Policy

The criminal history data used in this study do not offer a wide array of theoretically relevant variables, so our research cannot be used to explain why some youths begin their offending careers in the first place. We readily accept the characterization and the implied criticism offered by Sampson and Laub that, although the 1958 cohort study "has provided key information on criminal offending and has served as a stimulus for research, explanatory characteristics were limited largely to structural and demographic variables (such as poverty and race)" (1993: 23). We are not apologetic about this aspect of the data; rather, we hope we have adopted a realistic position about their strengths and weaknesses.

We believe that, despite the absence of explanatory variables, our wealth of criminal history data offer many other advantages. Further, the next phase of our research on the Philadelphia Birth Cohort will involve the examination of self-reported data for a carefully framed sample of the cohort members. From these interviews, rich and diverse information was obtained. The follow-up study may help us to inform theories about delinquency and crime, as well as to examine the value of various intervention strategies.

The strength of the data reported here lies in their unique ability to identify patterns of offending over a lengthy time frame, including all the juvenile years and the young adult period, consistently found to represent the highest risk of crime (i.e., ages 18 through 26). Indeed, the current yield from these data generates great potential to improve the effectiveness of juvenile justice policy, while some modest benefits for developments in the area of theory may be derived as well.

Implications for Theory

As we seek to improve the general understanding of crime and delinquency, the first utility of the findings of this study pertains to the issue of criminal careers. We noted earlier that, for a variety of reasons, prior research has not offered convincing evidence of the need to distinguish a single offense from a sequence of offending. Because of this, the concept of criminal careers, as well as the time, resources, and sustained professional effort needed for longitudinal observation of offending careers, have been called into question. Our data have fortunately enabled us to overcome many difficulties associated with other studies, and among the results of our research are findings showing quite discernible career patterns. There also are interesting variations that justify further attention to these criminal careers and how they begin, continue, escalate or stop.

For example, our results show that late adolescence is clearly a time of great risk, but knowing the reasons for vulnerability at this particular age requires more research. First-time adult offenders are also an interesting phenomenon as they begin crime as adults after escaping their adolescence without any record of delinquency. Equally puzzling are those delinquents who later desist while their delinquent colleagues continue careers in crime unabated. Despite these gray areas, we have discovered that particular delinquent experiences, including the ways in which the authorities responded to the delinquents in the 1958 cohort, represent highly salient pathways that lead to the continuation of a delinquent career into adulthood.

We hope these findings help to direct scholarly attention away from questioning whether the criminal career concept is a viable enterprise for criminology. Our wish is that the field focus instead on understanding the phenomenon and developing better explanations for the various life trajectories that delinquents and criminals seem to follow.

While the findings of this study may serve as a point from which to generate initial discussion, they offer only limited directions for areas in which theoretical explanations for criminal careers should be pursued. First, regarding the prevailing theories of the classical school of thought, rational choice and routine activities theories, we cannot comment on the thought processes, calculations, or presence of suitable targets, etc., inherent in these explanations. Our findings do, however, provide information that shows crime-specific models may not be necessary. The patterns of delinquency and corresponding odds of adult crime we observed indicate that it is ill-advised for theories to pursue the offense based focus of the classical perspective; rather, it appears a much wiser strategy to target the offenders and especially their career trajectories.

This is not to imply that we eschew all of the tenets of the classical school of thought, because such a declaration is beyond the scope of our study. It would, in any event, not be our inclination. In truth, we encourage scientific tests of the classical theories. The findings of our research suggest that the most fruitful efforts will be those that avoid strictly classical postulates of equal culpability and uniform sanctions in favor of neoclassical ideas that these dimensions must vary. Indeed, if science could isolate the reasons for specific criminal career paths, that knowledge could refine neoclassical theories and, with popular support, likely achieve more effective crime control policy interventions.

In terms of the positive school of thought, we can say little about social structure and offending, except that our measure of socioeconomic status was seldom a significant factor in helping to predict adult crime. The measure of socioeconomic status we used was ecological and fixed at one time, so we have interpreted it cautiously. When socioeconomic status was important in our analyses, lower socioeconomic status was associated with increased odds of adult offending, but typically among females only. And independent of socioeconomic status, there was a race effect indicating an escalated chance of adult offending among black youths in some of the analyses. These findings suggest that both gender-specific and race-specific differences merit greater attention in future tests of social disorganization, anomie and value or culture conflict theories.

The relationship shown between having co-offenders during delinquency and committing adult crime indicates that there should be more attention paid to understanding the dynamic process associated with youths who commit their offenses in the company of other youth. It would be short-sighted to conclude, as others have, that results such as these necessarily support a hypothesis that delinquent peers teach others to offend. This would suggest support for differential association or social learning theories, but the present data do not enable us to discern who the co-offenders were or what roles in the delinquencies they may have played.

For example, some co-offenders may be peers who are equally culpable for the misdeeds, in which case subcultural values and interests should be examined. Other co-offending alternatives could involve adults or gang members who coerced youths to believe that delinquency was the preferable choice among options presented to them, which may suggest rational choices or a differential association perspective. Reiss has discussed these issues far more effectively:

It should be abundantly clear that research on group offending not only is
disproportionately concentrated on juveniles but that it has focused almost
exclusively on documenting how pervasive it is and speculating on its role in
the etiology of delinquency. The etiological question therefore remains
murky and the consequences of groups for criminal career development remain unexplored. (1986: 156)

While suffering from a paucity of explanatory factors surrounding
delinquency and crime, one of the strengths of this research is its ability
to examine male versus female offending within a very large database.
This all too often receives minimal attention in criminology. It has been
argued that gender is actually the most important variable in understanding delinquency, yet gender receives the least attention in theory
development (Krisberg, 1992: 13). Of course, it was neither our intent
nor within the capability of the data to test any particular theoretical
tenet related to female offending. However, the magnitude of the
Philadelphia Birth Cohort data has offered greater possibilities of detect-
ing female delinquency than ever before. We have thus been able to generate population-based estimates of the prevalence, incidence, seriousness of delinquent conduct, and, most importantly, examination of
gender differences in the continuity between delinquent and criminal
careers.

Yet, despite our increased capability to document female offending,
the scarcity of both delinquency and adult crime among females is still
noteworthy. We observed distinct gender differences in the basic prevalence measures, but many of the more elaborate models we tested were
constrained by skewness in the distribution of female offending, especially delinquent recidivism and later adult criminality. However, we
did find that some factors were significant in their ability to distinguish
likely adult crime among females, and given the rare event of female offending, these effects should be considered all the more important. Further, because some of these factors held similar predictive utility for
males, it may well be that, although offending among females is much
less common than among males, female offending may not be as different from that of males as many may have thought.

We found for example, that the frequency of delinquency was a significant predictor of adult crime for both males and females. More importantly, we also found that major violence offenses and the severity of
the early career in delinquency were both significant factors in predicting the transition to adult crime for male and female delinquents. We
also discovered some effects unique to female delinquents. We observed
that any involvement in theft offenses or offenses involving drugs were
predictive of adult status for females. Further, we found that particular
concentration levels of female involvement in major violence, major

property, and theft offenses were similarly predictive. Rather than the usual race differences, we found that low social status was particularly disadvantageous for females and was at times a significant predictor of the female transition to adult crime status.

These findings confirm the validity of many of the arguments raised by Chesney-Lind and Shelden (1992), and because of the importance of the issues they raised, it is worth noting the major arguments here. Chesney-Lind and Shelden have correctly noted that some research suggests there are more similarities than previously imagined between female and male delinquency—in essence, most delinquency is trivial and the differences between the deviance of boys and girls are not pronounced (1992:209). However, they also raise the highly significant point that when research focuses on very serious violent offenses, such research tends to exaggerate the gender differences in delinquency because males are more likely to commit these offenses (1992:209).

We fully agree with Chesney-Lind and Shelden in their observation that, although both the similarities and differences between males and females are interesting from a theoretical standpoint, research generally tends to make more of the dissimilarities, especially the gender difference in the commission of violent crime (1992: 210). Naturally, the consequence of the disproportionate attention paid to male delinquents is that there has been a more extensive theoretical and programmatic focus on the plight of disadvantaged boys and their problems. This clearly ignores the victimization of girls and its relationship to girls' crime. Further, this necessarily ignores the central role the juvenile justice system plays in the sexualization of girls' delinquency and the criminalization of girls' survival strategies (1992: 214).

Criminology must admit that it has not fully appreciated the full range of issues surrounding male and female involvement in delinquency and crime. The offending behavior of females cannot be dismissed as merely a less frequent or less serious analog to that of males. Such a dismissal has two noteworthy consequences.

First, it precludes the development of common explanations where they are appropriate, but more important, it prevents the conceptualization and investigation of gender-specific perspectives where they are warranted and necessary. Second, it precludes the investigation of the differential processing that females receive in the juvenile justice system and the effects of such processing on career parameters.

Thus, we wholeheartedly endorse Chesney-Lind and Shelden's word of caution:

> Girls, in short, experience a childhood and adolescence heavily colored by their gender. It is simply not possible to discuss their problems, their delinquency, and what they encounter in the juvenile justice system without con-

sidering gender in all its dimensions. Girls and boys do not inhabit the same worlds, they do not have the same choices. This is not to say that girls do not share some circumstances and qualities with boys (notably class and race), but even the manner in which these affect the daily lives of young people is heavily mediated by gender. (1992: 212)

Implications for Policy

As we consider how our findings might properly be used to inform the debate surrounding juvenile justice policy and possibly guide the development of more effective juvenile court responses to juvenile offending, we first turn to representative recommendations offered by other scholars and practitioners. As might be expected, there are many ideas about how the system should respond to criminals. We will restrict our policy discussion to the realm of juvenile justice for two reasons.

First, this research has focused on the extent to which salient aspects of delinquency careers are associated with differential risks of subsequent adult crime. It would thus be inappropriate to offer policy recommendations here concerning the criminal justice process. Second, at least in this study, we have seen that "virgin" adult offenders are less prevalent and pose far fewer public safety concerns than do those who continue into adulthood the pattern of illegal conduct begun in their youth. It follows, therefore, that more effective interventions for these youths would diminish the necessity of the extensive criminal justice sanctions now commonplace in our society.

In reviewing the policy suggestions offered elsewhere, it is worth noting that the ideas originate among experts who have independently reached their respective conclusions following a variety of different perspectives, experiences, and research agenda. The similarities in the recommendations for juvenile justice policy are all the more remarkable given the diversity of the sources.

Social Policy: Reform Society

One of the principal recurring themes throughout the literature is the desirability of reforming society to eliminate the underlying causes of delinquency. Of course this is a familiar refrain that suggests that the most effective crime-fighting strategy is one that addresses the underlying social conditions that predispose some people to commit crimes in the first place. The important point here is that such calls for social reform have been at the very center of the juvenile justice policy debate for much longer than we may wish to admit.

Krisberg and Austin (1970), through a quotation from William Healy, have effectively reminded us that concern about societal conditions dates to the early history of juvenile justice advocacy. Healy, many years ago, clearly recognized that,

> If the roots of crime lie far back in the foundations of our social order, it may be that only radical change can bring any large measure of cure. Less unjust social and economic conditions may be the only way out, and until a better social order exists, crime will probably continue to flourish and society continue to pay the price. (cited in Krisberg and Austin, 1970: 30)

Ira Schwartz, a policy expert who has devoted his professional life to the juvenile justice system, has echoed Healy's concerns by noting that, "it is sheer folly to think that we will be able to tackle the juvenile crime problem effectively without addressing some of the country's broader domestic issues" (1989: 177). Likewise, Bernard has observed: "Solutions to juvenile crime problems cannot be accomplished merely by introducing a new juvenile justice policy. Rather, it requires changing the larger social conditions that gave rise to the problem in the first place" (1992: 186).

Sampson and Laub have more recently written:

> It is time to base crime policy on more than formal social control by the criminal justice system. Thus, it is time to take a more complex and long-term perspective that recognizes the linkages among crime policies, employment, family cohesion, and the social organization of inner-city communities. (1993: 256)

Most recently, Jones and Krisberg have suggested that,

> Long-range reductions in youth violence depend upon changing those factors that propel troubled youth toward violent behavior. Programs that deal only with offenders—that is, after the fact—will have little or no impact on levels of violence in America (1994: 6).

We are in complete agreement with the above views. It is abundantly clear that the most crucial societal problem to be addressed in the future is the amelioration of those circumstances which lead to poverty and differential social and economic opportunity, and, in turn, to poor school achievement. These are quite strongly related to early involvement with the police and juvenile courts. Society must find and implement prevention and intervention strategies that will uncover and eliminate the social, psychological, physiological, and other, as yet to be determined, influences which produce these unacceptable social and moral faults in the development of our youth. To be effective, this posture must take the form of a national policy that is given the highest possible priority and which enjoys the allocation of substantial and sustained resources.

But, it is one thing to recognize the need for societal reforms and quite another to deliver workable solutions, especially when the debate occurs within a policy-making process that is highly political, if not so ideological that effective discourse is vitiated. We might recall that the field of social work originally emphasized social reform, but the overall focus shifted quickly to casework, probably because of the impossibility of success (Bernard, 1992: 93, 101–102). Sampson and Laub have also acknowledged that, "these more complex crime policies are not easily translated into specific program initiatives." Indeed, Sampson and Laub do not venture to offer any such recommendations (1993: 256).

It is also clear that the various disciplines concerned with the problem of crime have embraced the important obligation of developing theories and conducting research that will provide useful information for the dual objectives of crime prevention and effective crime control. However, these efforts need to be tempered with the knowledge that our work, however diligent, may not have the expected yield, especially with respect to social reform and crime prevention. What if we were to develop a sufficiently comprehensive theory that perfectly isolated the early childhood and family predictors of delinquent behavior, and what if subsequent empirical tests of this theory confirmed its validity? What could or should we do with such information?

It would seem that the question is premature, if not moot, as the ultimate theory is a long way off. Long-term efforts to educate and improve communities are desirable, noble, laudatory, and may even seem viable to many, but the immediate crime problems posed by juveniles during their young careers, and the increased likelihood that many of these delinquents will continue to commit crimes as adults, deserve our attention now. Certainly, we should address the problems of society and the criminogenic influences that breed delinquency and crime. But until such time as social reform is possible, we must turn our attention to the juvenile system and to the countless numbers of young people who are caught up in its well-intentioned, yet largely ineffective, apparatus.

Juvenile Justice Policy

Foundations

The one aspect of juvenile justice that perhaps engenders the least amount of controversy concerns the original intents and purposes of a court system exclusively dedicated to the misbehavior of minors. Bernard (1992), Platt (1969), and Rothman (1971) have provided us with excellent commentaries on the emergence of the "child saving movement" and the discovery of the reformatory as a preferred method of social control. There may be disagreement regarding whether the social reformers who created the juvenile court were well intentioned or were even correct in their judgments about what would be the best way to handle delinquents. But there seems to be little disagreement over what their creation looked like.

The characteristic feature of crime control in the United States is the existence of a two-track justice system that bases jurisdiction on the age of the offender. There is one court system specifically designed to handle youthful offenders and a different court system for adult criminals. There is some variation across the states concerning the statutory age limit for the jurisdiction of "juvenile" or "family" courts, but most states use 16 or 17 as the cutoff (although some states use 14 or 15). Despite the absence of a uniform age for the boundaries of juvenile and adult justice, there is considerable consistency concerning the philosophy, goals, procedures, and thus, the raison d'etre of juvenile justice.

Since its inception in 1899 in Cook County, Illinois, the juvenile court has been easily distinguishable from its adult court counterpart. Fundamentally, juvenile courts are guided by a *parens patriae* doctrine in which the court acts as a surrogate parent for the welfare of the child. This *parens patriae* doctrine has resulted in a particular form and substance for juvenile justice. In principle, juvenile courts are (1) informal and nonadversarial; (2) guided by a philosophy of limited intervention; (3) oriented toward community-based treatment rather than institutional custody; and (4) concerned with rehabilitation and prevention rather than retribution or deterrence. These principles are in sharp contrast to the adult criminal justice system. The adult court is more: (1) formal and adversarial; (2) intrusive; (3) focused on crime control; and (4) punishment and deterrence-oriented.

The basic rationale for such a vastly different court philosophy and procedures for juveniles was the belief that delinquency is dissimilar from adult crime, not only because the acts themselves are different, but also because the offenders are believed to be very different from adult criminals.

The typical delinquents are assumed to be young and immature. Their misbehavior is generally believed to be infrequent and nonserious. Most important, the "condition" of delinquency is assumed to be temporary, a condition that can be remediated through appropriate court actions. This "usual" or "typical" delinquent is seen as requiring a justice model different from that of his or her adult counterparts.

Getting Tougher

This image of the prototypical delinquent and the appropriateness of the "benign hand" of juvenile justice has been challenged by an accumulation of contrary evidence that prompted many jurisdictions to reevaluate juvenile justice philosophy and procedures (see Forst and Blomquist, 1992). There had been a growing recognition that many juvenile offenders do not fit the stereotype described above, and in fact, these offenders are really indistinguishable from adult criminals except that they are younger.

The empirical evidence, however, does not support the public perception that juvenile crime was reaching epidemic proportions and drastic changes were necessary. Laub (1983) has provided analyses of National Crime Survey data for the period between 1973 and 1980 (i.e., the period just before the "get-tough" development begins in earnest) showing that the rates of serious juvenile crimes were very stable. Similarly, Snyder and Sickmund (1995) have shown that from 1973 through 1988, the juvenile arrest rates for violent crimes remained relatively constant.

Despite the absence of empirical data to support changes in juvenile justice policy, Schwartz has commented on what he termed the "winds of change" that characterized juvenile justice policy developments beginning in the 1970s.

> While the federal agenda and the voices of reformers were calling for deinstitutionalization and the emptying of the training schools, an entirely different agenda was emerging in the states. Public outrage over the juvenile crime problem was generating tremendous pressure on the states and local politicians, juvenile court judges, prosecutors, and others to take corrective action. The result was an avalanche of "get tough" policies and practices that were implemented throughout the mid and late 1970s and early 1980s (1989: 7).

Ohlin (1983) has similarly noted that the shift in juvenile justice policy reflected a strong conservative reaction to the liberal policies that had been advocated by the President's Commission on Law Enforcement and Administration of Justice (1967). In Ohlin's view, the growing fear of crime and increasing demands for repressive action led to more punitive sentencing and to a rapid escalation of incarcerations and the length of sentence to be served (1983: 231). Ohlin further argued that the "just deserts" approach began spreading to the juvenile system as well. He wrote:

> In many states we see increasing incarceration even as delinquency rates decline. Juvenile reform legislation now calls for more mandatory sentencing and more determinate sentences for juveniles, lowering of the upper age of

juvenile jurisdiction, greater ease in obtaining waivers to adult court for juvenile prosecution, and greater access to juvenile records (1983: 231).

Zimring has specifically noted that these attempts to reform sentencing practices in juvenile courts were "efforts to lead sanctioning models away from the jurisprudence of treatment and towards concepts of making the punishment fit the crime" (1981: 884). Indicating that the "get-tough" approach has persisted, Feld recently observed that "the influence of just deserts principles for sentencing adults has spilled over into the routine sentencing of juveniles as well" and that "despite persisting rehabilitative rhetoric, treating juveniles closely resembles punishing adult criminals" (1993: 263).

The consequences of the "get tough" approach have been well documented. Krisberg and Austin have contended, "The increase [in the proportion of young people processed through the juvenile court and juvenile corrections systems between 1980 and 1990] was due to more formal punitive juvenile justice policies that produced more court referrals and expanded use of detention and juvenile incarceration" (1993: 171). Schwartz (1989) has shown that between 1977 and 1985 the rates of juvenile detention increased by more than 50% and the rates of juvenile incarceration in training schools increased by more than 16%.

Future Directions

We are all aware that the conservative get tough model for juvenile justice has not been successful. Krisberg (1987) has noted that the available evidence indicates that the get tough approaches, which ignore subsequent correctional interventions, are expensive and counterproductive. In fact, Krisberg has observed that, "the large congregate training schools cannot cure and may actually worsen the problems of youth violence (1987: 51).

Naturally, suggestions for a "better" juvenile justice system run the gamut from no official intervention, to community level prevention, to traditional *parens patriae* treatment measures, to abolishing juvenile courts, to "criminalize" juvenile courts, and finally to punish all offenders in criminal courts regardless of age. At one extreme, Schur (1973) has advocated prevention programs with a community focus, voluntary community-based treatment, and the abolition of correctional institutions. Others have raised the issue of status offenders and the deinstitutionalization movement and questioned the role of the juvenile court aimed at youths deemed to be "at risk" (see, for example, Spiro, 1984; Murray, 1990).

Krisberg and Austin have been working to offer a reasonable basis on which to commence the next set of reforms for the juvenile justice system. They offer the following general view:

> We believe a more promising direction for the future of U.S. juvenile justice is the rediscovery and updating of the juvenile court's historical vision. Reforms that emphasize the best interests of children must pursue the true individualization of treatments and the expansion of the range of dispositional options available to the court. Incarceration, because of its expense and its lack of positive results, should remain a last resort. Large training schools must be replaced with a continuum of placements and services. These dispositional options should include small, service-intensive, secure programs for the few violent youths and community-based options for other offenders. Correctional caseloads must be low enough to ensure that individual needs are discovered and met (1993: 176).

In a similar vein, Bernard (1992) recommends a model of juvenile justice in which the objective is to communicate to youths that their actions have consequences. In this view, multistage treatment extends from "counsel and release" at the police encounter to criminal court punishment. He argues that the sanctions should be broadly applied and the vast majority of delinquents should be involved in an extensive network of community-based services. He also sees a need for small, treatment-oriented, secure juvenile facilities as the last resort, but with the potential for better results when used only for serious offenders.

Further along the continuum is Feld (1993), who believes that juveniles deserve more lenient treatment than adults, yet endorses a single criminal court system. He contends that the due process safeguards of criminal court would better eliminate differential processing based on race, sex, geographic location, and access to counsel, and that a graduated age–culpability sentencing scheme would accomplish reasonably discounted youth sentences (Feld, 1993: 280–288). Hirschi and Gottfredson (1993) also advocate a single system, though they want it structured like the traditional juvenile court model, with age posing little or no mitigating factor.

There is a movement to extend the network of control by holding parents accountable for the misdeeds of their children (for a critique see Geis and Binder, 1991). Others argue that the focus of resources should be on detection and incapacitation of chronic offenders (Greenwood, 1982; Regnery, 1985). A few scholars continue the call for the increased use of incarceration for offenders (see, for example, DiIulio, 1995). Even though the available evidence does not confirm the value of incarceration for juveniles, this "get-tough" approach has achieved hegemony in political debates and substantial popularity in legislative bodies.

We recognize that the public is often frustrated with the volume of crime in general, and currently with juvenile crime in particular, and that most hard-line political pronouncements of "a war on crime" are attempts to assuage the fears of the electorate. Reluctantly, but realistically, most policy initiatives are myopic in their expectations for crime control. We agree that efforts constitute mostly "marching to and fro" and that true encounters with the "enemy" are all too rare (Jacob, 1984). We also agree that disillusionment with traditional objectives of rehabilitation and punishment is helping to create situations within both juvenile and criminal justice in which all other goals are circumvented in lieu of efficient offender management systems, an approach Feeley and Simon (1992) call "the new penology."

In our view, this new trend is misguided and, especially given the current political milieu, we challenge criminology to be more forthcoming with information to support effective policy ideas. Adopting the popular strategic metaphor, we contend that it is important to choose the "battles" wisely, based on criteria that indicate a likely "win." Thus, we offer below only recommendations for which there is support available among our findings and among other informed researchers on the effectiveness of particular juvenile justice interventions.

In considering these various models, we are not so bold as to believe our findings can support a recommendation for total reform of any justice system. In fact, we are generally skeptical that the available evidence justifies any particular overall configuration of the juvenile justice process for all categories of youths. However, neither are we content to just stand back and wring our hands in frustration, hoping that society will offer future generations adequate and more equitable resources with which to prevent juvenile misconduct, or alternatively, respond to such conduct propitiously, effectively, and humanely. Of course, like many of our colleagues, we hope for these eventualities. Meanwhile, we are confident that we have information from which police, juvenile court officers, judges, and juvenile treatment specialists can embark on a reasonable set of reforms.

Policy Recommendations

We believe that the highest priority for addressing the crime problem in society is to recognize that the juvenile justice system must be accorded a much more significant role in the overall justice system. In fact, we believe that implementing a meaningful strategy for addressing the problem of juvenile offenders that proceeds comprehensively and strategically is a much more preferable and effective crime policy than the prevailing system, which gives the greatest priority and resources to the adult justice system. Generally, our recommendations for the juvenile justice system comprise the following essential elements:

1. Impose a structure of consistent intervention that is propitious and effective.
2. Require intervention as early as possible, so as to yield the greatest possible effectiveness.
3. Replace inconsistent interventions with a set of progressive sanctions, which gradually intensify the severity of the court's response.
4. Rely heavily on community-based interventions and supervision programs, rather than punitive detention and incarceration techniques.
5. Hold delinquent youth accountable for their actions; and
6. Convey to delinquents the need to assume individual responsibility for their misconduct.

These recommendations are based directly on the findings revealed in this research, and in particular, they arise from the sequence of findings that emerged as we examined the various delinquency factors for their predictive utility concerning a delinquent's transition to adult crime. Because these recommendations are result-based rather than emerging from speculation, abstract philosophy, or untested theories, it is necessary to ground these recommendations in their empirical context. Our context comprises the complete delinquency history of 27,160 persons, of whom 6,287 were official delinquents.

Higher Priority for Juvenile Justice

We argue in favor of significantly increasing the priority of the juvenile justice system, together with an accompanying substantial increase in the resources allocated to the juvenile as opposed to the adult system. The basis for this general recommendation is twofold.

First, the simple fact is that this research has conclusively shown that most of adult criminals, particularly the more frequent and more serious adult offenders who represent the greatest threats to society, begin their criminal careers, not as adults, but as juvenile delinquents. We found that the "virgin" adult offenders were neither a disproportionately frequent nor serious group of criminals. Rather, we found that such "adult only" offenders were a qualitatively and quantitatively different phenomenon compared to their counterparts who continue a career in crime begun in their youth. Further, these findings surrounding the virgin adult offenders bolstered our subsequent analyses directed at differentiating and understanding how adult offending might be linked with particular aspects of delinquency careers.

Second, this research not only confirmed that delinquents pose the highest risk of making the transition to adult crime, but also, our analyses revealed specific aspects of the frequency, timing, court handling, and severity of juvenile careers that significantly differentiated which delinquents would be most likely to continue the career in crime.

Thus it is clear that the juvenile justice process is the preferred venue in which to address the developing criminal career. The greatest yield for crime control therefore concerns delinquents who first establish a commitment to illegal conduct while they are young, a time when the system can either respond appropriately and dissuade such conduct from becoming reinforced and sustained, or the system can respond ineffectively or too late and too harshly. This consequently places these youth at disproportionate risks of becoming career criminals. Whether from the perspective of protecting society or the reform of the individual offender, accentuating the juvenile justice system's response to delinquents is both desirable and achievable.

Juvenile Justice Recommendations

This research has also uncovered specific aspects of delinquent careers that were conclusively associated with a continuing criminal career. Juvenile justice must take these factors into account and develop a consistent response to delinquents so that future misconduct of these "high risk" delinquents might be averted.

Our first recommendation concerns *the need for the juvenile justice system to impose a structure of consistent intervention that is propitious and effective*. That is, we found in the criminal history of delinquents in the 1958 cohort that most dispositions were applied sporadically and unevenly. Some delinquents were given "remedial" dispositions by the police, thereby allowing offenders at a point early in their careers to escape court hearings. We believe that police-based diversion programs, because they are likely to occur too arbitrarily, may send delinquents the wrong message. The "wrong" message is established as follows: (1) the delinquent can expect lenient treatment from authorities; (2) thus delinquents may believe that they will not be held accountable for their misconduct; and (3) this precludes the possibility that the delinquents will develop a sense of responsibility for their misconduct.

We believe consistent intervention requires a reduction in the ad hoc diversionary programs that are used by well-intentioned law enforcement and other officials on a daily basis. We propose instead that *all* youths accused of a delinquent offense be referred to court, where a consistent, and thus, more effective intervention can be achieved. But we are also concerned about the most promising time for the juvenile court's response to the delinquent—even those delinquents who are at the birth of their careers. This brings us to our second recommendation.

Our second recommendation *requires court intervention as early as possible so as to yield the greatest possible effectiveness*. This policy is justified by our finding that the frequency of delinquent activity is the most consistent and strongest predictor of adult crime status. This familiar aspect of the nature of delinquent careers and its relationship to adult crime provides interesting implications for policy development. For example, in response to the debate between Regnery (1985) on one side, who calls chronic delinquents "profiles in carnage" and attributes most of the violent juvenile crime to these offenders, and Brodt and Smith (1987) on the other extreme, who contend to the contrary that chronic delinquency primarily involves minor infractions, we confirm the accuracy of both positions. As such, rather than focusing on type of offense, our concern is that juvenile justice interventions address the persistent nature of delinquency.

We believe that the primary objective of a strategically planned and effective policy should be to inhibit chronic recidivism by responding to the delinquent before chronic delinquency status can be achieved. Apparently, chronic delinquents have established such a commitment to illegal conduct that their potential for continued delinquent recidivism and later adult criminality are greatly enhanced. Thus, every effort should be attempted to prevent chronic recidivism.

If, however, this early intervention effort should fail, then subsequent efforts should attempt to deter further delinquency and thus prevent adult crime through our third recommendation: *replace inconsistent and ineffective interventions with a set of progressive sanctions which gradually intensify the severity of the court's response*. We are concerned about the tendency in juvenile justice to respond to initial delinquency with lenient dispositions. This pattern is often repeated, until the delinquent engages in further criminal acts one time too often or commits a sufficiently serious offense that the court *finally* intervenes and imposes a serious sanction. Our concern is that when a punitive response is imposed only because the delinquent has taken advantage of the court's lenience, then the court is essentially acting retributively in a way that the delinquent had not been led to expect.

With a system of progressive sanctions, there should be noticeable success at each stage. Delinquents can expect to receive a progressively more restrictive disposition each and every time they commit an offense. When such sanctions are not only promised but in fact delivered, some youths may amend their behavior. Regardless of the exact degree of success achieved through progressive sanctions, they are far preferable to waiting until it is too late to be an effective remediation or deterrent, and the juvenile court response is thereby reduced to mere punishment rather than prevention.

Our faith in early intervention, together with a set of progressive sanctions, stems from our findings surrounding early probation. This leads to our fourth recommendation: *rely heavily on community-based intervention and supervision programs, rather than punitive detention and incarceration techniques*.

Specifically, we found that early probation dispositions did prevent some three-time delinquents from reinforcing their deviant tendencies and thus being more likely to become chronic delinquents. By achieving this reduction in delinquent recidivism, the early imposition of probation was also able to act as a significant inhibitor to adult crime status. The success of early probation intervention clearly shows that at least some youths do respond positively to community-based sanctions, and that consequently some adult crime is prevented. The success of probation was in sharp contrast to the use of incarceration dispositions, which were found to be highly ineffective.

Our fifth recommendation: *hold delinquent youth accountable for their actions*, and the sixth: *convey to delinquents the need to assume individual responsibility for their misconduct* are interrelated and arise from several aspects of the findings. For example, we observed an important effect surrounding the timing of delinquency and the need for an appropriate court response. Youth who began their delinquency careers early generally had longer careers and were at greater risk of continuity in offending as adults. Thus, despite what some might term a *tender* age, the early starters must receive court attention so that their delinquent conduct is not allowed to continue. These early starters are in the greatest need of "early" intervention, which, if it is certain and sufficiently firm, may avert subsequent delinquency.

Similarly, regardless of an absence of early childhood offending, when teenagers approaching the age of majority are involved in delinquency of any type, we found that it is equally important that juvenile justice authorities respond, and respond with more direct and frequent contact than that provided by traditional adjustment or consent decrees. This is very different from the minimal notice required of teens who may formerly have been active delinquents but who have desisted for some time later in their juvenile years. We are concerned about the tendency for the juvenile justice system to ignore the "older" delinquents and defer their handling to the adult system, which will soon have jurisdiction over their conduct. Older delinquents, whether they started early or began late, had significantly high chances of continuing their crimes when they became adults.

Thus, we are urging that regardless of either a very young age on the one hand, or being older and very near the point of moving beyond the jurisdiction of the juvenile system on the other, a delinquent's age should not provide juvenile authorities with the impetus to ignore these offenders and concentrate instead on those delinquents who are in the middle of the juvenile period at risk (e.g., ages 14, 15, or 16). Early intervention is likely to facilitate the emergence of the accountability process for the young delinquents when it may do the most good, and it may be an eleventh-hour reminder to the older delinquents that their period of more severe accountability is very close at hand indeed.

Besides the important effects surrounding frequency of juvenile offenses and the timing factors in predicting adult crime, we also observed offense severity as a significant predictive factor. Continuity to adult crime became more probable when the initial delinquency was a serious index crime, when escalation occurred early on, or even when any offense during the juvenile career involved major violence. These findings indicate some potential to prevent adult crime, including some of a serious nature, through appropriately targeted juvenile justice interventions. The findings surrounding the early severity of delinquency confirm the necessity to intervene with delinquents very early in their delinquent careers, especially when their conduct exceeds certain severity levels or appears to escalate, thus suggesting genuine risk behavior.

Our analyses, including offense types and delinquency specialization, suggest that beyond distinguishing certain average severity levels, placing too much reliance on crime-specific policies would not produce similarly effective results. Specialization in weapon offenses by male recidivists helped to predict adult crime, but a single weapon offense by any delinquent contributed nearly the same information. The odds of adult crime increased for males with any major violence, robbery, or weapon-related offenses as juveniles; similarly so for females with any major violence, larceny–theft, or drug-related referrals.

These findings suggest that juvenile justice should always respond actively to serious juvenile crime, especially when it involves violence or potential violence. In general, waiting for offense specialization, in which delinquents concentrate their offending within one general category of violations, would not be a prudent strategy. Concentration did not substantially help to identify those at risk of adult crime.

Our findings concerning co-offender involvement in juvenile crime indicate that the group context is somehow important in the continuity of criminal careers. We know, for example, that criminal career continuity as adults is more common among all male delinquents and females with at least three juvenile offenses and who commit any delinquency in concert with others. Although the absence of more detailed information on this issue prevents us from knowing who the co-offenders are, and how or why their involvement provided support for the deviant lifestyle, the data do lend support to the argument that juvenile justice should continue its efforts to intervene and disengage delinquents from their colleagues. Group misbehavior must be discouraged because it poses severe risks that such misconduct will lead to adult crime.

Surprisingly, perhaps, there was also sufficient evidence among our data to indicate that status offenses should not be ignored. The prevalence of adult crime among former status offenders leads us to conclude that there should be some requirement of accountability for this variant of juvenile misbehavior. We support the movement for deinstitutionalization of status offenders; our findings suggest institutional treatment does not work for most juveniles anyway. But apparently, status offending is part of a deleterious complex of behaviors. The juvenile system must respond to these behaviors in order to provide accountability and to prevent status offenders from developing a more serious delinquent life-style that places them at serious risk of adult crime.

We also recognize that status offending constitutes a complex issue often entwined with other personal and family problems. We are especially mindful of the gender differences surrounding status offending. Thus, it may prove necessary to expand our recommendation for conveying the importance of taking responsibility for the actions of the youths to include parents and schools, providing that family preservation remains a prime ingredient of this objective. We agree with Spiro (1984) and others that juvenile courts are currently the appropriate venue for this intervention, although we also believe that these problems are not ideally addressed by courts. We hope society would generally become more concerned and develop other alternatives.

There are at least two aspects of our recommendations that require additional elaboration. There are some who may argue that the system that we have been describing is too lenient, because it does not seem to include a sufficient dose of punishment. It generally eschews the use of incarceration for juveniles. Still others may object to what could be called a net-widening effect, albeit our recommendations carry only benign intentions. We are mindful of these concerns. Yet, we maintain that because our recommendations are based upon our findings, and because we are drawing upon a growing body of literature that is convincingly resisting the "get tough" crime control trend so popular in political bodies across the country, our vision for how the juvenile justice system can and must respond more effectively to juveniles is worthy of serious consideration.

In order for juvenile justice to fulfill these goals of accountability and personal responsibility, it is crucial that the responses to juvenile crime reflect a coordinated policy among police, courts, and corrections, a system in which information about initial decisions is communicated to those who might subsequently encounter the youths. This would enable an escalation in the intensity of the response when recidivism occurs. Regardless of the intensity of the sanction, a treatment objective should prevail. Juvenile justice interventions must be perceived by offenders as significant, and they need to be enacted early in delinquency careers when they can be of the greatest effect, not delayed until after the deviant life-style is reinforced.

We envision a system of interventions which escalates in the frequency, duration, and intensity of the youth contact with a supervisor or treatment workers. At the front end, police encounters should be professional, firm, and typically should lead to court referral. At the next stage there should be a range of informal court adjustments, each of which should be structured to include direct supervision of the youth. Traditional adjustment fails to provide supervision in any systematic way and too often represents a grab-bag of informal court responses that fail to hold youths accountable and promote responsibility. We did observe some merit associated with adjustment, however, and anticipate even greater benefits could ensue from a more explicit adjustment policy, which includes routine youth contact. We also believe adjustment should draw upon many of the aspects of formal court supervision because of its obvious value.

We are convinced that the primary mechanism by which juvenile courts should respond to delinquents is through community-based supervision, and our suggestion for progressive sanctions does nothing to detract from the primacy that we are according to community supervision. Our reliance on this particular form of intervention is grounded in several ways.

First, the potential value of probation was evidenced in the initial volume of the 1958 birth cohort series (Tracy, Wolfgang, and Figlio, 1990), which compared the males in the 1945 and 1958 cohorts. In attempting to explain the higher delinquency and recidivism rates, higher offense severity scores, and higher violent index rates that characterized the juvenile careers in the 1958 cohort, the authors found that very few of the delinquents had received a court disposition even as severe as probation for their first four acts of delinquency. Specifically, they noted that:

> Juvenile courts should more often consider the adoption of close probation supervision for perhaps first-time and certainly for second-time index offenders. When these offenses, although serious, occur early in the life of delinquents (as they do for chronic offenders), there is a temptation to be lenient and give the delinquent the benefit of the doubt. What is hoped for is that some process of spontaneous remission will occur, whereby the delinquent will desist from subsequent offenses on his own without the possible damaging effects of labeling that may be brought about by adjudication. Yet, we know that the chronic offender is detached from the schools and other community-based socialization and control agents. Failure to impose sanctions at all, or failure to impose necessary controls early on, can encourage further delinquency. This is apparently what happened in Cohort II. Initial index offenses were not singled out for severe dispositions early enough to have a deterrent effect. (Tracy et al., 1990: 295).

Second, it appears that this observation about probation was correct. Calling for its increased use was certainly justified then and is even more so now, because probation supervision has been shown to reduce the odds of adult crime in this research and confirms previous findings from a Puerto Rico cohort (Nevares, Wolfgang, and Tracy, 1990). This evidence moves us to assert that most juvenile offenders should receive this type of disposition, and they should receive it early. There is compelling evidence that even serious chronic juvenile offenders can be effectively treated without posing additional risk to public safety.

Third, the idea that probation supervision is workable even for chronic offenders comes from the valuable insight offered by Armstrong (1991) in his collection of important work on intensive interventions for high-risk youth. Armstrong noted that:

> [T]here has been considerable experimentation with programs and supervision strategies designed to maintain a subset of the serious juvenile offender population—defined in various ways in different jurisdictions—in the community either as an alternative to incarceration or after early release from secure correctional facilities. (1991: 2)

Concerning why community-based sanctions might hold potential for the chronic offender, Armstrong pointed out that the juvenile variants of community-based sanctions maintain a continuing adherence to treatment-rehabilitation as a fundamental part of intensive supervision (191: 4).

Fourth, our recommendation concerning an increased use of community-based sanctions would result in a larger and more diverse juvenile population to be served in the community. In the absence of a coherent strategy for treating these youths in the community, there could be genuine concern that such youths would pose a distinct danger to public safety. However, there have been impressive advances in the handling of juveniles in community-based supervision since members of the 1958 Philadelphia birth cohort received their court interventions (Greenwood, 1986). The Office of Juvenile Justice and Delinquency Prevention has sponsored numerous efforts to develop a comprehensive strategy for serious, violent, and chronic juvenile offenders (Wilson and Howell, 1993). These efforts are now producing impressive results.

The National Council on Crime and Delinquency has been at the forefront of the effort to evaluate the feasibility of community-based sanctions and develop new initiatives that would expand the range of services available to delinquents in the community. For example, Krisberg, Austin, and Steele (1989) have shown that Massachusetts has been able to close its training schools and replace them with secure and nonsecure community-based residential and nonresidential programs. Krisberg, Rodriguez, Bakke, Neuenfeldt, and Steele have further demonstrated the premise that the needs and problems of high-risk probationers could best be met in a noninstitutional setting if sufficient levels of control could be exercised over the behavior of these youths in the community (1989: 15). Most recently, Krisberg, Neuenfeldt, Wiebush, and Rodriguez (1994) have outlined an Intensive Supervision Program (ISP) which maintains that high-risk youth can be safely and effectively managed in the community after their behavior has been stabilized.

There are now effective community-based alternatives to incarceration that vary in the content of the programs and in the levels of supervision. The ISPs, for example, are community-based programs which use high levels of contact between the probation officer or caseworker and the delinquent. They incorporate strict conditions of compliance, so that both treatment/services and surveillance/control can be successfully integrated for the benefit of the community and the delinquent. Thus, there are now a range of strategies available to the juvenile justice system, which suggests that community-based sanctions, and especially Intensive Supervision Programs, are an integral part of a progressive sanction model that uses incarceration only as a last resort.

We are optimistic, but our prognosis is tempered by the reality that not all battles will be won. We recognize that at the back end of our treatment scheme, some juvenile offenders will need to be confined in juvenile facilities and still others, perhaps, will have to be handled by the criminal justice system. It is our belief that the number of such youths would be smaller than current practice, should our recommendations be implemented. Further, there is encouraging evidence to show that even those serious delinquents who require confinement can be effectively managed through intensive treatment in small, secure facilities (Fagan, Rudman, and Harstone, 1984a, 1984b; Greenwood, 1986).

We are encouraged that our suggestions are viable, but we are aware of the obstacles. For example, Schwartz and Van Vleet have shown:

> It is difficult to combat political arguments that detention centers and training schools are essential in the fight against juvenile crime for keeping dangerous and violent young offenders off the streets or that reducing the number of juveniles incarcerated by deinstitutionalization will jeopardize the community (1992: 160).

There is a significant need to marshall public support for community-based sanctioning programs so that a more effective response to juvenile crime can be realistically pursued. Fortunately, Schwartz has further informed us that "the public does not appear to be nearly as punitive and demanding of retribution toward juvenile offenders as many politicians, and in some instances, juvenile justice officials have made them out to be" (1992: 222). He cites results from a recent national survey on public attitudes toward juvenile crime, conducted by Alcser, Connor, and Heeringa (1991), in which the majority of respondents endorsed the treatment mission of juvenile justice, favored a system that largely relied on community-based services rather than institutions, and, most importantly, wanted their crime-fighting tax dollars targeted toward these kinds of programs. Specifically, Schwartz notes that:

> [B]y a wide margin, the public would embrace a youth correction system that restricted the use of training schools and incarceration to juveniles who are serious violent and chronic offenders. Only about half of the respondents to this survey believe that training schools have a deterrent effect or are effective in preventing juveniles from committing crimes in the future (1992: 223).

In addition, Schwartz reports that respondents would support a community-based system, as the public wants their juvenile crime-fighting dollars allocated to programs in which young offenders can repay victims and communities, receive job training and employment opportunities, have access to community-based educational programs, and receive counseling services and intensive community-based supervision (1992: 223–224)

Our recommendations are entirely consistent with others, but we readily acknowledge that our ideas perhaps parallel most closely those made previously by Bernard (1992). In addition to our mutual advocacy for a range of services with community-based supervision being the predominant mode, we share Bernard's interest in seeing a broad reach of juvenile justice. We specifically call for early intervention as a proactive stance for specific deterrence of later offending.

We also must applaud and endorse the efforts of the National Council on Crime and Delinquency (NCDD) to foster the use of community sanctioning models. These models, especially the Intensive Supervision Program, appear to have great potential for effectively responding to the problem of youth crime. While we were first guided in the direction of community-based sanctioning models by our findings, the work of NCCD has bolstered our confidence that the old style of probation supervision has been replaced with well-conceived new strategies for supervising the offender, even the chronic or serious offender, in the community. Effectiveness and public safety concerns are being blended cooperatively and harmoniously.

Given the evidence in support of the principle of criminal justice thermodynamics, this approach of widespread interventions of a more comprehensive and strategic, and thus, more effective nature, it is reasonable to suggest that many delinquents will never become chronic offenders, and consequently, many adult crimes will be prevented. Most important, criminal justice sanctions can routinely address a smaller population of adult criminals, thereby improving the chances of success.

We close this volume with a sobering caution. The forecasts for the next so-called wave of juvenile violence may not be just another set of erroneous predictions that never come to pass. This time, these forecasts offered by informed observers, which increasingly appear in the electronic and print media, may be prophetic. We draw upon the recent comments of DiIulio (1995) and Snyder and Sickmund (1995), who have provided chilling forecasts of the juvenile crime problem, especially juvenile violence, that awaits us in the not-so-distant future.

DiIulio (1995) has recently commented on the apparent effectiveness of select law enforcement, prosecutorial, and correctional programs to reduce overall crime rates in specific locations across the country. But, DiIulio (1995: 15) notes that "Americans are sitting on a demographic crime bomb" because current projections indicate that by the year 2000, we will have an additional 500,000 persons in the crime-prone age group of 14–17. "The consequence of this," according to DiIulio, is that "in five years we will have 30,000 more young murderers, rapists, and muggers on the streets than we do now" (1995: 15). DiIulio's prognosis is discouraging:

> This crime bomb probably cannot be defused. The larger population of seven to 10-year old boys, now growing up fatherless, Godless, and jobless—surrounded by deviant, delinquent, and criminal adults—will give rise to a new and more vicious group of predatory street criminals than the nation has ever known. We must therefore be prepared to contain the explosion's force and limit its damage. (1995: 15)

Snyder and Sickmund (1995), in a thorough and comprehensive analysis, made all the more impressive because it reviews both FBI arrest data and National Crime Survey data, have shown that, between 1988 and 1992, juvenile violence increased sharply after more than a decade of relative stability. But, Snyder and Sickmund have made projections using a "constant rate" assumption in which violent crimes by juveniles between 1992 and 2010 would increase by 22% and an "increasing rate" model in which the rates of juvenile violence would increase as they have prior to 1992. Under this increasing rate assumption, the number of juvenile violent crime arrests would double by the year 2010, with an increase of 145% for murder (1995: 7).

Whether one accepts the projections of DiIulio or the empirical estimates generated by Snyder and Sickmund, the future of juvenile crime appears to be a "growth industry." It is also clear from the present results that the majority of adult offenders are products of juvenile police recognition and juvenile court processing. Thus, juvenile delinquency causation must be thoroughly investigated, both theoretically and empirically, and appropriate measures taken. Large resource allocations will be necessary for research and implementation. We need to know more about the causal processes that induce delinquency.

But, because most eventual adult criminals can be first addressed while they are still juveniles, the arena of juvenile justice must be accorded primacy in the battle against crime. We cannot ignore that our past response to that small cadre of serious juvenile offenders has not been effective. They have continued their delinquency careers and most have made the transition to adult crime without missing a step. We must heed the research literature and the accumulating evidence that provides an optimistic response to the famous question, what works? Fortunately, some efforts do work and these community-based initiatives must be expanded to encompass a broader range of offenders and must be implemented early in a delinquent's career.

In addition to the problem of delinquents becoming criminals is the problem of the virgin adult arrestee. These persons were never recorded as being delinquent, either because they never committed delinquent acts, or because they did and never got caught. Regardless, virgin adult offenders would seem to have their own set of causal processes, and we need to develop appropriate responses to these offenders. The problem becomes even more paramount when one realizes that these "new" offenders will come under the aegis of an already overcrowded criminal justice process, and this population of "new" offenders could be quite large in the years ahead, as the teenagers currently under 17 make the transition to adult life.

The juvenile career parameters developed in this research clearly highlight the magnitude of the problem of juvenile delinquency, its strong relation to adult crime, and to the understudied entity—the first-time adult criminal. When one augments our findings with the future forecasts, the magnitude of the problem clearly becomes one of significant proportions, and policy-makers must take urgent notice.

References

Akerstrom, M. (1985). *Crooks and squares: Lifestyles of thieves and addicts in comparison to conventional people.* New Brunswick, NJ: Transaction Books.

Alcser, K.H., Connor, J.H., & Heeringa, S.G. (1991). *National study of attitudes toward juvenile crime: Final report.* Ann Arbor, MI: Survey Research Center, Institute for Social Research, University of Michigan.

American Bar Association (1977). *Report on juvenile justice standards.* Cambridge, MA: Ballinger.

Anderson, N. (1923). *The hobo: The sociology of the homeless man.* Chicago: University of Chicago Press.

Armstrong, T.L. (Ed.) (1991). *Intensive interventions with high-risk youths: Promising approaches in juvenile probation and parole.* Monsey, NY: Criminal Justice Press.

Barnett, A., Blumstein, A., & Farrington, D. P. (1987). Probabilistic models of youthful criminal careers. *Criminology, 25,* 83–107.

Becker, G. (1968). Crime and punishment: An economic approach. *Journal of Political Economy, 76,* 169–217.

Becker, H. (1957). *Race and career problems of the Chicago public school teacher.* New York: Arno Press (1980 edition).

Becker, H. (1963). *Outsiders.* New York: Free Press.

Becker, H., Geer, B., Hughes, E. & Strauss, A.L. (1961). *Boys in white.* Chicago: University of Chicago Press.

Bernard, T. (1992). *The cycle of juvenile justice.* New York: Oxford University Press.

Bernard, T.J., & Ritti, R.R. (1990). The Philadelphia birth cohort and selective incapacitation. *Journal of Research in Crime and Delinquency, 28,* 33–54.

Black, D., & Reiss, Jr.; A.J. (1970). Police control of juveniles. *American Sociological Review, 35,* 63–77.

Blumstein, A. (1983). Crime control: The search for the predators. In K.R. Feinberg (Ed.), *Violent crime in America.* Washington, DC: National Policy Exchange.

Blumstein, A., & Cohen, J. (1979). Estimation of individual crime rates from arrest records. *Journal of Criminal Law and Criminology, 70,* 561–585.

Blumstein, A., Cohen, J., & Farrington, D.P. (1988a). Criminal career research: Its value for criminology. *Criminology, 26,* 1–35.

Blumstein, A., Cohen, J., & Farrington, D. P. (1988b). Longitudinal and criminal career research: Further clarifications. *Criminology, 26,* 57–74.

Blumstein, A., & Greene, M.A. (1979). Analysis of crime-type switching in recidivism. Pittsburgh, PA: Carnegie-Mellon University.

Blumstein, A., Cohen, J. & Hsieh, P. (1982). *The duration of adult criminal careers.* Washington, DC: US Department of Justice.

Blumstein, A., Cohen, J., & Nagin, D. (Eds.) (1978). *Deterrence and incapacitation: Estimating the effects of criminal sanctions on crime rates.* Washington, DC: National Academy Press.

Blumstein, A. & Moitra, S. (1980). The identification of "career criminals" from "chronic offenders" in a cohort. *Law & Policy Quarterly, 2,* 321–334.

Blumstein, A., Cohen, J., Roth, J. A., & Visher, C. A. (Eds.) (1986). *Criminal careers and career criminals,* vols. 1 & 2. Washington, DC: National Academy Press.

Boland, B., & Wilson, J. Q. (1978). Age, crime, and punishment. *The Public Interest, 51,* 22–34.

Braithwaite, J. (1989). *Crime, shame and reintegration.* Cambridge, UK: Cambridge University Press.

Brodt, S.J., & Smith, J.S. (1987). Public policy and the serious juvenile offender. *Criminal Justice Policy Review, 2,* 20–31

Brown, M. (1981). *Working the street: Police discretion and the dilemmas of reform.* New York: Russell Sage.

Buikhuisen, W., & Jongman, R.W. (1970). A legalistic classification of juvenile delinquents. *British Journal of Criminology, 10,* 109–123.

Bursik, R.J. (1980). The dynamics of specialization in juvenile offenses. *Social Forces, 58,* 851–864.

Bursik, R.J. (1989). Erickson could never have imagined: Recent extensions of birth cohort studies. *Journal of Quantitative Criminology, 5,* 389–396.

Cameron, M.O. (1964). *The booster and the snitch.* New York: Free Press.

Campbell, D.T., & Stanley, J.C. (1966). *Experimental and quasi-experimental designs for research.* Chicago: Rand-McNally.

Chaiken, J., & Rolph, J. (1978). *Selective incapacitation strategies based on estimated crime rates.* Santa Monica, CA: Rand Corporation.

Chaiken, J. & Chaiken, M. (1982a). *Varieties of criminal behavior.* Santa Monica, CA: Rand Corporation.

Chaiken, J., & Chaiken, M., with Peterson, J. (1982b). *Varieties of criminal behavior: summary and policy implications.* Santa Monica, CA: Rand Corporation.

Chaitin, M., & Dunham, H. (1966). The juvenile court in its relationship to adult criminality: A replicated study. *Social Forces, 45,* 114–119.

Chambliss, W.J., & Seidman, R.B. (1971). *Law, order, and power.* Reading, MA: Addison-Wesley.

Chesney-Lind, M., & Shelden, R.G. (1992). *Girls delinquency and juvenile justice.* Pacific Grove, CA: Brooks/Cole.

Christensen, K.O., Elers-Nielsen, M., LeMaire, L., & Sturup, G. (1965). Recidivism among sexual offenders. In K.O. Christensen (Ed.), *Scandinavian studies in criminology,* Vol. 1. London: Tavistock.

Cicourel, A.V. (1968). *The social organization of juvenile justice.* New York: Wiley.

Clarke, R. (1980). Situational crime prevention: Theory and practice. *British Journal of Criminology, 20,* 136–147.

Clarke, R., & Cornish, D. (1985). Modeling offenders' decisions: A framework for research and policy. In M. Tonry & N. Morris (Eds.), *Crime and justice,* Vol. 6. Chicago: University of Chicago Press.

Clarke, R., & Cornish, D. (1987). Understanding crime displacement: An application of rational choice theory. *Criminology, 25,* 933–947.

Clarke, R., & Mayhew, P. (1980). *Designing out crime.* London: H.M.S.O.

Clarke, S.H. (1975). Some implications for North Carolina of recent research on juvenile delinquency. *Journal of Research on Crime and Delinquency, 12,* 51–60.

Clinard, M., & Quinney, R. (1967). *Criminal behavior systems: A typology*. New York: Holt, Rinehart & Winston.

Cline, H. (1980). Criminal Behavior over the Life Span. In O. Brim & J. Hagan (Eds.), *Constancy and change in human development*. Cambridge, MA: Harvard University Press.

Cloward, R. A., & Ohlin, L. (1960). *Delinquency and opportunity*. New York: Free Press.

Cohen, A. (1955). *Delinquent boys: The culture of the gang*. New York: Free Press.

Cohen J. (1986). Research on criminal careers: Individual frequency rates and offense seriousness. In A. Blumstein, J. Cohen, J.A. Roth, & C. A. Visher (Eds.), *Criminal careers and career criminals*, Vol. 1. Washington, DC: National Academy Press.

Cohen, L., & Felson, M. (1979). Social change and crime rate trends: A routine activities approach. *American Sociological Review, 44*, 588–608.

Collins, J.J (1977a). *Offender careers and restraint: Probabilities and policy implications*. Washington, DC: US Department of Justice.

Collins, J.J. (1977b). *Deterrence by restraint: Two models to estimate its effect in a cohort of offenders*. (Doctoral dissertation), University of Pennsylvania.

Conklin, J. (1972). *Robbery and the criminal justice system*. Philadelphia: Lippincott.

Criminal Law Reporter, 12 August 1992.

Cullen, F., & Link, B. (1980). Crime as an occupation. *Criminology, 18*, 399–410.

Davis, K.C. (1975). *Police discretion*. St. Paul, MN: West.

DiIulio, J.J. (1995). Why violent crime rates have dropped. *The Wall Street Journal*, September 6, A.17.

DiIulio, J.J. (1995). Arresting ideas: Tougher law enforcement is driving down crime. *Policy Review, 74*, 12–16.

Dinitz, S., & Conrad, J. (1984). Who is in that dark alley? In S. Mednick, M. Harway, & K. Finello (Eds.), *Handbook of longitudinal research: Teenage and adult cohorts*. New York: Praeger.

Dunham, H., & Knauer, M. (1954). The juvenile court in its relationship to adult criminality. *Social Forces, 32*, 290–296.

Ehrlich, I. (1973). Participation in illegitimate activities: An economic approach. *Journal of Political Economy, 81*, 521–567.

Elliott, D.S., & Ageton, S.S. (1980). Reconciling race and class differences in self-reported and official estimates of delinquency. *American Sociological Review, 45*, 95–110.

Elliott, D.S., Ageton, S., & Canter, R. (1979). An integrated theoretical perspective on delinquent behavior. *Journal of Research in Crime and Delinquency, 16*, 3–27.

Elliott, D.S., Huizinga, D., & Ageton, S. (1985). *Explaining delinquency and drug use*. Beverly Hills, CA: Sage.

Emerson, R. (1969). *Judging delinquents: Context and process in juvenile court*. Chicago: Aldine.

Empey, L., & Rabow, J. (1961). The provo experiment in delinquency rehabilitation. *American Sociological Review, 26*, 679–695.

Fagan, J., Forst, M., & Vivona, T.S. (1987). Racial determinants of the judicial transfer decision: Prosecuting violent youth in criminal court. *Crime & Delinquency, 33*, 259–286.

Fagan, J., Rudman, C.J., & Hartstone, E. (1984a). System processing of violent juvenile offenders: an empirical assessment. In R.A. Mathias, P. DeMuro, & R. S. Allinson (Eds.), *Juvenile offenders—An anthology*. San Francisco, CA: National Council on Crime and Delinquency.

Fagan, J., Rudman, C.J., & Hartstone, E. (1984b). Intervening with violent juvenile offenders: A community reintegration model. In R.A. Mathias, P. DeMuro, & R. S. Allinson (Eds.), *Juvenile offenders—An anthology*. San Francisco, CA: National Council on Crime and Delinquency.

Farrington, D.P. (1973). Self-reports of deviant behavior: Predictive and stable? *Journal of Criminal Law and Criminology, 64,* 99–110.

Farrington, D.P. (1979). Longitudinal research on crime and delinquency. In N. Morris & M. Tonry (Eds.), *Crime and justice,* Vol. 1 (pp.289–348). Chicago: University of Chicago Press.

Farrington, D.P. (1981). Longitudinal analyses of criminal violence. In M. E. Wolfgang & N.A. Weiner (Eds.), *Proceedings of a workshop on interdisciplinary approaches to the study of criminal violence.* Beverly Hills, CA: Sage Publications.

Farrington, D.P. (1982a). *Stepping stones to adult criminal careers.* Presented at the Conference on Development of Antisocial and Prosocial Behavior, Voss, Norway.

Farrington, D.P. (1982b). Delinquency from 10 to 25. In S. Mednick (Ed.), *Antecedents of aggression and antisocial behavior.* Boston: Hingham-Kluwer.

Farrington, D.P. (1983). *Further analyses of a longitudinal survey of crime and delinquency.* Cambridge, UK: Institute of Criminology, Cambridge University.

Farrington, D.P. (1985). Chairman's letter. *Division of Criminological & Legal Psychology, 17,* 2–8.

Farrington, D.P. (1986). Age and crime. In N. Morris & M. Tonry (Eds.), *Crime and justice,* Vol. 7. Chicago: University of Chicago Press.

Farrington, D.P. (1994). *The nature and origins of delinquency.* Presented at the 2nd European Conference of the Association for Child Psychology and Psychiatry, Winchester, UK.

Farrington, D.P., Ohlin, L.E., & Wilson, J.Q. (1986). *Understanding and controlling crime: Toward a new research strategy.* New York: Springer-Verlag.

Farrington, D.P., Osborn, S.G., & West, D.J. (1978). The persistence of labelling effects. *British Journal of Criminology, 18,* 277–284.

Farrington, D.P., Snyder, H.N., & Finnegan, T.A. (1988). Specialization in juvenile court careers. *Criminology, 26,* 461–485.

Farrington, D.P., & West, D.J. (1981). The Cambridge study in delinquent development. In S. Mednick & A. Baert (Eds.), *Prospective longitudinal Research.* Oxford, UK: Oxford University Press.

Feeley, M.M., & Simon, J. (1992). The "new penology": Notes on the emerging strategy of corrections and its implications. *Criminology, 30,* 449–474.

Feld, B.C. (1988). In re Gault revisited: A cross-state comparison of the right to counsel in juvenile court. *Crime & Delinquency, 39,* 393–420.

Feld, B.C. (1992). Criminalizing the juvenile court: A research agenda for the 1990s. In I. Schwartz (Ed.), *Juvenile justice and public policy* (pp. 59–88). New York: Lexington Books.

Feld, B.C. (1993). *Justice for children: The right to counsel and the juvenile courts.* Boston, MA: Northeastern University Press.

Felson, M. (1986). Linking criminal choices, routine activities, informal control, and criminal outcomes. In D. Cornish & R. Clarke (Eds.), *The reasoning criminal.* New York: Springer-Verlag.

Figlio, R. M. (1981). Delinquency careers as a simple Markov process. In J.A. Fox (Ed.), *Models in quantitative criminology.* New York: Academic Press.

Forst, B. (1983). Selective incapacitation: An idea whose time has come? *Federal Probation, 46,* 19–21.

Forst, M.L. & Blomquist, M.E. (1992). Punishment, accountability, and the new juvenile justice. *Juvenile & Family Court Journal, 43,* 1–10.

Frazier, C.E., Bock, E.W., & Henretta, J.C. (1980). Pretrial release and bail decisions. *Criminology, 18,* 162–181.

Frum, H.S. (1958). Adult criminal offense trends following juvenile delinquency. *Journal of Criminal Law, Criminology & Police Science, 29*–49.

Geis, G., & Binder, A. (1991). Sins of their children: Parental responsibility for juvenile delinquency. *Notre Dame Journal of Law, Ethics & Public Policy, 5*, 303–322.

Gibbons, D. (1965). *Changing the lawbreaker*. Englewood Cliffs, NJ: Prentice-Hall.

Gibbons, D. (1975). Offender typologies—Two decades later. *British Journal of Criminology, 16*, 140–156.

Glaser, D. (1978). *Crime and our changing society*. New York: Holt, Rinehart & Winston.

Glaser, D. (1979). A review of crime-causation theory and its application. In N. Morris & M. Tonry (Eds.), *Crime and justice,* Vol. 1 (pp. 203–237). Chicago: University of Chicago Press.

Glueck, S., & Glueck, E.T. (1930). *Five hundred criminal careers*. New York: Knopf.

Glueck, S., & Glueck, E.T. (1934). *One thousand juvenile delinquents*. Cambridge, MA: Harvard University Press.

Glueck, S., & Glueck, E. T. (1937). *Later criminal careers*. New York: Commonwealth Fund.

Glueck, S., & Glueck, E. T. (1940). *Juvenile delinquents grown up*. New York: Commonwealth Fund.

Glueck, S., & Glueck, E. T. (1943). *Criminal careers in retrospect*. New York: Commonwealth Fund.

Glueck, S., & Glueck, E. T. (1945). *The after conduct of discharged offenders*. London: Macmillan.

Glueck, S., & Glueck, E. T. (1950). *Unraveling juvenile delinquency*. New York: Commonwealth Fund.

Glueck, S., & Glueck, E. T. (1964). *Ventures in criminology: Selected recent papers by Sheldon and Eleanor Glueck*. Cambridge, MA: Harvard University Press.

Glueck, S., & Glueck, E. T. (1968). *Delinquents and non-delinquents in perspective*. Cambridge, MA: Harvard University Press.

Glueck, S., & Glueck, E. T. (1974). *Of delinquency and crime: A panorama of years of search and research*. Springfield, IL: Charles C Thomas.

Goffman, E. (1961). *Asylums*. Garden City, NY: Doubleday/Anchor Books.

Goffman, E. (1963). *Stigma: Notes on the management of spoiled identity*. Englewood Cliffs, NJ: Prentice-Hall.

Gottfredson, D. (1989). Criminological theories: The truth as told by Mark Twain. *Advances in Criminological Theory 1*, 1–16.

Gottfredson, G. (1975). Organizing crime: A classification schema based on offense transitions. *Journal of Criminal Justice, 3*, 321–332.

Gottfredson, M., & Hirschi, T. (1986). The true value of lambda would appear to be zero: An essay on career criminals, criminal careers, selective incapacitation, cohort studies, and related topics. *Criminology, 24*, 213–233.

Gottfredson, M., & Hirschi, T. (1987). The methodological adequacy of longitudinal research on crime. *Criminology, 25*, 581–614.

Gottfredson, M., & Hirschi, T. (1988). Science, public policy, and the career paradigm. *Criminology, 26*, 37–55.

Gottfredson, S., & D. Gottfredson (1985). Selective incapacitation. *The Annals, 478*, 135–149.

Greenberg, D. (1975). The incapacitative effect of imprisonment: Some estimates. *Law & Society Review, 9*, 541–580.

Greenberg, D. (1985). Age, crime, and social explanation. *American Journal of Sociology, 91*, 1–21.

Greenwood, P. (1986). Promising approaches for the rehabilitation or prevention of chronic juvenile offenders. In P. Greenwood (Ed.), *Intervention strategies for chronic juvenile offenders*. Westport, CT: Greenwood Press.

Greenwood, P., with Abrahamse, A. (1982). *Selective incapacitation*. Santa Monica, CA: Rand Corporation.

Guggenheim, M. (1984). The right to be represented but not heard: Reflections on legal representation for children. *New York University Law Review, 59,* 76–155.

Guttmacher, M. (1960). *The mind of the murderer.* New York: Farrar, Straus & Giroux.

Habenstein, R.W. (1955). *The history of American funeral directing.* Milwaukee: Bulfin Printers.

Hagan, J. (1989). *Structural criminology.* New Brunswick, NJ: Rutgers University Press.

Hagan, J., & Palloni, A. (1988). Crimes as social events in the life course: Reconceiving a criminological controversy. *Criminology, 26,* 87–100.

Hamparian, D.M., Davis, J.M., Jacobson, J.M., & McGraw, R.T. (1985). *The young criminal years of the violent few.* Washington, DC: US Government Printing Office.

Hamparian, D.M., Schuster, R., Dinitz, S., & Conrad, J. (1978). *The violent few.* Lexington, MA: Lexington Books.

Havighurst, R. J., Bowman, P. H., Liddle, G. P., Matthews, C. V., & Pierce, J. V. (1966). *Growing up in river city.* New York: Wiley.

Healy, W., & Bronner, A. (1926). *Delinquents and criminals: Their making and unmaking.* New York: Macmillan (reprinted Montclair, NJ: Patterson Smith, 1969).

Healy, W., & Bronner, A. (1936). *New light on juvenile delinquency.* New Haven, CT: Yale University Press.

Heuser, J.P. (1979). *Are Status Offenders Really Different?* Salem, OR: Oregon Law Enforcement Council.

Hindelang, M. (1971). Age, sex, and the versatility of delinquent involvements. *Social Problems, 18,* 522–535.

Hindelang, M. J., Hirschi, T., & Weis, J. G. (1979). Correlates of delinquency: The illusion of discrepancy between self-report and official measures. *American Sociological Review, 44,* 995–1014.

Hirschi, T. (1985). *On the compatibility of rational choice and social control theories of crime.* Presented at the Home Office Conference on Offender Decisionmaking, Cambridge, UK, July 24.

Hirschi, T., & Gottfredson, M. (1983). Age and the explanation of crime. *American Journal of Sociology, 89,* 552–584.

Hirschi, T., & Gottfredson, M. (1993). Rethinking the juvenile justice system. *Crime & Delinquency, 39,* 262–271.

Hirschi, T., & Selvin, H. (1967). *Delinquency research: An appraisal of analytic methods.* New York: Free Press.

Hughes, E. (1952). The sociological study of work: An editorial foreword. *American Journal of Sociology, 57,* 5.

Irwin, J. (1970). *The felon.* Englewood Cliffs, NJ: Prentice-Hall.

Jackson, B. (1969). *The thieves primer.* New York: Macmillan.

Jacob, H. (1984). *The frustration of policy: Responses to crime by American cities.* Boston: Little, Brown.

Jencks, C. (1992). *Rethinking social policy: Race, poverty, and the underclass.* Cambridge, MA: Harvard University Press.

Jones, M.A., & Krisberg, B. (1994). *Images and reality: Juvenile crime, youth violence, and public policy.* San Francisco: National Council of Crime and Delinquency.

Kalton, G. (1983). *Introduction to survey sampling.* Beverly Hills, CA: Sage.

Kamin, L.J. (1986). Is the crime in the genes? The answer may depend who chooses what evidence. *Scientific American, 254,* 22–27.

Kempf, K. (1983). *Assessment of the relationship between economic status and delinquency using the 1958 Philadelphia birth cohort.* Presented at the Annual Meetings of the American Society of Criminology.

Kempf-Leonard, K., Pope, C., & Feyerherm, W. (1995). *Minorities in juvenile justice*. Thousand Oaks, CA: Sage.

Kenney, D., Pate, A., & Hamilton, E. (1990). *Police handling of juveniles: Developing model programs of response*. Washington, DC: Police Foundation.

Klein, M. (1971). *Street gangs and street workers*. Englewood Cliffs, NJ: Prentice-Hall.

Klein, M. (1975). On the front end of the juvenile justice system. In R.M. Carter & M.W. Klein (Eds.), *Back on the street: The diversion of juvenile offenders* (pp. 307–313). Englewood Cliffs, NJ: Prentice-Hall.

Klein, M. (1979). Deinstitutionalization and diversion of juvenile offenders: A litany of impediments. In N. Morris & M. Tonry (Eds.), *Crime and Justice*, Vol. 1 (pp. 145–201). Chicago: University of Chicago Press.

Klein, M. (1984). Offense specialisation and versatility among juveniles. *British Journal of Criminology, 24*, 185–194.

Klein, M.W., Tielmann, K.S., Styles, J.A., Lincoln, S.B., & Lubin-Rosenweig, S. (1976). The explosion in police diversion programs: Evaluating the structural dimensions of a social fad. In M.W. Klein (Ed.), *The juvenile justice system* (pp. 101–120). Beverly Hills, CA: Sage.

Klockars, C. (1976). *The professional fence*. New York: Free Press.

Kobrin, S., Hellum, F.R., & Peterson, J. (1980). Offense patterns of status offenders. In D. Shichor & D.H. Kelly (Eds.), *Critical issues in juvenile delinquency*. Lexington, MA: Lexington Books.

Krisberg, B. (1987). Preventing and controlling violent youth crime: the state of the art. In I. Schwartz (Ed.), *Violent juvenile crime: What do we know about it and what can we do about it?* Minneapolis: Center for the Study of Youth Policy, University of Minnesota.

Krisberg, B. (1992). Youth crime and its prevention: A research agenda. In I.M. Schwartz (Ed.), *Juvenile Justice and Public Policy*. New York: Lexington Books.

Krisberg, B., & Austin, J.F. (1970). *The children of Ishmael*. Palo Alto, CA: Mayfield.

Krisberg, B., & Austin, J.F. (1993) *Reinventing juvenile justice*. Newberry Park, CA: Sage.

Krisberg, B., Austin, J.F., & Steele, P. (1989). *Unlocking juvenile corrections*. San Francisco: National Council of Crime and Delinquency.

Krisberg, B., Neuenfeldt, D., Wiebush, R., & Rodriguez, O. (1994). *Juvenile intensive supervision: Planning guide*. Washington, DC: US Government Printing Office.

Krisberg, B., Rodriguez, O., Bakke, A., Neuenfeldt, D., & Steele, P. (1989). *Demonstration of postadjudication nonresidential intensive supervision programs: Assessment report*. San Francisco: National Council of Crime and Delinquency.

Langan, P., & Farrington, D.P. (1983). Two-track or one-track justice? Some evidence from an english longitudinal survey. *Journal of Criminal Law and Criminology, 74*, 519–546.

Langan, P., & Greenfeld, L. (1983). *Career patterns in crime*. Washington, DC: Bureau of Justice Statistics (Special Report NCJ-88672).

Laub, J. H. (1983). Trends in serious juvenile crime. *Criminal Justice and Behavior, 10*, 485–506.

Laub, J.H., & R.J. Sampson (1988). Unraveling families and delinquency: A reanalysis of the Gluecks' data. *Criminology, 26*, 355–380.

Lemert, E. (1951). *Social pathology*. New York: McGraw-Hill.

Lemert, E. (1962). *Human deviance, social problems, and social control*. Englewood Cliffs, NJ: Prentice-Hall.

Letkeman, P. (1973). *Crime as work*. Englewood Cliffs, NJ: Prentice-Hall.

Loeber, R., & LeBlanc, M. (1990). Toward a developmental criminology. In M. Tonry & N. Morris (Eds.), *Crime and justice*, Vol. 12. Chicago: University of Chicago Press.

Loftin, C., & McDowell, D. (1981). One with a gun gets you two: Mandatory sentencing and firearms violence in Detroit. *Annals, AAPS, 445:* 158–68.

Long, J.V.F., & Vaillant, G.E. (1984). Natural history of male psychological health, XI: Escape from the underclass. *American Journal of Psychiatry, 141,* 341–346.

Lundman, R. (1974). Routine police practices: A commonwealth perspective. *Social Problems, 22,* 127–141.

McCaghy, C. (1967). Child molesters: A study of their careers as deviants." In M. Clinard and R. Quinney (Eds.), *Criminal behavior systems.* New York: Holt, Rinehart & Winston.

McClintock, F. (1963). *Crimes of violence.* London: Macmillan.

McCord, J. (1978). A thirty-year follow-up of treatment effects. *American Psychologist, 33,* 284–289.

McCord, J. (1979). Some child rearing antecedents of criminal behavior in adult men. *Journal of Personality and Social Psychology, 37,* 1477–1486.

McCord, J. (1981). A longitudinal perspective on patterns of crime. *Criminology, 19,* 211–218.

McCord, J., & McCord, W. (1959). A follow-up report on the Cambridge–Somerville youth study. *The Annals, March,* 89–96.

McCord, W., McCord, J., & Zola, I.K. (1969). *Origins of crime.* New York: Columbia University Press.

Martin, J.B. (1952). *My life in crime: The autobiography of a professional thief.* New York: Knopf.

Matza, D. (1964). *Delinquency and drift.* New York: Wiley.

Maurer, D. (1940). *The big con.* Indianapolis, IN: Bobbs-Merrill.

Maurer, D. (1964). *Whiz mob.* New Haven, CT: College and University Press.

May, D. (1981). The Aberdeen delinquency study. In S. Mednick & A. Baert (Eds.), *Prospective longitudinal research: An empiricial basis for the primary prevention of psychological disorders.* Oxford: Oxford University Press.

Merton, R.K. (1938). Social structure and anomie. *American Sociological Review, 3,* 672–682.

Messner, S.F., & Rosenfeld, R. (1994). *Crime and the American dream.* Belmont, CA: Wadsworth.

Miller, C. (1978). *Odd jobs: The world of deviant work.* Englewood Cliffs, NJ: Prentice-Hall.

Miller, W. (1958). Lower class culture as a generating mileu of gang delinquency. *Journal of Social Issues, 14,* 5–19.

Morash, M. (1984). Establishment of a juvenile record. *Criminology, 22,* 97–111.

Murray, J.P. (1990). Status offenders: Roles, rules, and reactions. In R.A. Weisheit & R.G. Culbertson (Eds.), *Juvenile delinquency: A justice perspective.* Prospect Heights, IL: Waveland Press.

Murray, C., & Cox, L. (1979). *Beyond probation.* Beverly Hills, CA: Sage.

Myerhoff, H.L. & Myerhoff, B.G. (1964). Field observations of middle class gangs. *Social Forces, 42,* 328–336.

Nagin, D. & Farrington, D.P. (1992). The stability of criminal potential from childhood to adulthood. *Criminology, 30,* 235–245.

Neustatter, W. (1967). *The mind of the murderer.* New York: Philosophical Library.

Nevares, D., Wolfgang, M. E., & Tracy, P. E. (1990). *Delinquency in Puerto Rico: The 1970 birth cohort study.* Westport, CT: Greenwood.

Office of Juvenile Justice and Delinquency Prevention (OJJDP) (1993). *Children in custody.* Washington, DC: US Government Printing Office.

Ohlin, L.E. (1983). The future of juvenile justice policy. *Crime and Delinquency, 29,* 463–472.

Park, R.E. (1915). The city: Suggestions for the investigation of behavior in the city environment. *American Journal of Sociology, 20,* 579–83.

Park, R.E., Burgess, E., & McKenzie, R. (1925). *The city*. Chicago: University of Chicago Press.

Petersilia, J. (1980). Criminal career research: A review of recent evidence. In N. Morris & M. Tonry (Eds.), *Crime and justice*, Vol. 2 (pp. 321–379). Chicago: University of Chicago Press.

Petersilia, J., Greenwood, P., & Lavin, M. (1977). *Criminal careers of habitual felons*. Santa Monica, CA: Rand.

Peterson, M., Braiker, H., & Polich, S. (1980). *Doing crime: A survey of California inmates*. Santa Monica, CA: Rand.

Peterson, R.A., Pitman, D.J., & O'Neal, P. (1962). Stabilities of deviance: A study of assaultive and non-assaultive offenders. *Journal of Criminal Law, Criminology, and Police Science, 53*, 44–48.

Phillip, L., & Votey, H. (1987). The influence of police interventions and alternative income sources on the dynamic process of choosing crime as a career. *Journal of Quantitative Criminology, 3*, 251–274.

Piliavin, I., & S. Briar (1964). Police encounters with juveniles. *American Journal of Sociology, 70*, 206–14.

Platt, A. (1969). *The child savers*. Chicago: University of Chicago Press.

Polk, K., Adler, C., Bazemore, G., Blake, G., Cordray, S., Coventry, G., Galvin, J., & Temple, M. (1981). *Becoming adult: An analysis of maturational development from age 16 to 30 of a cohort of young men*. Final Report of the Marion County Youth Study. Eugene, OR: University of Oregon.

Polsky, N. (1969). *Hustlers, beats and others*. Garden City, NY: Doubleday/Anchor Books.

Powers, E. Witmer, H. (1951). An experiment in the prevention of delinquency. New York: Columbia University Press.

President's Commission on Law Enforcement and Administration of Justice. (1967). *The challenge of crime in a free society*. Washington, DC: US Government Printing Office.

Prus, R., & Sharper, B. (1977). *Road hustler*. Lexington, MA: Lexington Books.

Quay, H.C., & Blumen, L. (1968). Dimensions of delinquent behavior. *The Journal of Social Psychology, 61*, 273–277.

Quinney, R. (1970). *The social reality of crime*. Boston: Little, Brown.

Reckless, W. (1961). A new theory of delinquency. *Federal probation, 25*, 42–46.

Regnery, A.S. (1985). Getting away with murder: Why the juvenile justice system needs an overhaul. *Policy Review, 34*, 465.

Reiss, Jr., A.J. (1951). Unraveling juvenile deinquency. II. An appraisal of the research methods. *American Journal of Sociology, 57*, 115–120.

Reiss, Jr., A.J. (1986). Co-offending influences on criminal careers. In A. Blumstein, J. Cohen, J. A. Roth, & C. A. Visher (Eds.), *Criminal careers and career criminals*, Vol. 2 (pp. 121–160). Washington, DC: National Academy Press.

Robins, L. (1966). *Deviant children grown Up*. Baltimore: Williams & Wilkins.

Robins, L., & Hill, S.Y. (1966). Assessing the contribution of family structure, class, and peer groups to juvenile delinquency. *Journal of Criminal Law, Criminology, and Police Science, 57*, 325–334.

Robins, R., & O'Neal, P. (1958). Mortality, mobility and crime: Problem children thirty years later. *American Sociological Review, 23*, 162–171.

Roebuck, J. (1966). *Criminal typologies*. Springfield, IL: Charles C Thomas.

Roebuck, J., & Cadwaller, M.L. (1961). The Negro armed robber as a criminal type: The construction and application of a typology. *Pacific Sociological Review, 4*, 21–25.

Rojek, D.G., & Erickson, M.L. (1982). Delinquent careers: A test of the career escalation model. *Criminology, 20*, 5–28.

Rothman, D.J. (1971). *The discovery of the asylum*. Boston: Little, Brown.

Ryder, N. (1965). The cohort as a concept in the study of social change. *American Sociological Review, 30*, 843–861.

Sampson, R.J., & Laub, J.H. (1990). Crime and deviance over the life course: The salience of adult social bonds. *American Sociological Review, 55*, 609–627.

Sampson, R.J., & Laub, J.H. (1993). *Crime in the making: Pathways and turning points through life*. Boston: Harvard University Press.

Schall v. Martin (1984). 467 U.S. 253.

Schrag, C. (1944). *Social types in a prison community*. Seattle, University of Washington, M.A. thesis.

Schrag, C. (1961). A preliminary criminal typology. *Pacific Sociological Review, 4*, 11–16.

Schur, E.M. (1973). *Radical non-intervention: Rethinking the delinquency problem*. Englewood Cliffs, NJ: Prentice-Hall

Schwartz, I.M. (1989). *(In) justice for juveniles: Rethinking the best interests of the child*. Lexington, MA: Lexington Books.

Schwartz, I.M. (1992). Juvenile crime-fighting policies: What the public really wants. In I.M. Schwartz (Ed.), *Juvenile Justice and Public Policy* (pp. 214–248). New York: Lexington Books.

Schwartz, I.M., & Van Vleet, R. (1992). Public policy and the incarceration of juveniles: directions for the 1990s. In I.M. Schwartz (Ed.), *Juvenile justice and public policy* (pp. 151–164). New York: Lexington Books.

Sellin, T. (1938). *Culture conflict and crime*. New York: Social Science Research Council.

Sellin, T., & Wolfgang, M. E. (1964). *The measurement of delinquency*. New York: Wiley.

Shannon, L.W. (1968). Scaling juvenile delinquency. *Journal of Research, 5*, 52–65.

Shannon, L. W. (1978). A longitudinal study of delinquency and crime. In C. Wellford (Ed.), *Quantitative studies in criminology*. Beverly Hills, CA: Sage.

Shannon, L. W. (1980). *Assessing the relationship of adult criminal careers to juvenile careers*. Washington, DC: US Government Printing Office.

Shannon, L. W. (1988). *Criminal career continuity: Its social context*. New York: Human Sciences Press.

Shaw, C. (1930). *The jackroller*. Chicago: University of Chicago Press.

Shaw, C. (1931). *Natural history of a delinquent career*. Chicago: University of Chicago Press.

Shaw, C. (1936). *Brothers in crime*. Chicago: University of Chicago Press.

Shaw, C. (1947). *Subsequent criminal careers of juvenile delinquents, school truants, and special school pupils*. Unpublished manuscript, Department of Sociology, University of Chicago.

Shaw, C., & McKay, H. (1942). *Juvenile delinquency and urban areas*. Chicago: University of Chicago Press.

Shine, J., & Price, D. (1992). Prosecutors and juvenile justice: new roles and perspectives. In I. Schwartz (Ed.), *Juvenile justice and public policy* (pp.101–133). New York: Lexington Books.

Shinnar, R., & Shinnar, S. (1975). The effect of the criminal justice system on the control of crime: A quantitative approach. *Law and Society Review, 9*, 581–611.

Short, J.F. (1969). Book review of *Delinquents and nondelinquents in perspective*. *American Sociological Review, 34*, 981–983.

Shover, N. (1985). *Aging criminals*. Beverly Hills, CA: Sage.

Sinclair, I. & Clarke, R. (1982). Predicting, treating, and explaining delinquency: The lessons from research on institutions. In P. Feldman (Ed.), *Development in the study of criminal behavior: The prevention and control of offending*. New York: Wiley.

Smith, D.R., & Smith, W.R. (1984). Patterns of delinquent careers: An assessment of three perspectives. *Social Science Research, 13*, 129–158.

Smith, D., & Visher, C. (1981). Street-level justice: Situational determinants of police arrest decisions. *Social Problems, 29,* 267–277.

Smith, D.S., Visher, C., & Jarjoura, R. (1991). Dimensions of delinquency: Exploring the correlates of participation, frequency, and persistence of delinquent behavior. *Journal of Research in Crime and Delinquency, 28,* 6–32.

Snyder, H. (1990). *Update on statistics, growthg in minority detentions attributed to drug law violators.* Washington, DC: US Department of Justice.

Snyder, H.N., & Sickmund, M. (1995). *Juvenile offenders and victims: A focus on violence.* Washington, DC: Office of Juvenile Justice and Delinquency Prevention.

Soothill, K.L., & Pope, P.J. (1973). Arson: A twenty-year cohort study. *Medicine, Science and Law, 16,* 62–69.

Spector, P.E. (1981). *Research designs.* Beverly Hills, CA: Sage.

Spiro, B.E. (1984). Abolishing court jurisdiction over status offenders: Anticipating the unintended consequences. In S.S. Decker (Ed.), *Juvenile justice policy: Analyzing trends and outcomes* (pp.77–94). Beverly Hills, CA: Sage.

Stott, D., & Wilson, D. (1977). The adult criminal as juvenile. *British Journal of Criminology, 17,* 47–57.

Sutherland, E. (1937). *The professional thief.* Chicago: University of Chicago Press.

Sykes, G. (1958). *The society of captives.* Princeton, NJ: Princeton University Press.

Taylor, I., Walton, P., & Young, J. (1973). *The new criminology.* London: Routledge & Kegan Paul.

Thornberry, T.P. (1987). Towards an interactional theory. *Criminology, 25,* 863–881.

Thornberry, T.P., Lizotte, A., Krohn, M., Farnworth, M., & Jang, S.J. (1991). Testing interactional theory: An examination of reciprocal causal relationships among family, school, and delinquency. *Journal of Criminal Law and Criminology, 82,* 3–35.

Thrasher, F. (1927). *The gang.* Chicago: University of Chicago Press.

Tielman, K.S., & Peterson, I. (1981). What works for whom: the use of deinstitutionalization. In S. Kobrin & M. Klein (Eds.), *National Evaluation of the Deinstitutionalizatoin of Status Offenders Programs.* Los Angeles, CA: University of Southern California.

Tittle, C.R. (1988). Two empirical regularities (maybe) in search of an explanation: Commentary on the age/crime debate. *Criminology, 26,* 75–85.

Tracy, P.E. (1981). *Ecology and delinquency: Developing a composite measure of social class.* Philadelphia, PA: Center for Studies in Criminology and Criminal Law, University of Pennsylvania.

Tracy, P. E. (1987). Race and class differences in official and self-reported delinquency. In M.E. Wolfgang, T.P. Thornberry, & R.M. Figlio (Eds.), *From boy to man, from delinquency to crime.* Chicago: University of Chicago Press.

Tracy, P.E., Wolfgang, M.E., & Figlio, R.M. (1985) *Delinquency in two birth cohorts, executive summary.* Washington, DC: US Government Printing Office.

Tracy, P.E., Wolfgang, M.E., & Figlio, R.M. (1989). *Patterns of delinquency and adult crime in the 1958 Philadelphia birth cohort, executive summary.* Washington, DC: US Government Printing Office.

Tracy, P.E., Wolfgang, M.E., & Figlio, R.M. (1990). *Delinquency careers in two birth cohorts.* New York: Plenum Press.

Violent crime control and law enforcement act of 1994. P.L. 103–322, 103rd Congress, Second Session, September 13, 1994.

Visher, C. A. (1986). The rand inmate surveys: A reanalysis. In A. Blumstein, J. Cohen, J. A. Roth, & C. A. Visher, (Eds.), *Criminal careers and career criminals,* Vol. 2 (pp. 161–211). Washington, DC: National Academy Press.

Vold, G. (1958). *Theoretical criminology.* New York: Oxford University Press.

Walker, S. (1983). *Police in society.* New York: McGraw-Hill.

Walker, S. (1985). *Sense and nonsense about crime*. Pacific Grove, CA: Brooks Cole.

Wallerstedt, J. (1984). *Returning to prison*. Washington, DC: Bureau of Justice Statistics.

Weis, J.G. (1986). Issues in the measurement of criminal careers. In A. Blumstein, J. Cohen, J. A. Roth, & C. A. Visher (Eds.), *Criminal careers and career criminals*, Vol. 2 (pp.1–51). Washington, DC: National Academy Press.

Weis, J.G., & Hawkins, J. D. (1981). *Reports of the national juvenile justice assessment centers, preventing delinquency*. Washington, DC: US Department of Justice.

Weis, J.G., & Sederstrom, J. (1981). *Reports of the national juvenile justice assessment centers, the prevention of serious delinquency: What to do*. Washington, DC: US Department of Justice.

West, D.J. (1969). *Present conduct and future delinquency*. London: Heinemann.

West, D.J. (1982). *Delinquency: Its roots, careers and prospects*. London: Heinemann.

West, D.J., & Farrington, D.P. (1973). *Who becomes delinquent?* London: Heinemann.

West, D.J., & Farrington, D.P. (1977). *The delinquent way of life*. London: Heinemann.

Wilkins, L.T. (1969). Data and delinquency. *Yale Law Journal, 78,* 731–737.

Wilson, J.J., & Howell, J.C. (1993). *Comprehensive strategy for serious, violent, and chronic juvenile offenders*. Washington, DC: Office of Juvenile Justice and Delinquency prevention.

Wilson, W.J. (1987). *The truly disadvantaged: The inner city, the underclass, and public policy*. Chicago: University of Chicago Press.

Wolfgang, M.E. (1977). *From boy to man—from delinquency to crime*. Presented to the National Symposium on the Serious Juvenile Offender, Minneapolis, MN.

Wolfgang, M.E. (1995). Transition of crime in the aging process. In J. Hagan, (Ed.), *Current perpsectives on aging and the life cycle*. New York: JAI Press.

Wolfgang, M.E., Figlio, R.M., & Sellin, T. (1972). *Delinquency in a birth cohort*. Chicago: University of Chicago Press.

Wolfgang, M. E., Figlio, R. M., Tracy, P. E., & Singer, S. I. (1985). *The national survey of crime severity*. Washington, DC: US Government Printing Office.

Wolfgang, M.E., Thornberry, T.P., & Figlio, R.M. (1987). *From boy to man, from delinquency to crime*. Chicago: University of Chicago Press.

Wright, R., & Decker, S.H. (1994). *Burglars on the job*. Boston: Northeastern University Press.

Wright, R., Logie, R.H., & Decker, S.H. (1995). Criminal expertise and offender decision making: An experimental study of the target selection process in residential burglary. *Journal Research in Crime and Delinquency, 32,* 39–53.

Zimring, F.E. (1981). Kids, groups, and crime: Some implications of a well known secret. *Journal of Criminal Law and Criminology, 72,* 867–885.

Zorbaugh, H.W. (1929). *Gold coast and sun: A sociological study of Chicago's near north side*. Chicago: University of Chicago Press.

Name Index

Subject Index

Aberdeen cohort, 60
Age-at-first delinquency, and adult
   offender status, 110–118, 137–138, 208
Age-at-last delinquency, and adult
   offender status, 110–118, 137–138, 208

Birth cohort, 1958
   data limitations of, 75–77, 219
   data sources for, 63–65
   eligibility for, ix, 1, 55–56
   importance of, 1, 203–204
   representativeness of, 54–57, 205
   variables in, 65–70
Birth cohort, 1945
   acclaim for, 10
   and chronic delinquents, 6, 10
   and desistence from delinquency, 47–
      48
   and juvenile offense severity, 49, 182
   and juvenile offense specialization,
      50–52
   follow-up of, 7, 43–45

Cambridge Study in Delinquent
   Development, 8, 41, 42, 49, 74
Cambridge–Somerville Youth Study, 39, 58,
   74
Chicago School, 3, 5, 35
Continuity and discontinuity
   definitions of, 35
   issues surrounding, 44–54
   and prior research, 37–44, 58–63, 73–75
   and research designs, 55–56
Criminal career research
   concepts in, 2
   critique of, 11–13

Criminal career research (*cont.*)
   focus of, 8–11
   origins of, 3–8
Criminal justice policy, implications for,
   31–34

Delinquency status, and adult offender
   status, 79–87, 206–208
Delinquency groups
   and adult offender status, 86–90
   and adult offender groups, 90–94
Delinquent careers
   length of, and adult offender status,
      110–118, 137–138, 208
   typology of, 36–37
Delinquent offense concentration
   definition of, 161–164
   and adult status
      for males, 164–171, 176–179, 211–214
      for females, 171–176, 177–179, 211–
         214
Delinquent offense severity
   definition of, 181–183
   measurement of, 67–69
   and adult status
      for males, 183–189, 215–216
      for females, 194–196, 215–216
   early offenses, and adult status
      for males, 193–194, 217–218
      for females, 199–200, 217–218
   timing of, and adult status
      for males, 189–193, 216–217
      for females, 196–199, 216–217
Delinquent offense types
   definitions of, 144–145
   and adult status

261

ISBN 0-306-45347-9

90000